Railway Track Diagrams
Book 4: Midlands & North W

Editor: Gerald Jacobs

C000254417

Preface to the Second Edition

Quail Track Diagrams have been published since 1988 and provide a reference to Enthusia........ ....ey contain information which may exist elsewhere and in other forms but are unique in making it all available in one easily portable volume.

The idea was not new as other similar information had been published in the past. However, not until Gerald Jacobs as editor joined forces with John Yonge of the Quail Map Co as cartographer and publisher did the principle find two people with the knowledge and the attention to detail to put it into full and effective practice. The Railway Track Diagrams, as a result, have become standard reference works for a wide range of users from train staff and infrastructure managers to railway enthusiast and modellers.

The first book to be published detailed Scotland and gradually coverage of the whole of the UK mainland was completed including private railways and London Underground. The books cover the network roughly on the basis of the original British Rail regions. The information included is a combination of historical sources collected by Gerald Jacobs during his 40 years with British Railways, added to subsequently, kept up to date with reference to Network Rail and its predecessors and supplemented by other data, by the kind assistance of other persons and by field observation.

Until recently, all the books were drawn by the careful hand of cartographer John Yonge but the demands of more frequent updating and the opportunity presented by the use of colour has necessitated a change. In September 2004, Trackmaps took over the responsibility for updating and publishing the books and this volume, Midlands and North West, Book 4 in the series, is the first to be produced by electronic cartography. It reflects a tremendous amount of work by Gerald Jacobs in bridging the 15 years that have passed since this title was last published.

This volume has been a long time coming. Everyone involved believes that it is worth the wait.

March 2005

Introduction

The Track Diagrams in this book cover the lines forming the LNW Territory of Network Rail, also parts of LNE, South Eastern, Western and Scotland Territories, together with a number of private railways and industrial layouts. They are, in general, up date as at March 2005.

However, records are wonderful things. They can both inform and confuse. Nowhere is this more certain than on the UK Railway Network. Built up, as it has been, over more than 180 years, managed as individual companies, as a nationalised industry and now as individual train operating companies with a single infrastructure owner, it has grown, stagnated, declined and grown again more than once within that time. Many persons have produced records and maps at different times for different parts, both within the industry and outside. Many record systems compete for information or act in a complementary manner to each other. The Track Diagrams attempt to collate these diverse sources into one publication but, even so, space precludes the inclusion of much detail including, for example, signals. These may be the subject of later publications.

Track Diagrams also try to put down a standard where discrepancies occur; mileages are typical. Mileages often vary slightly between different official records but, in general, those given in Sectional Appendix have been used. Station mileages are usually taken from the mid-point of the platforms or, in the case of a terminus, the buffer stops. The Railway is continually changing and, because of its diverse nature and varied history, discrepancies often arise between seeming accurate sources. In such circumstances, the Editor's judgement is applied.

Acknowledgements

A large number of people have contributed to the information in this publication, some in a significant way providing layouts, site checking or proofing details and some in a small way giving personal observations, answering individual questions or giving access to engineering drawings and construction diagrams. The assistance of all is gratefully acknowledged, especially persons at Network Rail (including its predecessors), at EWS Railways, at London Underground, together with Iain Scotchman, Michael Oakley and Fred Howes. Other acknowledgements are due to the Branch Line Society, the Railway Correspondence & Travel Society and many other correspondents, other railway societies and also representatives of the other private and preserved systems featured.

The digital production of this book could not have proceeded without the efforts of the team at ESR Cartography Ltd but special thanks must also be given to two people; firstly, to John Yonge, the originator of the track diagram artwork, whose cartography and advice provided a sound basis of the maps in the book; and, secondly, to Elvina Jacobs for her forbearance and continuous support given throughout the Editor's long and arduous task.

Gerald Jacobs

1st Edition 1990
Reprinted 1996
2nd Edition 2005

ISBN 0-9549866-0-1

Published by Trackmaps
Little Court, Upper South Wraxall, Bradford on Avon BA15 2SE (Tel: 0845 300 1370 Fax: 0845 300 1375)
Web: www.trackmaps.co.uk Email: sales@trackmaps.co.uk

Edited by Gerald Jacobs

Original Cartography by John Yonge

Digital Conversion & Design by ESR Cartography Ltd
Maidenhead, Berkshire SL6 8BR

Printed by Victoria Litho Ltd,
Hayes, Middlesex UB8 4SA

KEY

————	Running Line
————	Siding
————	Electrified overhead
————	Electrified 3rd rail
————	Electrified 3rd rail (Underail contact, DLR)
————	Electrified 4th rail (LU)
————	Electrified, overhead & Conductor rail

A broken line indicates 'in situ' but out of use, proposed or under construction.

——●——	Line obstructed
——○——	Line out of use
——·——	Change of Signalling mandate
LNW ‖ LNE	Network Rail Territory boundary
Preston (PN) | Carlisle (CE)	Signal Box / centre area limits
—)---(—	Tunnel
	Bridge under Rail or Viaduct
—Y—	Selected Motorway / Trunk Road bridges over rail
—+—	Network Rail operated level crossing
	User-worked crossing with Telephone
←——→	Track signalled in both directions (a double arrow indicates normal direction of travel) (On single lines 'DN' indicates down direction)
—⋈—	Private siding boundary, often marked by a gate
———⅃	Sand Drag
—⊘—	Turntable
············	Gantry Rails (Freightliner Terminal)
ᴧᴧᴧᴧᴧᴧᴧ	Wall / Bank
	Hot Axle Box Detector (HABD), Wheel Impact Load Detector (WILD) or Wheelchex Device

LEC	ELR-Engineer's Line Reference (Prefix and suffix numbers indicate sub-divisions and their boundaries)
[MD 101]	Line of Route Code
◇1◇	Metro Service Number
| 93	Whole mileposts, shown on the appropriate side of the line
| 32	Whole kilometre posts
81.3⌐	End of mileage run
113.76 / 105.70 COM	Lineside mileage change
3	Platform with number (May be supplemented by sub-divisions. e.g. (a), (b), (c), 'N' or North etc)
⑦	Indicates number of carriages per platform (approx 20m lengths)
⌐⌐⌐	Provisional proposed platform
▭	Former Royal Mail platform
▭	Platform out of use
⌐⌐	Other feature (labelled)
▨	Loading bank
Preston (PN) ⊠	Signal Box or Signalling Centre, with code (underlined text relates to SB or SC)
⊡	Control Panel
⊠	Gate Box
⊡ ⊙	Ground Frame/Ground Switch Panel or Shunting Frame. Ⓢ Indicates 'Shut in' facility
✳	Radio electronic token block / Token exchange point
¶	Proposed closure
○	Water tower
∧	Summit, height in feet
(Irchester) ●	Indicates a former Jn, Station or Signal Box
86.34 (Not italic if Station mileage)	Distance in Miles and chains from specified zero 1 Mile = 1760 yards / 1.6km 80 chains = 1 Mile 1 chain = 22 yards / 20.11m
57.60 km	Distance in Kilometres

Guide references are given to pre-nationalisation, pre-grouping and sometimes pioneer railways e.g. LMS : LNW (London & Birmingham)

Traditional Line Descriptions may be quoted, e.g. **CREWE and BIRDSWOOD LINE (Grand Junction)**

Publisher's Note

Every effort has been made by the editor to ensure the accuracy of the information in the book is as correct as possible at the time of going to press. Notwithstanding, the Publishers welcome corrections, updates or suggestions for application to future editions

GENERAL ABBREVIATIONS

AA	Acid Application	FP	Fuelling Point or Footpath	PW	Permanent Way
ABP	Associated British Ports	ft	Feet	Qy	Query concerning distances etc, unresolved
AC	Alternating Current	GB	Gate Box	REC	Reception
ARR	Arrival	GC	Gantry Crane	RETB	Radio Electronic Token Block
ASC	Area Signalling Centre i/c IECC, Power Box	GDS	Goods	REV	Reversing or Reversible line
bdy	boundary	GF	Ground Frame	RR	Run-Round
BCH	Branch	GL	Goods Loop	S	South
BR	British Rail	GS	Goods Shed	S & T	Signal & Telegraph
CCTV	Closed Circuit Television	GSP	Ground Switch Panel	SB	Signal Box or Southbound
CET	Controlled Emission Toilet Discharge	H	Headshunt	SC	Signalling Centre
CL	Crossing Loop on Single Line	HABD	Hot Axle Box Detector	SCC	Signalling Control Centre
COM	Change of Mileage	HH	Hopper House	Sdg(s)	Siding(s)
CR	Cripple Siding	HST	High Speed Train	SD	Sand Drag
CW	Carriage Washer	IECC	Intergrated Electronic Control Centre	SF	Shunting Frame
C&W	Carriage & Wagon	Jn	Junction	SIMBIDS	Simplified Bi-Directional Signalling
D	Connections Disconnected	Jt	Joint	SN	Shunt Neck
DA	Down Avoiding	km	kilometres	SP	Switch Panel
DC	Direct Current	L	Wheel Lathe	SS	Shunt Spur
DE	Down Electric	LC	Level Crossing (manned, automatic or open)	TA	Tamper siding
DED	Diesel Electric Depot	LHS	Locomotive Holding Siding	TB	Turnback Siding
DEP	Departure	LP	Loop	TEP	Token Exchange Point
DF	Down Fast	LPG	Liquified petroleum gas	TL	Traffic Lights
DG	Down Goods	LS	Locomotive Shed	TMD	Traction Maintenance Depot
DGL	Down Goods Loop	LW	Locomotive Washer	T&RSMD	Traction & Rolling Stock Maintenance Depot
DL	Down Loop	M	Middle	U&D	Up & Down
DM	Down Main	M ch	Miles and Chains	UA	Up Avoiding
DMD	Diesel Maintenance Depot	M&EE	Mechanical & Electrical Engineer	UE	Up Electric
DMUD	Diesel Multiple Unit Depot	MGR	'Merry-go-round'	UF	Up Fast
DN	Down	MN	Main	UFN	Until Further Notice
DPL	Down Passenger Loop	MOD	Ministry of Defence	UG	Up Goods
DR	Down Relief	MU	Maintenance Unit	UGL	Up Goods Loop
DRS	Down Refuge Sidings	N	North	UH	Unloading Hopper
DS	Down Slow	NB	Northbound	UL	Up Loop
DSB	Down Surburban	NIRU	Not in regular use	UM	Up Main
DT	Down Through	NR	Network Rail	UPL	Up Passenger Loop
E	East	OHC	Overhead Crane	UR	Up Relief
e	elecrified	OHLE	Overhead Line Equipment	URS	Up Refuge Siding
EB	Eastbound	OOU	Out of Use	US	Up Slow
EGF	Emergency Ground Frame	ONS	Overhead Neutral Section	USB	Up Suburban
EMD	Electric Maintenance Depot	OTM	On-track Maintenance	UT	Up Through
EMUD	Electric Multiple Unit Depot	P	Points padlocked	V or Vdct	Viaduct
Engrs	Engineers' Sidings	PAD	Prefabricated Assembly Depot	W	West
eol	End of Line	PL	Passenger Loop	WB	Westbound or Weighbridge
ESP	Emergency Signalling Panel	PS	Private Siding	WD	War Department or Wheelchex Device
EWS	English Welsh & Scottish Railway Ltd	PSB	Power Signal Box	WILD	Wheel Impact Load Detector
FA	Flushing Apron			yds	yards

SUPPLEMENTARY ABBREVIATIONS FOR THIS BOOK

Cal	former Caledonian Railway	LUL	London Underground Limited
CTRL	Channel Tunnel Rail Link	MD&HC	Mersey Docks & Harbour Co.
CLC	former Cheshire Lines Committee	M&C	former Maryport and Carlisle Railway
GC	former Great Central Railway	MSC	Manchester Ship Canal
GE	former Great Eastern Railway	MSJ&A	former Manchester South Jn & Altrincham Railway
GN	former Great Northern Railway	Met	former Metropolitan Railway
GSW	former Glasgow & South Western Railway	Mid	former Midland Railway
GW	former Great Western Railway	NB	former North British Railway
LBSC	former London, Brighton and South Coast Railway	NE	former North Eastern Railway
LCD	former London, Chatham and Dover Railway	NS	former North Staffordshire Railway
LMS	former London Midland and Scottish Railway	N&SWJn	former North and South Western Jn Railway
LNE	former London and North Eastern Railway	S	former Southern Railway
LNW	former London and North Western Railway	SE	former South Eastern Railway
LPTB	former London Passenger Transport Board	WL	former West London Joint Railway
LSW	former London and South Western Railway	WLE	former West London Extension Joint Railway
L&Y	former Lancashire and Yorkshire Railway		

LEVEL CROSSING ABBREVIATIONS

STANDARD	Supplementary	Description	STANDARD	Supplementary	Description
(ABCL) *		Automatic Barrier Crossing, Locally monitored		(MWLO)	Miniature Warning Lights at Open crossing
(AHBC) *		Automatic Half-Barrier Crossing	(OC)	(O) (OPEN)	Open Crossing (non-automatic), without barriers, gates or road traffic signals
(AOCL) *		Automatic Open Crossing, Locally monitored			
	(AOCR)	Automatic Open Crossing, Remotely monitored	(RC)		Remotely Controlled crossing with barriers
	(BW)	Bridle Way	(R/G)		User-worked crossing with Red and Green warning lights operated by approaching trains
(CCTV)		Manually controlled barrier crossing with Closed Circuit Television			
			(TMO)		Traincrew Operated crossing
	(FP (B)(G)(K)(W))	Footpath crossing (only shown if telephone provided)		(TMOB)	Traincrew Operated Barrier
		(B) Barriers, (G) Gates, (K) Kissing Gate, (W) Wickets		(TMOG)	Traincrew Operated Gates
(MCB)	(MB)	Manually controlled Crossing with Barriers	(UWC)	(UWCP)	User-Worked Crossing of occupation, accommodation or bridleway status with telephone
	(MCBR)	Manually controlled Crossing with Barriers, Remotely controlled			
(MG)	(MCG)	Manually controlled Crossing with Gates	(UWB)		User-Worked Barriers
	(MGH)	Manned Gates, Hand worked		(UWCM)	User-Worked Crossing with miniature Red and Green warning lights
	(MGW)	Manned Gates with Wickets			
	(MSL (B)(F)(G))	Miniature Stop Light with (B) Barriers, (F) Footpath, (G) Gates	(UWG)		User-Worked Gates
	(MWL)	Miniature Warning Lights	(UWK)		User-Worked with Kissing Gates
	(MWLB)	Miniature Warning Lights with Barriers	(UWS)		User-Worked Stile
	(MWLF)	Miniature Warning Lights at user-worked Footpath	(UWW)		User-Worked Wickets
	(MWLG)	Miniature Warning Lights with Gates	(WL)		Barrow or Foot Crossing with White Light indicators

* (-X) shown after these abbreviations e.g. (AHBC-X) indicates that the crossing works automatically for movements in the wrong direction.

In some cases, the code of the controlling signal box may be shown e.g. (AHBC-X) (KS).

If no abbreviation is shown, the level crossing is either operated locally by a Signaller or Crossing Keeper, or privately but equipped with a telephone.

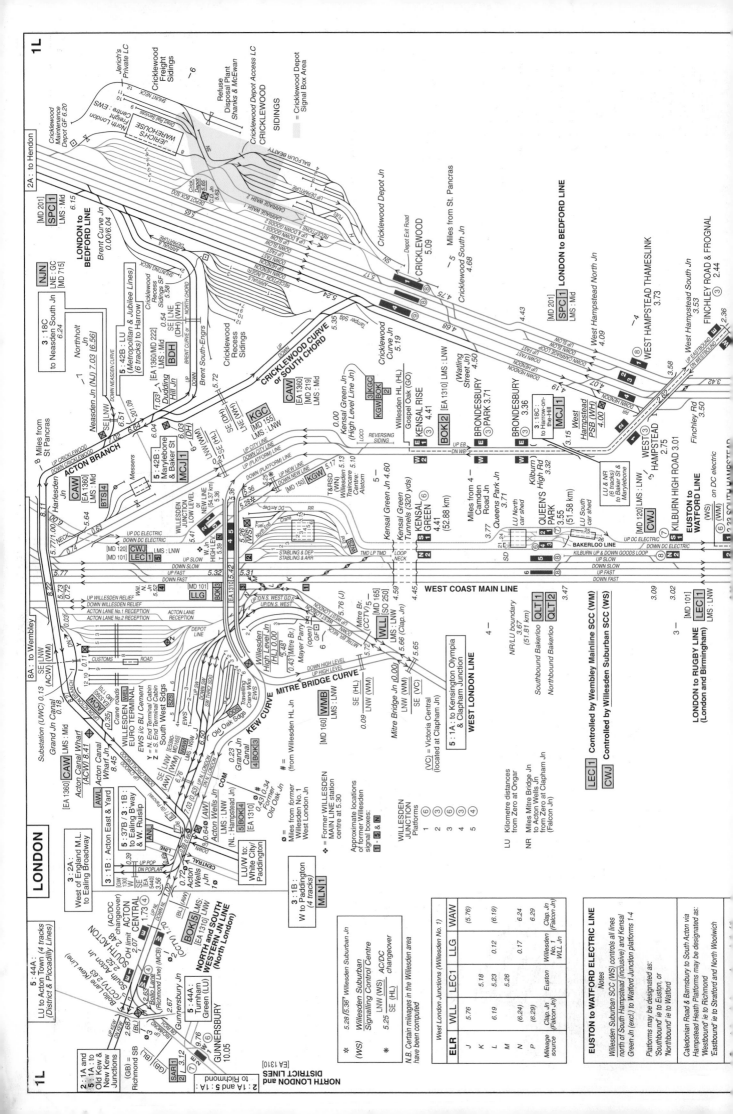

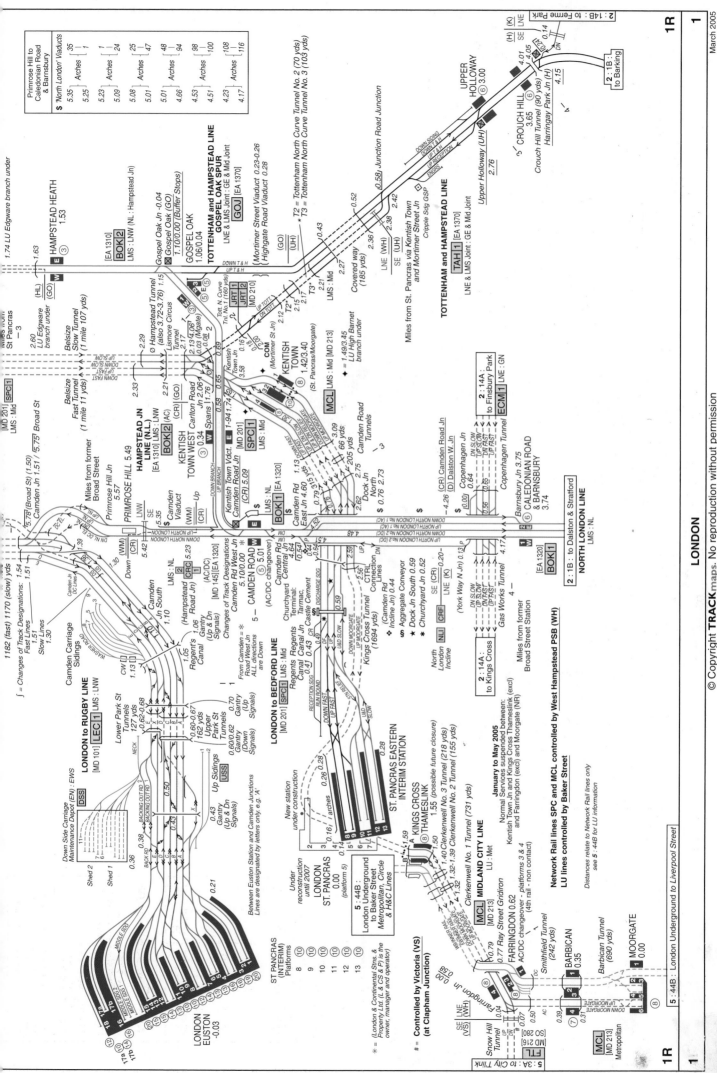

LONDON

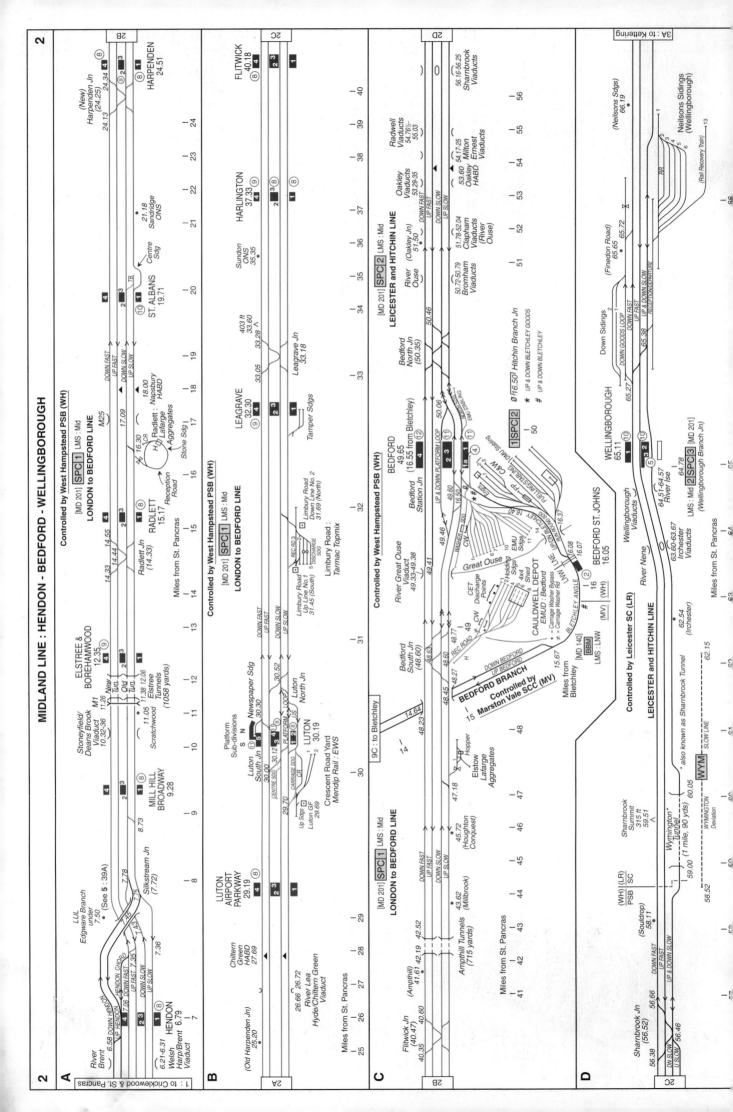

MIDLAND LINE : KETTERING - LEICESTER - SYSTON JN ● CORBY LOOP ● WIGSTON - HINCKLEY - (NUNEATON)

A — LEICESTER and HITCHIN LINE

Controlled by Leicester SC (LR)

KETTERING

Harrowden Jn
HABD 67.36
Harrowden Jn 67.00

Isham & Burton Latimer 69.27
(Finedon) 68.18

SPC 3 [MD 201]
LMS : Mid
DN MAIN
UP MAIN
DOWN FAST
UP FAST
UP & DOWN SLOW

Kettering South Jn 70.51
70.60
70.60

Kettering Station Jn 72.23
Kettering 72.01

Engrs/Hot Box Siding

Kettering North Jn 74.00
74.02
73.73
(Glendon North Jn) 74.77

Glendon Viaduct 75.22-75.26
(R. Ouse) 75.22-75.26

Geddington/ Harpers Brook Viaduct 77.38-50
Geddington HABD 77.08

Desborough Summit 436 ft 78.39

Market Harborough 82.74
Market Harborough Jn 82.47
82.01
NIRU

MARKET HARBOROUGH

Little Bowden 81.83 (LR)

KETTERING and MANTON LINE
LMS : Mid GSM1 [MD 601]

DN CORBY
UP CORBY
85.00 (Harringworth)
Harringworth Vdct max height 70 ft 82 arches
Welland Viaduct

Saton (206 yds, 82yds) 86.24-86.33
86.18-76

East Langton HABD 86.20

Seaton Tunnel (206 yds) 87.30

Glaston Tunnel (1mile, 82yds) 88.33

Watkins (UWC) 87.12

D — CORBY CORUS BRANCH

BSC BR
Corby North Jn 79.32 0.0
NFR 0.16
Warehouse Sdgs

Wincanton Distribution "Eurohub" [MD 610]
A6086 1.10
Water Works LC
A427

CORBY: CORUS Scrap
CORBY: CORUS Coil Unloading Pad
Overhead Crane

G. E. F. Co. Sdgs
Exchange & Oil Sdgs
Autolink Sdgs
Ramps

A6086 2.05
Signal MJ19

CORBY: AUTOMOTIVE TERMINAL
AUTOMOTIVE BRANCH
Controlled by Manton Jn (MJ)

Corby North Jn 79.32

CORBY 79.45
Corby 79.32
3D CORBY

Corby North Jn 79.58 79.49
RECEPTION RR

Corby Tunnel (1mile, 160yds) 80.74

LEICESTER and HITCHIN LINE
LMS : Mid SPC 3 [MD 201]
DOWN MAIN
UP MAIN
UP & DOWN CORBY

357 ft 78.65

Controlled by Manton Jn (MJ)

B — Controlled by Leicester SC (LR)

Corby North Jn 79.32 0.0

Kibworth 88.74
(Kibworth) 88.74
89.54 89.22 89.39
Cooks Lane (UWC) 92.35
93.49 Hills (UWC)

Kilby Bridge 93.40
DOWN MAIN UP MAIN
DOWN WC UP WC
UP & DOWN SLOW
UP FAST
DOWN FAST

Wigston South Jn 95.37
Wigston SOUTH CURVE
3 SPC4 [MD 201] LMS : Mid

WIGSTON SOUTH CURVE
WGP LMS : Mid [MD 231]

Glen Parva Jn 96.07
Glen Parva Jn 14.53
Brook's River Viaduct 13.58-55
(Blaby Jn) 13.40
(LR) SC

SOUTH WIGSTON 14.57 (5)
WNS [MD 232]
WIGSTON NORTH CURVE LMS : LNW
15.31 Wigston North Jn
96.02 [15.36]

AVOIDING LINE

95.76
DOWN MAIN UP MAIN

RUGBY and LEICESTER LINE

NARBOROUGH 11.67
(NB) Narborough 11.64
M1 Narborough 11.30
Narborough HABD
12.17
12.15
12.75 former GC Overbridge (107.24)

Hinks 13.55 (UWC)
(NH) SB

LEICESTER and BURTON LINE
KSL LMS : Mid [MD 525]
UP & DOWN BURTON

Knighton Old Sdgs-Engrs

former London Rd Jn

Knighton Jn (ex Knighton South Jn)
97.45 98.02
Knighton Tunnel (104 yds)

Leicester South Jn 98.07 98.36
98.74

Carriage Sidings

4 SPC5
LEICESTER 99.01 99.07

Leicester North Jn 99.30

Leicester SC 99.03

LMS : LNW

Croft Sidings 10.04
Croft Quarry : Bardon Aggregates
Loading Hopper 9.44

Lugons 10.31 (UWC)
Dunhams 11.05 (UWC)
[MD 232] WNS LMS : LNW

SOUTH LEICESTERSHIRE LINE

Thornmields 7.64 (UWC)
M69 7.46
Hollis 8.76 (UWC)
O'Neals 7.21 (UWC)

Fedge Hall 2.24 (UWC)
DN LEICS UP LEICS
Jericho 3.31 (UWC)
(HY) 3.70
HINCKLEY 4.00
HINCKLEY LINE (HY) (NW)

11B : to Nuneaton

Miles from Nuneaton (South Jn)

River Soar

M69 7.40

C — CADEBY LIGHT RAILWAY 2' 0" gauge 5 chains
5' gauge 2 chains Nov 2004

Loco Sdgs
CADEBY
Sutton Lane
UP N CURVE

3 — to Loughborough
4A : to Loughborough

SEN [MD 234] 0.17
SPC 5 [MD 201] GSM6 [MD 615]

Syston North Jn 104.25
UP N CURVE
DOWN FAST
UP FAST
DOWN MAIN UP MAIN
DN & UP PETERBORO
104.22 Syston East Jn
104.25
Syston South Jn 103.72
SYSTON 103.63
GSM6 [MD 615]

Thurmaston Wheelchex 101.78

Humberstone Road 100.20
UP DN GOODS
DOWN FAST UP FAST
SHUNT NECK
Humberstone Jn (100.20)
100.31

Bell Lane 99.59
No. 5 TOP SDG
REC No. 1
UP DN SLOW

Leicester Sidings

A Under the Box
B Accident Van Road
C Old Shed Side
D Coal Road 1
E Coal Road 2
F Coal Road 3
G Slip Road
H Pass Pit Road
J Goods Pit Road
K Fuel Road 1
L Fuel Road 2
M Shop Road
N Long Coal Road

Platforms 1 (13)
2-4 (14)
* All Platforms subdivided (a) south (b) north

7B : to Coalville & Burton

Leicester North 99.07

Loco Sidings (LR) EWS

SYSTON and PETERBOROUGH LINE

Mills from St Pancras via Leicester
2 GSM3 [MD 615]
(Leics) 113.36 meet
(Corby) 105.70 meet mileage

MELTON MOWBRAY 105.22
Melton Stn 105.27
Melton Jn
DALBY JN

SPC5 [MD 201]
DN FAST
UP FAST
UP & DN SLOW

River Eye

Langham Jn (MCB) 96.47
Ashwell Gate House (MCBR) 96.47
Ashwell (MCB) 96.67
Ashwell 99.69
Teigh (FPG) 99.01
(Ashwell) 99.15
River Eye 99.15

Whissendine 99.15

Oakham (CCTV) (O) 93.56
Brooke Road (CCTV) 92.00
(MCB) (O)
OAKHAM 93.61
Egleton (UWB) 92.27
Patersons (UWC) 91.24
Gunthorpe (UWC) 91.24

2 24D Peterborough (P)

Whissendine 99.15

Whitwell 99.67
(WCB) 99.67

Wymondham (MCB) 99.01

Miles from St Pancras via Corby

Manton North Jn 91.05
Manton Tunnel (749 yards)
Manton Jn GF
Manton South
Manton Jn (MJ) 90.18
1 GSM2 [MD 615]
Manton 0.00/90.25
(UWC) (R)
Manton Viaduct 88.65-89.09
(Great Glen) 91.44

KETTERING and MANTON LINE
LMS : Mid

Wing Tunnel (353 yards)
Wing Viaduct (River Chater)
89.54 89.22 89.39

PMJ LMS : Mid (Syston & Peterborough)

Castle Cement Co.
Loading Silos
Ketton Cement Works

Meadows Exchange Sdgs
Wards Sdgs GF
Ketton (K) 6.60

River Chater 1.03
Wing (UWC) 1.03

Manton Jn GF 0.14
0.50

Rutland Water

Luffenham (CCTV) 4.11
Luffenham (CCTV)
Naylors (UWC) 5.46

STAMFORD 10.11
Stamford Tunnel (341 yds)
1 STAMFORD 10.20-36
4 2 STAMFORD
River Welland
Hoods Mill (UWC) 11.08
Stapes (UWC) 11.67
Uffington 12.75
Cemetery Sdg
Brassey (UWC) 13.08
Ashmoke (UWC) 13.57
13.60
(UN) 2 24D

Miles from Manton Jn

4C : to Alstom Midlands Test Centre

March 2005
© Copyright TRACKmaps. No reproduction without permission

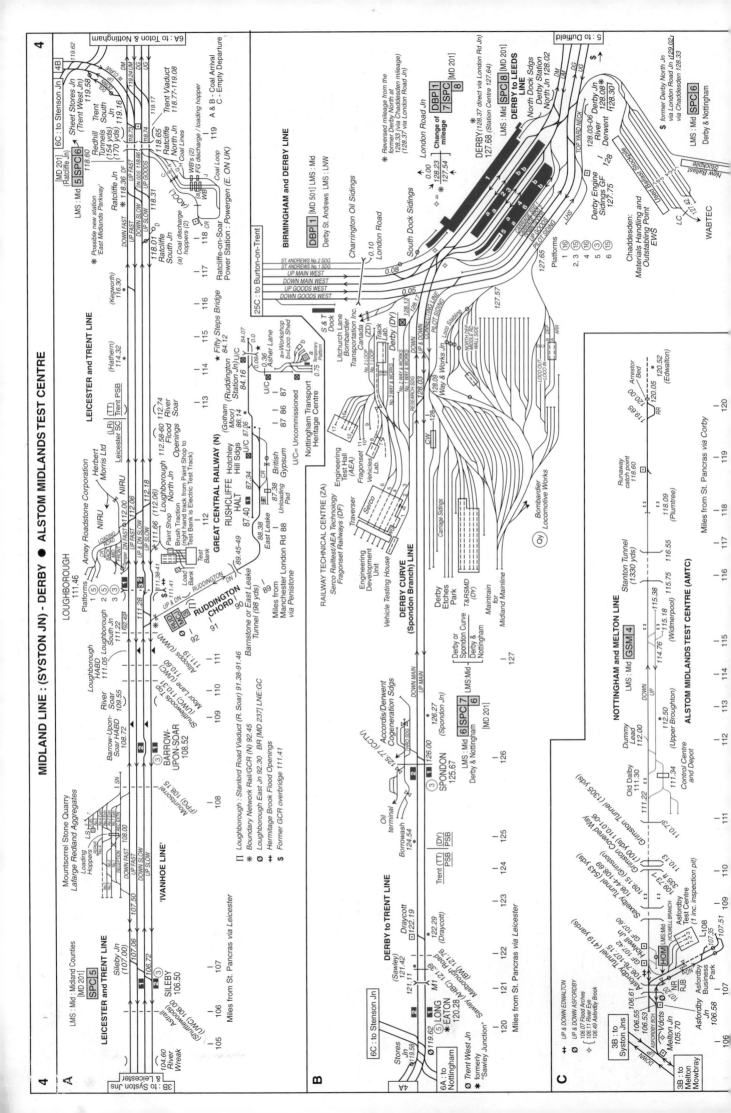

5

MIDLAND LINE : (DERBY) / LANGLEY MILL - CLAY CROSS - (CHESTERFIELD) ● WIRKSWORTH & MATLOCK BRANCHES ● NEWSTEAD - MANSFIELD

5

MATLOCK

7D : to Rowsley South

Peak Rail Sdg — Peak 145.24
Boathouse — GF
Bridge Road

CROMFORD 143.10 — Whitsey Tunnel (764 yards) 143.48
MATLOCK BATH 143.73
High Tor Tunnels

RAVENSTOR HALT
Lea Wood Bridge 141.58
Lea Wood Tunnel (315 yards)

WIRKSWORTH

WIRKSWORTH 142.04
WHATSTANDWELL 140.13
Whatstandwell Tunnel (149 yds)
High Peak Junction

AMBERGATE and ROWSLEY LINE

Miles from St Pancras via Leicester & Chaddesden

RD* = Derailer
C* = Cromford Viaduct 143.03-06
1* = High Tor No. 1 Tunnel (321 yards) 144.06-21
1A* = High Tor No. 1A Tunnel (59 yards) 144.21-24
2* = High Tor No. 2 Tunnel (378 yards) 144.24-41
H* = Holt Lane Tunnel (126 yards) 144.65-70

DERBY and LEEDS LINE
LMS : Mid

1 AJM

WIRKSWORTH BRANCH
Under Restoration (re-opening planned 2008)

(Hazelwood) 134.77
(May 2005)
Idridgehay 138.05

DJW [MD 243]

Ecclesbourne Valley Railway
(Wyvern Rail plc)
"MyTestTrack.com"

Controlled by Derby PSB (DY)

AMBERGATE
Ambergate South Jn
Ambergate North Jn

BELPER 135.55

BUTTERLEY 135.57
Midland Railway Trust Ltd

GOLDEN VALLEY LIGHT RAILWAY
2' 0" gauge

DUFFIELD 132.79
Milford Tunnel (855 yards)

SWANWICK JN 134.78

EREWASH VALLEY LINE
LMS : Mid

ALFRETON 136.07
Alfreton Tunnel (840 yards)

AVENUE COKING PLANT (closed)

2 : 28E : to Chesterfield

DERBY and LEEDS LINE (North Midland)
LMS : Mid

Clay Cross Tunnel (1 mile, 24 yards)
Clay Cross North Jn 142.10
Clay Cross South Jn

Coney Green Jn 141.24

SPC 9

Miles from St Pancras via Leicester & Toton

"ROBIN HOOD LINE"
LMS : Mid

SHIREBROOK 145.06
Shirebrook East Jn 145.62
W H Davis Wagon Works

LANGWITH-WHALEY THORNS 147.14

2 : 30A : to Worksop

Doe Hill Disposal Point
H. J. Banks

MANSFIELD WOODHOUSE 142.17
MANSFIELD 140.44

SUTTON PARKWAY 137.60

KIRKBY-IN-ASHFIELD 138.38
Kirkby Tunnel (198 yds)
Kirkby Summit

PINXTON BRANCH
PBS 1

LANGLEY MILL 129.68

NEWSTEAD 134.20

ROBIN HOOD LINE
RAC [MD 255] NRLINE: GC/GN

6D : to Hucknall & Nottingham

4B : to Derby
7A : to Toton

March 2005

© Copyright TRACKmaps. No reproduction without permission

TRENT JNS - NOTTINGHAM - (NEWARK) / BINGHAM ● TRENT JNS - STENSON JN ● NOTTINGHAM - NEWSTEAD

NOTTINGHAM EXPRESS TRANSIT (NET) 750dc

Controlled by Trent PSB (TT)

NOTTINGHAM Platforms
- a 1 b ⑳
- 2 ⑤
- a 3 b ⑳
- a 4 b ⑱
- a 5 b ⑱
- 6 ⑭

Trent Lane (footpath) 0.36
Snenton (MCB) 0.35

Nottingham TMD (NM)
Maintrain for Central Trains
Eastcroft Depot : Engrs 0.15

LNER : GN Nottingham London Road LL
(near Ø former London Road Jn)
PARCELS SDG

Gregory Boulevard
The Forest (Park & Ride)
High School
Nottingham Trent University
Royal Centre
Old Market Square
Lace Market
Broadmarsh (proposed)

* former GCR over at 123.43
Station St
Nottingham West Jn 123.52
Nottingham East Jn 123.27
NOTTINGHAM 123.39

(from St. Pancras via Corby and Plumtree)
Change of mileage 123.23

[MD 204] 2 TSN NOB1 NOTTINGHAM and LINCOLN LINE
LMS : Mid [MD 625] DERBY and NOTTINGHAM LINE

1 TSN 2 Mansfield Jn 124.22 (mileage meet)
[MD 252] LMS : Mid
MJT 1 Lenton North Jn 124.56
Radford Jn 125.55

NOTTINGHAM and MANSFIELD LINE
[MD 252] RAC 2 MJT 1 Lenton South Jn 125.27
LSN [MD 249] Lenton South Jn

RADFORD and TROWELL LINE
Moor Farm 128.7

Beeston South Sdgs (Non-operational)
Beeston South Jn 123.62
BEESTON 123.22
La Farge (Non-operational)
European Recycling
Attenborough Jn (AHBC) (CCTV) 121.38 / 121.70
ATTENBOROUGH 121.76
Barton Lane (AHBC) (CCTV) 121.61 [MD 264]
Meadow Lane (CCTV) 120.31
THL [MD 264]
AML [MD 264]
Meadow Lane Jn 121.02

7A : to Toton Yard & Trowell Jn
TOTON HIGH LEVEL GOODS LINE

EREWASH VALLEY LINE
Long Eaton (CCTV) 120.53
Long Eaton Town (CCTV) 120.36
Trent East Jn 119.69
North Erewash (CCTV)
COM 119.56
TES [MD 228]
SPC6 [MD 201]
Sheet Stores Jn 119.58
4B : to Derby
4A : to Loughborough
Trent South Jn 119.17

Controlled by Trent PSB (TT)

NOB1 LMS : Mid [MD 625]
GEDLING COLLIERY 126.45
Gedling Colliery 126.38
BURTON JOYCE (AHBC-X) 5.00 / 4.77
Netherfield CARLTON (Mid) Jn 2.35
Netherfield Jn (NL) 125.17
Netherfield (GN) 125.08
Colwick West Jn 119.62
2 NOG COM 125.25
DEX NGC [MD 645]
Derbyshire Extn (TMOG) 0.23
Victoria Road 0.00
Stoke Lane (AHBC-X) 3.54

NOTTINGHAM and LINCOLN LINE
LOWDHAM 7.31
Lowdham (AHBC-X) 7.27
THURGARTON 9.43
Gonalston (AHBC) 6.31
BLEASBY 10.55
Rolleston Jn 13.13
FISKERTON 12.46
Fiskerton Jn 12.03
ROLLESTON 12.46
Gorsey Lane (UWC) 11.36
Morton Lane (MGW) 12.43
Staythorpe Crossing 14.20
Averham Weir Viaduct
Arnolds Flood Bridge
Old Trent Dyke Vdct
Newark Castle 16.02
2 : 2BB : to Grantham & Sleaford
2 : 27D : to Newark Castle

Controlled by Trent PSB (TT)

NOTTINGHAM BRANCH (GN) [MD 635] NOG1 LINE : GN
RADCLIFFE (Notts) 123.08
Radcliffe Rectory Jn 123.71-53
BINGHAM 119.39
Bingham 119.57
Saxondale (UWC) 120.71
to former COTGRAVE COLLIERY
Cotgrave Colliery West Jn
CCBI1 [MD 640]
NR boundary

DERBYSHIRE EXTENSION BRANCH LINE : GN
Branch Sdgs Rectory Jn 123.72
Trent Fields Vdct 0.18
Rectory Jn (RJ) 123.76

[MD 625] NOB1 LMS : Mid NOTTINGHAM and LINCOLN LINE

ASLOCKTON 117.22
ELTON & ORSTON 115.34
BOTTESFORD 112.68
West Jn (BW) 113.78
Allington Jn 112
Bottesford West Jn 111.60
BW Allington Jn
Staythorpe Crossing
MAIN LINE
Newark Castle

Phoenix Park (Park & Ride)
Cinderhill Highbury Vale
David Lane
Basford
Wilkinson St (Park & Ride) & Depot
Shipstone St
Radford Rd
Beaconsfield St
Hyson Gm
Market
Radford Rd 125.55

"ROBIN HOOD LINE"
former GC over 132.76
Linby (ABCL) 132.24
Linby (FP) 132.00
Moss & Plums (FP) 132.00
HUCKNALL 131.65
Hucknall No. 3 (UWC) 131.11
Hucknall No. 4 (UWC) 131.04
Butler's Hill 131.21
Moor Bridge (Park & Ride)
Bulwell Forest 129.52
Bulwell Forest Crossing (CCTV)
BULWELL 128.76
Bulwell South Jn 128.65
Bestwood Park Jn 130.20
Bayles & Wylies (FPW) 130.32
River Leen 130.68
CALVERTON OOU
NEWSTEAD 134.20
5 : to Kirkby-in-Ashfield
4 : to Kirkby

Miles from St. Pancras via Corby
Miles from Kings Cross 124
Miles from Kings Cross via Leicester

NOTTINGHAM EXPRESS TRANSIT (NET) 750dc
Alongside Network Rail
RAC [MD 255] LMS : Mid : Nottingham & Mansfield

WILKINSON STREET TRAM DEPOT AND CONTROL ROOM (NET)
Wheel Lathe
Sanding
CW
Car Park
LC

NR Controlled by Trent PSB (TT)
RAC [MD 255] LMS : Mid : Nottingham & Mansfield

River Trent Viaduct 121.35
Whites (UWC) 121.35
Lock Lane Crossing (MCG)
Sheet Stores Jn 119.58
Trent West Jn 119.62
4B : to Derby
Sawmers (UWC) 120.88-59
Flood arches 120.44
Castle Donnington
Back Lane (LWCM) 123.63
Castle Donnington 123.28
DOWN CHELLASTON 123.33
Derby DY (TT) Trent TT
Elton (UWC) 124.57-50
R. Trent Vdct 124.49-47
Flood arches 124.66-62

2 SSJ MSJ1 SSJ1 [MD 520]
(Chellaston W. Jn) (Chellaston E. Jn) 127.34
'Stenson & Weston' LMS.MI 'Sawley & Weston' Derby and Melbourne
(Weston on Trent) 126.19
STENSON JN 127.27
UP STENSON
DOWN STENSON
132.18 Stenson Jn
25C : to Peartree & Derby
25C : to N. Stafford Jn & Burton-on-Trent
4B : to Derby
6A

Panel A

LMS : Mid [MD 207] TCC
EREWASH VALLEY LINE

Meadow Sidings
Network Rail Virtual Quarry

145.24 NR – PR
145.39 WL – PR
Used Ballast Sidings

Long Eaton Sdgs (OOU)

Former Down Marshalling Sidings
North Yard *(two systems of numbering)*

STAPLEFORD and SANDIACRE

Sandiacre Ballast Sidings EWS

Balfour Beatty Railway Engineering

Minor Materials Depot

FA = Fuel Avoiding Line
F1, F2 = Nos 1 and 2 Fuel Roads
T = Tank Road
5 & 6 NR Maintenance Sdgs
WL = Wheel Lathe
WP = Washing Plants

Weightwell Machine RR

Toton
TMD (TO)
EWS

Toton No.1
LC

Traction Maintenance School

Loco Stabling WP

Wagon Repair Sdg

Load Test Road

DN SHUNT NECK
DOWN MAIN
UP MAIN
DOWN HIGH LEVEL GOODS
UP HIGH LEVEL GOODS
UP & 8 INDEPENDENT

Old Bank Sdgs - West Storage

HUMP AVOIDING LINE
LOCO LINE
(former Hump)

New Bank Sidings
(former Up Arrival Lines)

Arrival Sidings

former Fan No. 2

TOTON YARDS

West Yard

Toton Centre GF

RECEPTION SDG No.2
RECEPTION SDG No.1

Wagon Repair Depot

TOTON HIGH LEVEL GOODS LINE

THL [MD 264] TCC

Long Eaton Town (CCTV) 120.52

Saffron Lane GF 98.02

DOWN
UP
UP SHUNT NECK

Miles from St. Pancras

6A : to Trent Junctions

Panel D

AJM 1 LMS : Mid 'Ambergate & Rowsley'

5 : to Matlock and Belper

PEAK RAIL *(Nov 2004)*
MATLOCK RIVERSIDE 145.32

Bridge 35 145.36
River Derwent 145.39

DARLEY DALE 147.10 147.15

South Yard Jn 146.76
South Yard
North Yard 147.26
Church Lane Crossing 147.47
147.30 147.47

ROWSLEY SOUTH 148.29
148.17
Loco Shed Engrs

Nanny Goat Crossing 143.43
Rowsley (A6) 148.39
Ash Pit
LC 148.39
Rowsley c.149.30

5 : to Langley Mill

TCC [MD 207] LMS : Mid DEX
EREWASH VALLEY LINE

Bennerley Viaduct (Shipley Gate) 128.57
Pollet's Lock No. 2 127.31
Awsworth Jn (former LNE : GN) (Derbyshire Extn) 128.09
Erewash Canal
Bennerley HABD 127.00
Erewash Viaduct No. 1 125.78

Stanton Works : Saint – Gobian Pipelines plc

REC LINE
(Trowell) 125.14
Trowell Jn 125.09 (via Nottingham)
[†30.56] 129.74 M1
–130

M1 DOWN

6A : to Radford Jn & Nottingham

MJT 2 [MD 252] LMS : Mid
RADFORD and TROWELL LINE

SIDING WHM TCC [MD 287]
124.00 M1

Stanton Gate SF (SG) 123.65 (OOU)

Stanton Gate North Jn 123.56
Stanton Gate SF (SF) (OOU) 123.72
(Stanton Gate)

Down Sdgs

Stanton Gate South

Up Sdgs (OOU)

Mapperley Goods Branch Line Jn WHM TCC
122.70

Mapperley Goods Branch

DOWN MAIN 123.46
DOWN HIGH LEVEL GOODS
RECEPTION LINES
UP GOODS

MAPPERLEY GOODS BRANCH

Stapleford & Sandiacre 122.47
Stapleford & Sandiacre SF 122.35
122.52 B5010
Overbridge 9

Overbridge 8D
122.32 A52

LC's
122.36 122.40

Miles from St. Pancras *via Leicester*
Controlled by Trent PSB (TT)

Panel B

KSL [MD 525] LMS : Mid LEICESTER and BURTON LINE

(River Soar) Aylestone Viaduct 98.36-42
98.53 former GC line (104.03)

Leicester (LR) (BH)

Kirby Muxloe 102.23 M1
Kirby Muxloe 102.36
101.49

BELVOIR ROAD HALT 1ch

SNIBSTON COLLIERY RAILWAY *(June 2004)*
2' 6" gauge 4' 8½' gauge
SNIBSTON CENTRAL 53ch 30ch

Desford (Sdgs) Desford Colliery 106.57
Lindridge Farm (UWB) 105.84
Desford (UWC) 104.65
Watsons (AJBC) 104.68

Bagworth (Bagworth & Ellistown) 109.16
Bagworth Jn 110.00
565 ft 109.77
REFUGE SDG

New Cliffe Hill : Stud Farm Quarry
Tarmac Roadstone
Midland Quarry Products 1.24

Cliffe Hill No.1 GF 110.63
Cliffe Hill No.2 GF 110.42
Old Cliffe Hill Sdg

Weighbridge 0.62
A511 (AOCL)
Overhead Loading point 1.10

Bardon Hill (BH) 111.23
Bardon Hill GF 111.40
(BOW)

Repair Sdgs

Bardon Hill Quarries
Workshop
Aggregate Industries

Coalville Jn 112.13

Coalville Station (ML) 112.66 (Coalville)

DN GOODS
UP GOODS

7C

DRAKELOW 'C' Power Station *(Closed)*
Hoppers WBs
River
C.Canal
buried
KGB LOOP
(open)

DRAKELOW PowerGen

a = South Dep
b = South Arr
c = North Arr
d = North Dep

Miles from St. Pancras

3B : to Knighton Jn

Panel C

KSL [MD 525] LMS : Mid LEICESTER and BURTON LINE

COALVILLE TOWN

Coalville Station (CCTV) 112.82 7B

Mantle Lane (ML) 113.05

RECEPTION
NECK DGL
Holding Sdgs

113.21
113.30
113.39
113.10

NIRU
EWS
OOU

(Station) 112.66
(Swannington)
Swannington (AJBC) 114.01
Swannington 114.04

Lounge Jn 116.60 116.67
UK Coal
Lounge Disposal Point
UK Coal
LOADING RR
CRIPPLE SDG
Pad
117.47 (Ashby)

Moira West Jn (MW) 120.67
DOWN GOODS
120.04 (Moira)
Hicks
Pad Lodge Sdg 119.40
UK Coal

Swains Park Sdgs Hepworth Properties
(ex Rawdon Colliery area)

Gresley (Gresley) 122.44
121.62 122.10 (DY) Derby
Gresley Tunnel (623 yds)
121.12
Pad
DN LEICESTER GOODS
UP LEICESTER GOODS

Nadins Swadlincote GF 124.200.00
Nadins Disposal Point 0.41
(ex Cadley Hill Colliery area)
UK Coal
Loading pad 0.22 0.45
WB

DRAKELOW East Curve Jn 125.17
Drakelow Power Sdgs

EAST CURVE
WEST CURVE
WEST CURVE
Drakelow West Curve Jn 125.76-126-00

River Trent Vdct 125.59
River Trent Jn 125.61-70
Flood Viaduct

Birmingham Curve Jn 126.40
125.22 125.55
DEP ARR

25C : to Branston Jn :: to Burton on Trent

Miles from St. Pancras

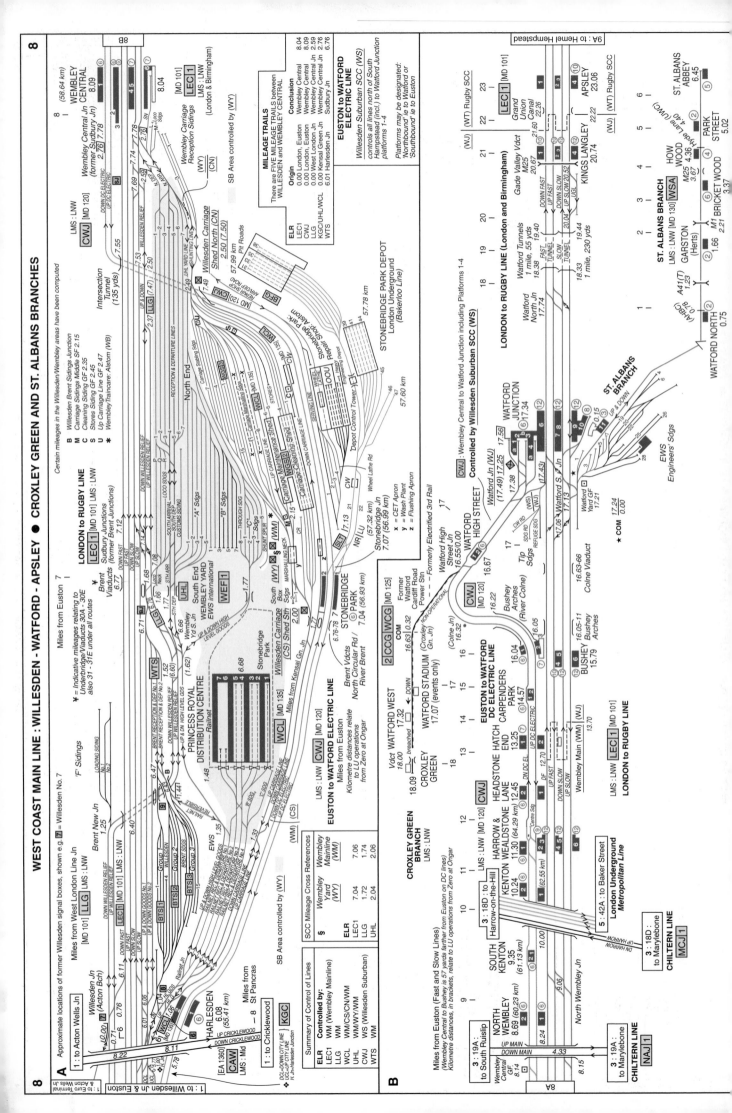

WEST COAST MAIN LINE : HEMEL HEMPSTEAD - WOLVERTON ● BLETCHLEY - (BEDFORD)

A

8B : to Watford Jn

HEMEL HEMPSTEAD (12) 24.39
BACK RD Boxmoor Sdgs 24.14

Miles from Euston

Bourne End Jn 25.40
Grand Union Canal 25.21
25.22
25.64
(a) Point ends (b)

BERKHAMSTED (12) 27.75
28.76
Northchurch HABD 29.47
FAST LINES
Northchurch Tunnels (349 yds) 29.12
DS US

Controlled by Rugby SCC (WT)

Rugby SCC (WT) (TK)
TRING 31.50
Tring South Jn 31.30
H RELIEF
TRING Platforms 1 2 3-5
Tring Sdgs

Tring North Jn 32.00

LEC 1 [MD 101]
DOWN FAST
UP FAST
DOWN SLOW
UP SLOW

CHEDDINGTON (12) 36.08
Ledburn Jn (37.35) 37.15 37.58
Grand Union Canal 34.53
34.60 Cheddington Wheel Chex
(a) Point ends (b)

LONDON to RUGBY LINE (London & Birmingham) LMS : LNW

Controlled by Rugby SCC (TK)

LEIGHTON BUZZARD (12) 40.14
Linslade Tunnels (287 yards) (down fast 283 yds)
40.60 40.73 MIDDLE DF US

Stoke Hammond HABD's 42.68 42.60
(TK) (BY) 43.43 (TK) (BY)

9B

B

3 : 13A : to Oxford
Miles from Bletchley Station 1.28
1.29 Stop blocks & gate Line closed to 11m 79c
Swanbourne Siding 1—
0.64 COM 0.00
(former Bletchley Chord Jn) 46.08

OXD [MD 735]
OXFORD BRANCH LMS : LNW
Bletchley Flyover Junction
UP OXFORD
DOWN OXFORD
BR BFO [MD 735]
(0.06) (MD 735)

Bletchley South Jn (45.46) 45.46

LEIGHTON BUZZARD RAILWAY LTD 2' 0" gauge

Nov 2004

PAGE'S PARK 0.00
Loco. & Carriage shed
Western Avenue
Stanbridge Road
Vandyke Road
(VANDYKE ROAD HALT)
2.08
Appenine Way
Leedon Loop 1.10
Hocklffe Road
Fifty Penny Curve
Stanley Hill
Redlands

STONEHENGE WORKS

Shed
Works
Stonehenge
Mundays Hill 3.00

BLETCHLEY

BLETCHLEY Platforms
1 (12)
2 (12)
3 (9)
4 (9)
5 (6)
6 (6)

Bletchley PSB (BY) 46.46
46.54/0.04
46.38
46.43 46.56
a b c
a = Bletchley Sth. or Cambridge Jn
b = Bletchley Middle
c = Bletchley East Jn 0.17
z = Ready Mixed Concrete Discharge Point

Parcels Sdgs
Miles from Euston
LEC 1 [MD 101]
Bletchley Nth 47.33
Up Yard
DOWN FAST
DOWN SLOW
UP SLOW
UP FAST
DOWN GOODS
UP GOODS
Carriage Sdgs
Up CW
Up Arrival
EWS
Wagon M'tce Sdgs
BDL
BLTD
Field Sdgs
DHE [MD 735]
BR
TMD Silverlink (BY)
Engrs'
Refuelling Road
EMU Stabling
BLT 2 [MD 135]
Bletchley Yard
Top Yard
S&T
Bletchley Cambridge GF 0.52
Bletchley Cambridge GF 0.49
BBM
DOWN CAMBRIDGE 0.40
UP CAMBRIDGE 0.23
BFO [MD 740]
BR
CAMBRIDGE FLYOVER 1.23
Cambridge Flyover Single Line Jn
Cambridge Single Line Jn
LEC BBM 46.46 0.00 COM
Summit of Flyover Jn 0.68
0.66

Denbigh Hall South Jn 47.52
Denbigh Hall North Jn (48.48) 48.53 48.31
A5(T) 47.72
A5(T) Flyover Jn 1.71
NECK
0.53 0.36 0.17 1.00 1.37

9C

9A

WOLVERTON WORKS (ZN) Alstom Railcare Ltd (Not Verified)

a = Cell shop
b = Tin Shop
c = Brass Shop
d = Traction Shop
e = High Voltage Test Bay
f = Final Inspection
g = Paint Shop

Timber Shed
Timber Store
Road Vehicle Shop
Wheel Shop
Lifting Shop
Heavy Repair Shop
West Repair
East Repair
Press Bay
Rebuilding Shop
Trimming Shop
Initial Examin'n
No. 30 Stores
No. 20 Stores

WKS 1
WKS 2

LC's Church Lane
Train Store
Bibby Transport & Warehousing Facilities Ltd

UNDER THE ROAD

Wolverton HABD 51.72
Wolverton 51.66 51.60
SDG
INCLINE
WOWM Wolverton Centre GF 52.05
Wolverton South GF 51.66
CENTRE SDGS
Wolverton Deviation 51.40 - 52.72 (35 Yards Longer)
WOLVERTON (12) 52.33
52.18 52.40 52.42
Grand Union Canal
B = Back of the wall

Rugby SCC (KR)
(KR) (BY) 52.68
52.72-53.01 Wolverton / Haversham Viaduct
DF DS US

Castlethorpe 54.60 54.24

10A : to Northampton

Milton Keynes CENTRAL 49.65
5 (15) 4 (15) 3 (15) 2 (15) 1 (14)
DOWN FAST
UP FAST
DOWN SLOW
UP SLOW

LONDON to RUGBY LINE (London & Birmingham) LMS : LNW

Controlled by Bletchley PSB (BY)

C — BEDFORD BRANCH "MARSTON VALE LINE" LMS : LNW BBM [MD 140]

Controlled by Marston Vale SCC (MV)

Miles from Bletchley
A = Grand Union Canal
B = A5(T)

Fenny Stratford Bletchley Flyover Jn
0.76
A B
0.9 1.36 CAMBRIDGE
(CCTV) UBD
(CCTV) 1.13
FENNY STRATFORD 1.05
1.42
BOW BRICKHILL 2.05 (2)
1.48 (4)
WOBURN SANDS 4.08 (2)
DM UM
ASPLEY GUISE 5.04 (2)
Berry Lane (WMV) (CCTV) 4.71
RIDGMONT 6.59
Marston Vale SCC (MV)
Marston Vale (NLC) 6.9
M71 6.41
Brogborough (MMV) 5.33
(CCTV)
LIDLINGTON 8.49 (3)
Marston (AHBC-X) 9.02 (CCTV)
MILLBROOK (Beds) 10.05 (3)
STEWARTBY 11.17 (2)
Stewartby Brickworks (CCTV) 11.33
Green Lane (AHBC-X) (CCTV)
FORDERS SIDINGS
Shanks & McEwan Waste Disposal Terminal
Local Distribution Centre EWS
Maintenance
NBS New Ballast Stockpile
Loading Dock Sdg 11.55
CR LC
Woburn Broadmead (CCTV) 12.08
KEMPSTON HARDWICK 12.76
AHBC-X (CCTV) 12.17
SPUR ON BED UP BED DN MAIN UP MAIN

2C : to Bedford

© Copyright TRACKmaps. No reproduction without permission

9

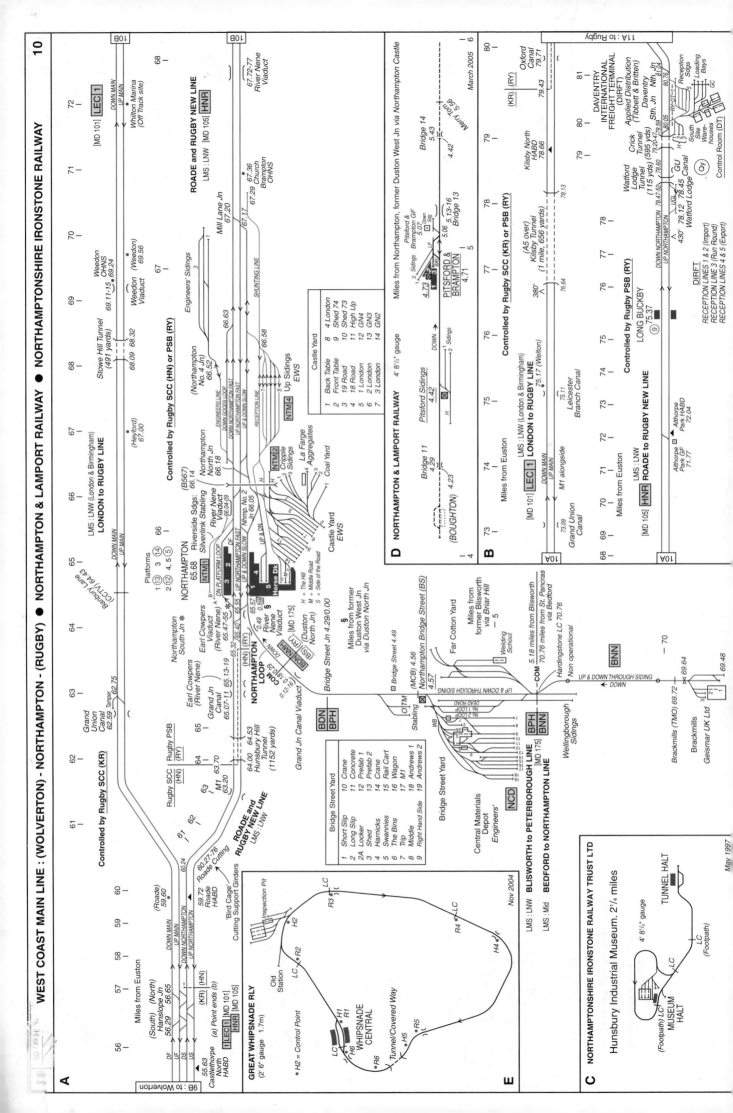

WEST COAST MAIN LINE : (WOLVERTON) - NORTHAMPTON - (RUGBY) ● NORTHAMPTON & LAMPORT RAILWAY ● NORTHAMPTONSHIRE IRONSTONE RAILWAY

10

WEST COAST MAIN LINE : RUGBY - NUNEATON - TAMWORTH

A

LONDON to RUGBY LINE (London & Birmingham)

[MD 101] LEC 1

LMS : LNW

Controlled by Rugby SCC (KR) or PSB (RY)

Routes in close proximity:
LEC1 80.00 (LEC1) and
HNR 82.15 to Rugby Flyover
former Hillmorton SB at
80.30 (LEC1) and
82.58 (HNR),
controlled both routes

Platforms
1 ㉑
2 ⑳
3 ⑥
6 ⑥
7 ⑥
8 ⑧

Miles from Euston
80 · 81 · 82 · 83

Daventry North Jn 80.76
Oxford Canal 81.04
§ former Hillmorton
81.16
82* MP's on other side of line
83*
84*
Miles from Euston via Northampton

(KR) (TK) (WT) (HN)

10B : to Northampton & Roade

Clifton Rd Line overbridge
Northamp. Line Jn
Former GC line overbridge
Peterborough Branch Sdg

Rugby South Jn 82.26
Rugby PSB (RY) 82.25
RUGBY 82.40
84.68
Rugby North Jn 82.70
Carriage Sidings

DOWN FAST
UP FAST
DOWN SLOW
UP SLOW
UP GOODS
DOWN GOODS
UP & DOWN ENGINE
Depot Line

RGY1 1
RGY2
LEC2 1 RBS 1
RBS 1

Rugby SCC 82.60
LHS FRONT SDG 1
ARRIVAL SDG
New Ballast Stockpile
North Side
Up Sidings
EWS

(KR) Wolverton (excl) – Kilsbury Tunnel
(TK) Tring – Leighton Buzzard
(WT) Kings Langley (excl) – Tring
(HN) Hanslope – Northampton (excl)

Minor Variations occur concerning
the junction mileages with ELR's ❖

Rugby Trent Valley Jn 83.18

Rugby PSB (RY)

Controlled by Rugby PSB (RY)

RUGBY and BIRMINGHAM LINE (London and Birmingham)

TRENT VALLEY LINE
LMS : LNW

Miles from Euston
84 · 85 · 86 · 87 · 88 · 89 · 90 · 91 · 92 · 93

14B : to Coventry

[MD 101] LEC 2

Avon Viaduct 84.04–09
High Oaks 85.20
Oxford Canal 85.46
Brinklow 87.72 DPL
Oxford Canal 88.00
Oxford Canal 89.61
Shilton HABD's 91.26–30
Nettle Hill Viaduct 89.51
M6 91.30
M69 91.63

(RY) (NN) Rugby (RY) (NN) Nuneaton

11B

RUGBY and LEAMINGTON LINE
LMS : LNW

New Bilton Jarvis 0.79
Bilton West 0.71
Bilton East 0.58
UP BIRMINGHAM
DOWN BIRMINGHAM

83.52 · 83.53 · 83.47 · 83.29 · 83.28 · 83.23 · 83.32 · 83.20 · 83.15 · 83.14 · 83.08 · 0.20 · −0.05

Rugby On Track machines
Wiring Train

ROADE and RUGBY NEW LINE
LMS : LNW

HNR [MD 105]

B

Saltley PSB (SY)
18 : to Water Orton

Miles from Whitacre Jn
Abbey Jn 9.60
Miles from Water Orton 9.20
(NN)

DOWN ARLEY
UP ARLEY

[MD 555] DNW

Ashby Jn 97.51

Hartshill Sidings
Non-operational
South GF 99.36
North GF @ 99.48

Miles from Coventry North Jn
5 · 6 · 7

Hawkesbury Lane (HL) 4.71
Hawkesbury La Up Side Frame 4.50
M6 REC SDG

Chivers Coton Vdct 8.66–70
Attleborough Road Vdct 9.26–32

Bedworth 6.29
Murco Petroleum (Calor Gas)
Calor Gas Sdgs GF 5.37

COVENTRY and NUNEATON LINE
LMS : LNW

CNN [MD 410]

Miles from Coventry
4 · 5 · 6

14B : to Coventry

NUNEATON 97.10 · 97.11
10.15 · 10.44 · 10.45

Nuneaton South Jn
Nuneaton PSB (NN) 96.65

COM 0.00 10.61
WNS NSA

Platforms
1 ⑧
2 ⑰
3 ⑮
4 ⑰
5 ⑲
6,7 ⑦

NSA [MD 232]
LMS : Mid

COM WNS NSA
Horse Coventry landing
Down Sdgs

DOWN SLOW
UP SLOW
DOWN FAST
UP FAST
DOWN MAIN
UP MAIN

96.64
95.49
94.61

Bedworth 5 · 6 · 7
Platforms
1 5 6 7

SOUTH LEICESTERSHIRE LINE
LMS : LNW
WNS [MD 232]

DN & UP LEICESTER
DOWN LEICESTER
UP LEICESTER

Ashby Canal 94.61
River Anker Viaduct 96.36–38

(former Nuneaton Midland Jn) 0.58
Miles from former Nuneaton South Jn

TRENT VALLEY LINE
LMS : LNW

11A

Saltley PSB (SY)
18 : to Water Orton

Miles from Euston
99 · 100 · 101 · 102 · 103 · 104 · 105 · 106 · 107 · 108 · 109 · 110

[MD 101] LEC 2 **TRENT VALLEY LINE**
LMS : LNW

ATHERSTONE
102.23 (Baddesley) 103.05
Coventry Canal 102.68
Coventry Canal 105.59
POLESWORTH 106.39
M42 106.72
Polesworth North Viaduct 106.49–53
Polesworth South Viaduct 105.71–75 (River Anker)

(NN) (TH)

TAMWORTH (HIGH LEVEL)
Tamworth Vdct 109.70 (River Anker) 23.58
109.73 · 109.43 · 109.54 · 109.78 · 110.01 · 110.23 · 110.12

TAMWORTH (LOW LEVEL) (TH)
(NN) (TH)

Tamworth Low Level (TH)
18 : to Water Orton
12A : to Lichfield

Platforms
1 ⑭
2 ⑩
3, 4 ⑫

18 : to Wichnor Jn
DBP [MD 501]

BIRMINGHAM and DERBY LINE
LMS : Mid

Controlled by Saltley PSB (SY)

11

March 2005

© Copyright **TRACK**maps. No reproduction without permission

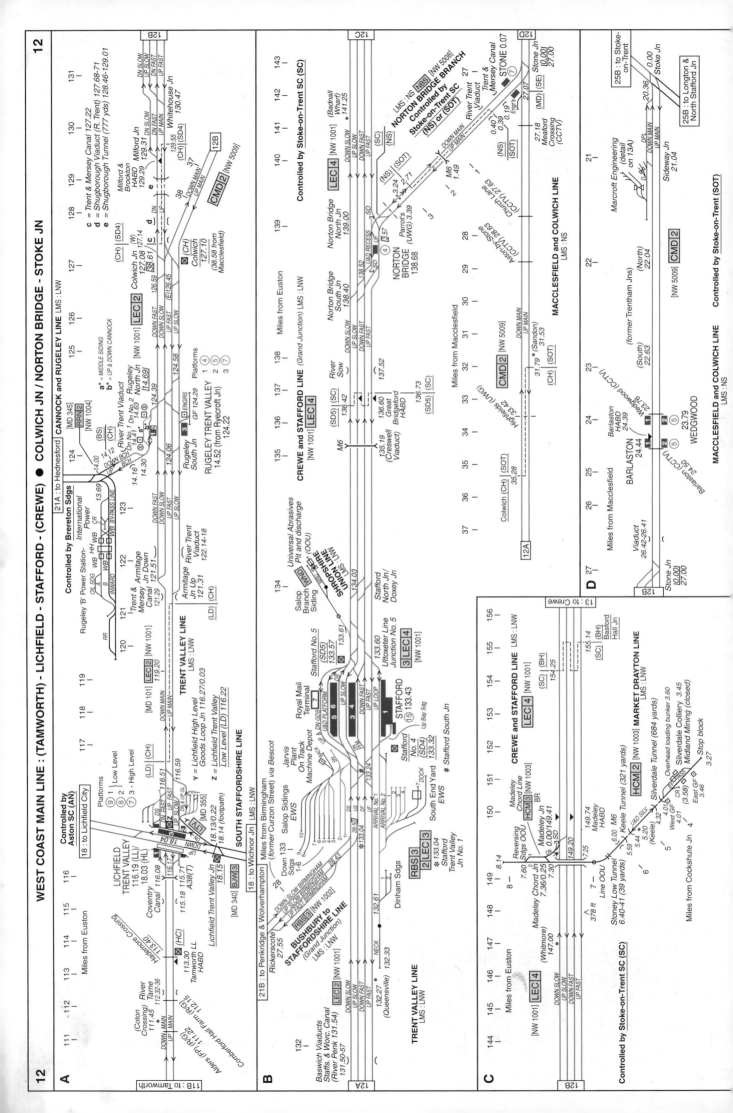

13

12D : to Stoke

12D : to Wedgewood

Trent & Mersey Canal

STOKE ON TRENT
Wagon Works

Marcroft Engineering

CMD 2
[NW 5009]

Sideway Jn
21.04

Traversers

Wheel Bay
Bogie Shop
Main Workshop one
Wshop two
Paint Shop

DOWN PASSENGER LOOP
DOWN MAIN UP MAIN

Gas
freeing,
purging
& steaming
sidings

p = Paint Booth
s = Shotblast Booth
z = Hoist

100 metres

35C : to Chester

Traverser
Brakes
Engine Services
Electrical
Wheel Shop
Electrical Reprs
Core Plant
Bogie Shop
Repairs

CREWE WORKS (ZC)
Bombardier Transportation

Crewe Steelworks
(SW) 159.41

UP MAIN
DOWN MAIN
159.55

Works Training School
158.77 159.01
THRO'
West Side
East Side
Wheel Lathe
159 —

* 1 also equipped with DC conductor Rail
Z = WISTASTON ROAD 159.24 (EMD Platform)
5-8 = SHED ROADS 1-4
11 = ELEC LOCO RR

Crewe Electric EMD (CE) EWS

CNH1 [NW 3001]

23A : to Nantich & Shrewsbury

CREWE and SHREWSBURY LINE LMS : LNW

Sdgs 5, 10, 11 Jarvis
6, 9 Marcroft
7, 8 Wabtec

Gresty Lane : Western Sidings

SYC [NW 1007]

Gresty Down Sidings GF

Gresty Lane Sdgs

Gresty Green Sidings
EWS Maintenance

Gresty Lane (GL)
Gresty Road Engrs
Gresty Road S & T

CSG SYC GSG

Salop Goods Jn

CREWE and CHESTER LINE LMS : LNW

Railway Age Heritage Centre

Exhibition Hall

Crewe Signalling Centre (CE) 158.21

LMS · LNW
CREWE and BIRDSWOOD LINE (Grand Junction)

LEC 5 CGJ1

Crewe Coal Yard (CY) 158.68

26A : to Winsford

43B : to Sandbach

BHI 1 CMP1

Sydney Bridge Jn
159.03

Thomas Street Engrs'

CREWE and STOCKPORT LINE LMS : LNW

Crewe North Jn 158.18

LLI Tunnel (394 yards)

CMP1 [NW 5001]

CREWE 158.03

Platforms

CREWE JUNCTIONS
A Stoke Line Jn
B Shrewsbury Line Jn
C Chester Line Jn
D Manchester Line Jn

Crewe Diesel Depot (CD) EWS

Crewe Down Holding Sdgs

Crewe South Jn 157.60

Coal Sidings (DRS)

Direct Rail Services EWS (Res)

South Yard

Crewe Carriage Sheds (1 & 2) LNW (CP)

Brook Carriage Sdgs

North Stafford Jn (Crewe) 7.52

CREWE BRANCH (NS) LMS : NS

KCS 1&2 [NW 1005]

Miles from Kidsgrove

CREWE and STAFFORD LINE (Grand Junction) LMS : LNW

LEC 4 [NW 1001]

Basford Hall Jn (BH) 156.23

Basford Hall Wood GF 157.03

New Middle Sdgs

CREWE LOCAL DISTRIBUTION CENTRE
(except Siding 17)

Carillon : On Track Plant
Crewe Wagon Shop
Track Materials Handling

Basford Hall Up Sdgs

Basford Hall Down Sdgs

Crewe Sorting Sidings North SB (NY) 157.23
Crewe Sorting Siding Middle 156.66

(A500)

Miles from Euston

LEC 4

43A : to Kidsgrove

RADWAY GREEN 4.03

Lower Radway Green (UWG) 4.26

Barthomley Jn 4.67

Barthomley (MWLG) 4.77

12C : to Stafford

UP & DOWN POTTERIES

© Copyright TRACKmaps. No reproduction without permission

March 2005

13

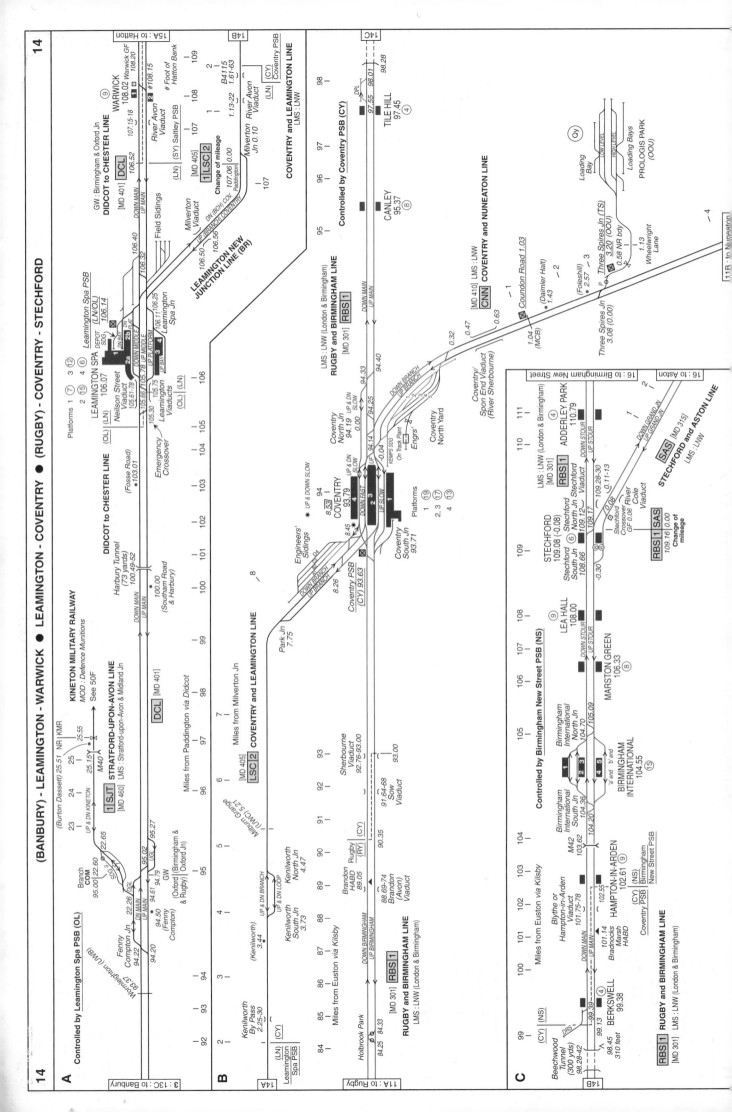

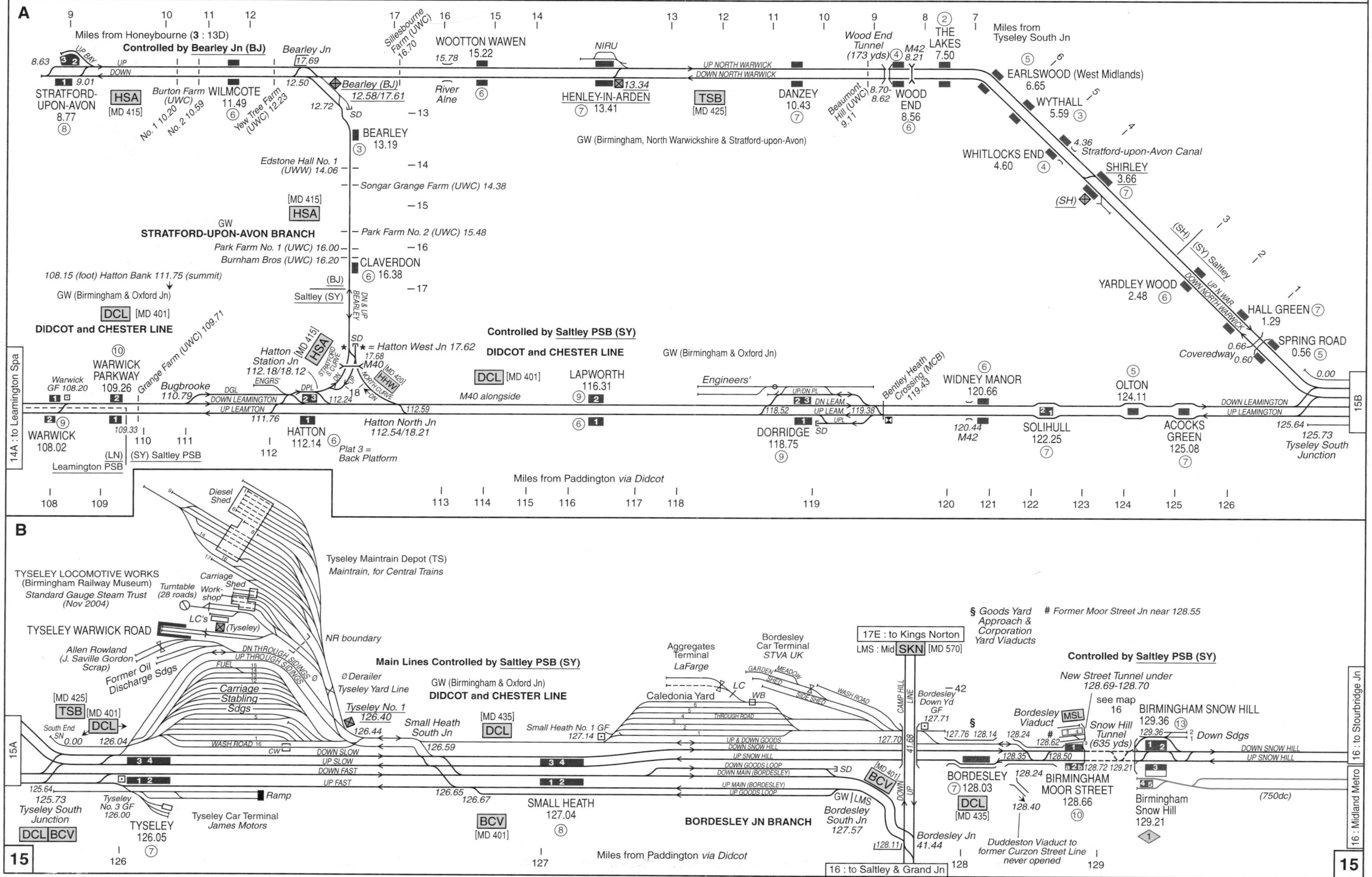

This is a detailed railway track diagram (schematic map) of the North Warwick Line and Warwick–Tyseley area. The diagram is rendered as a technical line map with track layouts, station names, mileages and signalling box control annotations.

Key locations and annotations labelled on the diagram include:

Panel A (upper section):
- SPRING ROAD 0.56 (5) 0.00
- HALL GREEN (7) 1.29
- SHIRLEY (7) 3.66
- YARDLEY WOOD (6) 2.48
- WHITLOCKS END 4.60
- WYTHALL 5.59 (3)
- EARLSWOOD (West Midlands) 6.65 (5)(6)
- THE LAKES (2) 7.50
- WOOD END 8.56 (6), Wood End Tunnel (173 yds)
- DANZEY 10.43 (7)
- HENLEY-IN-ARDEN 13.41 (7), NIRU
- WOOTTON WAWEN 15.22 (6), River Alne 15.78
- BEARLEY 13.19 (3), Bearley Jn 17.69, Bearley (BJ) 12.58/17.61
- WILMCOTE 11.49 (6)
- STRATFORD-UPON-AVON 8.77 (8)
- ACOCKS GREEN 125.08 (7)
- OLTON 124.11 (5)
- SOLIHULL 122.25 (7)
- WIDNEY MANOR 120.66 (6)
- DORRIDGE 118.75 (9)
- LAPWORTH 116.31
- HATTON 112.14 (6), Hatton Station Jn, Hatton West Jn 17.62, Hatton North Jn
- WARWICK PARKWAY 109.26 (10)
- WARWICK 108.02 (9)
- Tyseley South Junction 125.73 / 125.64

Panel B (lower section):
- BIRMINGHAM SNOW HILL 129.36 (13), Snow Hill Tunnel (635 yds) 128.69-128.70
- BIRMINGHAM MOOR STREET 128.66 (10)
- BORDESLEY 128.03 (7), Bordesley Jn 41.44
- SMALL HEATH 127.04 (8), Small Heath South Jn 126.59
- TYSELEY 126.05 (7), Tyseley No.1 126.40
- TYSELEY WARWICK ROAD
- TYSELEY LOCOMOTIVE WORKS (Birmingham Railway Museum), Standard Gauge Steam Trust (Nov 2004)
- Tyseley Maintrain Depot (TS), Maintrain, for Central Trains
- Bordesley Car Terminal STVA UK
- Aggregates Terminal LaFarge, Caledonia Yard
- Midland Metro 16 : to Stourbridge Jn

Control / signalling annotations:
- Controlled by Bearley Jn (BJ)
- Controlled by Saltley PSB (SY)
- DIDCOT and CHESTER LINE
- GW (Birmingham & Oxford Jn)
- GW (Birmingham, North Warwickshire & Stratford-upon-Avon)
- Miles from Honeybourne (3 : 13D)
- Miles from Tyseley South Jn
- Miles from Paddington via Didcot
- New Street Tunnel under 16 see map
- 17E : to Kings Norton LMS : Mid [SKN] [MD 570]
- 16 : to Saltley & Grand Jn
- 14A : to Leamington Spa
- 15A / 15B

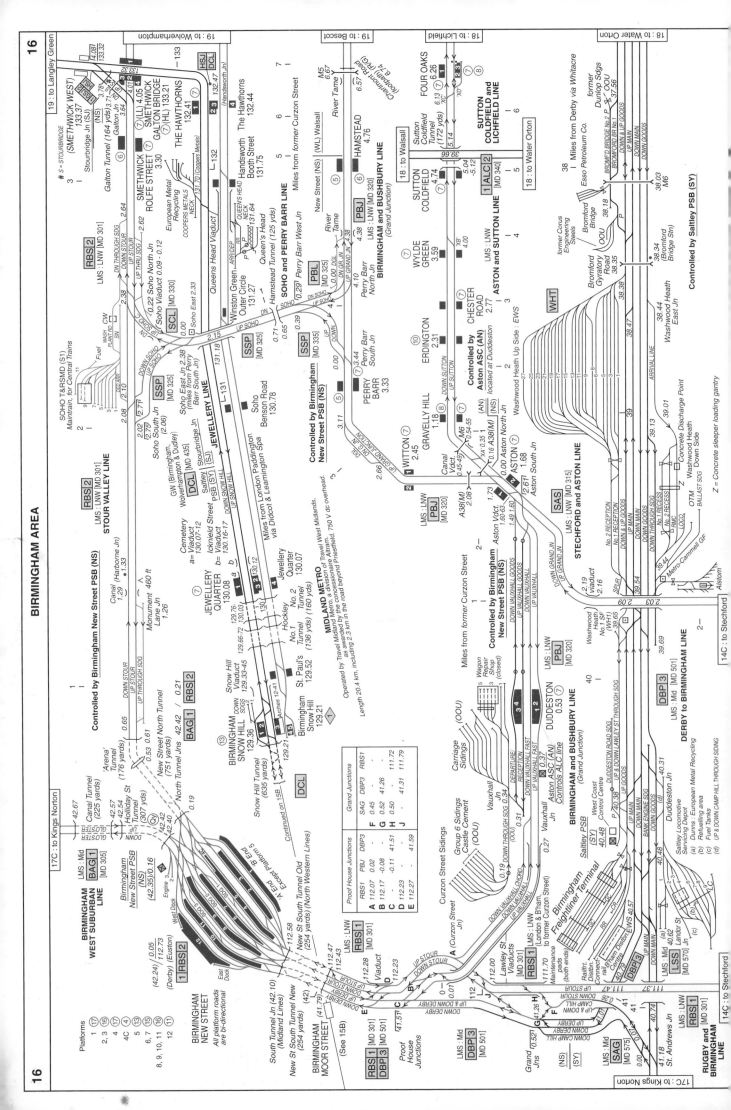

A LLANGOLLEN RAILWAY

Miles from Llangollen Line Junction

Jan 2005

Llangollen Station
5.38
LLANGOLLEN 5.44
5.35

Pentrefelin Sidings

Ffordd Jn 5.75

Berwyn Viaduct (77 yds) 7.10-07
BERWYN 7.05
7

Carriage Works 6.37-33
River Dee 6.04
Llangollen Goods Jn

Berwyn Tunnel (689 yds)
7.56
8.07 Deeside 8.62
DEESIDE HALT 8.64

DOWN

GLYNDYFRDWY 10.57
10.52 / 10.53

Carrog 12.63
CARROG 12.66
13

Proposed extension to Corwen 15.50
12.75

B GREAT CENTRAL RAILWAY

Miles from Manchester London Road (GC) via Penistone

May 2005

Former Belgrave & Birstall Station 100.44
LEICESTER NORTH 100.59

100

Rothley Carriage Works
ROTHLEY 97.72
97.73
P = Paintshop

Swithland Sidings 97.18
UP GOODS LOOP
UP MAIN
DOWN MAIN
DOWN GOODS LOOP

Swithland Dock

Swithland Viaducts (Sw. Reservoir)
96.52-55 96.61-68

ANNESLEY and QUAINTON ROAD LINE
LNE : GC
MCJ3

Quorn 95.16
LIE-BYE
QUORN & WOODHOUSE 95.06

95

94

A6 (T) 93.61
UP LOOP
UP MAIN
DOWN MAIN

LOUGHBOROUGH CENTRAL 93.02

Loughborough South Carriage Sdgs

Loco Shed
Loughborough North 92.66
92.59

93

C BIRMINGHAM WEST SUBURBAN LINE / BIRMINGHAM and GLOUCESTER LINE

16 : to Saltley & Grand Jn
16 : to Birmingham New Street

Qy

Bath Row Tunnel (210 yards)
Granville Street Tunnel (225 yards)
Canal Tunnel (81 yards)
42.40
Holliday Street Tunnel (307 yards) 42.54
43.07-01
42.42-17
42.38-25
41

Bordesley Jn 41.44
St. Andrews Jn
41.18
41.68
122.70 122.71
DCL BCV
15B : to Tyseley
15B : to Birmingham Snow Hill
42.29

FIVE WAYS 43.18
43.46
43.61-56 / 43.46
42

Granville Street Tunnel (225 yards)

Miles from Derby via Whitacre & New Street
LMS : Mid BAG 1 [MD 305]
BIRMINGHAM WEST SUBURBAN LINE

Worcester & Birmingham Canal
UNIVERSITY 44.73
Church Road Tunnel (106 yards)

New St (NS)
Saltley (SY) 44
Miles from Derby via Whitacre
43.54 43.47
43

Moseley Tunnel (155 yards)

SKN [MD 570]

Selly Oak Viaduct 45.42-32
SELLY OAK 45.50
45.74
45

BOURNVILLE 46.58
for Cadbury World

BIRMINGHAM and GLOUCESTER LINE
LMS : Midland

HAZELWELL 45.07
45

UP CAMP HILL
DOWN CAMP HILL

Lifford East HABD 46.00
Lifford West Jn 46.36
LEL
[MD 580]

Lifford East Jn 46.11

Pershore Road Tunnel (62 yards)
47.37-34
Kings Norton Jn 46.59
KINGS NORTON 46.42
COM
BAG 2 SKN
*Kings Norton Jn
*48.02 via New Street
*46.77 via Camp Hill
47.64
47.48
2 BAG 1
2 BAG SKN
46.42

On-track Plant Depot
RAMP ROAD
NECK
ARR & DEP

48
LMS : Mid [MD 305] BAG 2

NORTHFIELD 48.12
47.53

LONGBRIDGE and HALESOWEN BRANCH

West Sidings

MG Rover Group Ltd.

Longbridge East Shunt Frame 0.26
LINE 2 0.49

North Sdg
North Works
GF 0.06
LS
UP FAST
DOWN FAST
UP SLOW
DOWN SLOW

LONGBRIDGE 49.12
Halesowen Jn 49.21
49.26

South Works

LONGBRIDGE CAR TERMINAL
0.34
A38
REVERS'G RD
REC & DEP
ARR & DEP
UP SDG 1
LINE 1
0.60
0.70

HND 1

LMS : Mid & GW Jt

UP GOODS
UP MAIN
DOWN MAIN
DOWN GOODS

Cotton
BIRMINGHAM and GLOUCESTER LINE
LMS : Midland
50.34
BAG 2 [MD 305]

51

Worcester & Birmingham Canal

BARNT GREEN 51.67
Barnt Green Jn 51.58 51.52
(Plat. 3) 7
52.11 (Plat. 3)

ALVECHURCH 53.40
53.03

[MD 310]
BARNT GREEN, EVESHAM and MALVERN LINE
LMS : Midland
BEA

REDDITCH 56.60

Blackwell Summit (564 ft)
Blackwell 52.35 52.17
M42 52.60
LICKEY INCLINE
LNW
Saltley PSB (SY)
Gloucester PSB (G)
(Blackwell) 53.25
52.40
52.59
M42
DOWN MAIN
UP MAIN
BAG 2
[MD 305]
LMS : Mid

Bromsgrove 266 ft
3 : 15B : to Bromsgrove
Miles from Derby via Whitacre & Camp Hill Line
Controlled by Saltley PSB (SY)
Nov 2004

D WELSH HIGHLAND RAILWAY

1' 11½" / 597mm gauge

24J
March 2005

PORTHMADOG 20.00
WHR Porthmadog (44 ch to Pen-y-Mount) See 50H

PONT CROESOR 18.00

NANTMOR 15.10

Aberglaslyn Tunnels

HAFOD Y LLYN

Proposed re-instatement

BEDDGELERT 12.60
Proposed re-instatement

RHYD DDU 9.35

Pitt's Head Summit 10.30

SNOWDON RANGER

Glan yr Afon Viaduct
6.20

Plas-y-Nant

WAUNFAWR 3.70
(BETTWS GARMON) 4.65

(TRYFAN JUNCTION) 2.15
(open)

DINAS 2.58
0.00
Museum
Carriage Shed

BONTNEWYDD 1.50
0.74 Hendy (open)

CAERNARFON 0.05
0.00

Caernarfon - Dinas on trackbed of LNW standard gauge line to Afon Wen
(former Mch shown but new km to be installed)

© Copyright TRACKmaps. No reproduction without permission

17

18

25C : to Burton-on-Trent

Miles from Derby

Central Rivers Depot
Arblasters (UWC) 14.55
14.50 114.01
Barton North Jn
DERBY to BIRMINGHAM LINE
DBP1 [MD 501] LMS : Mid

Wichnor Jn 23.33/15.65
16.22 15.73 Barton North Jn
Barton South Jn 16.22
Wichnor Jn 22.65-78
Wichnor Viaduct 16.79-58
(Rivers Tame & Trent)

(AS) (DY)
(R. Trent) Little Viaduct 22.53-54
Wichnor Viaduct 22.12
Alrewas 22.09
Controlled by Derby PSB (DY)

CENTRAL RIVERS DEPOT (CZ)
Bombardier Transportation for Virgin Cross-Country
Barton-under-Needwood
Bombardier (Central Rivers) (BD)

Heavy Maintenance
Light Maintenance
Servicing
UC = Underframe Cleaning
NR limit
NORTH ARRIVAL ROAD
14.55
Wheel Lathe
Stores
Cleaning
Platforms
Refuelling points
SOUTH ARRIVAL ROAD
Barton SD 15.65
NR limit
Barton South Jn 15.73

11B : to Nuneaton

9.20
(SY) (NN)
Saltley PSB (SY) NN
Nuneaton PSB NN
6.22 6.55 7.21
Arley Tunnel (709 yards)
A = ARLEY
[MD 555] NWO LMS : Mid
WHITACRE and NUNEATON LINE

Brookhay (AHBC) 19.4
Fime Lane (MCRH) 20.32
Waterworks (UWC) 20.13
Elford GF 19.40
Elford Loop
20.17
Roddige (MCRH) 21.16
22.40 Tamworth HABD

LNW LINE
DOWN WALSALL
UP WALSALL
LMS : LNW [MD 340] BJW3

19.00
Corks Farm 18.66

SOUTH STAFFORDSHIRE LINE
Lichfield High Level Goods Loop Jn 116.27/0.03
0.22, LC (footpath) 18.14
Lichfield Trent Valley Jn 18.14
Hollands (Street) 18.41
Lichfield (Street) 18.13
Lichfield HL TV Jn 18.15
LEC2 [MD 101]
WEST COAST MAIN LINE

TNT VW Group Logistics
Birch Coppice Exchange Sdgs
2.20 Hall End Jn
2.40

KBC KINGSBURY BRANCH
Warwickshire Oil Storage Co.
Kingsbury SF (KY)
Kingsbury 0.35 DOWN
European Metal Recycling
28.260.03 Kingsbury Jn
Down Sidings
LMS : Mid DBP1 KJW 2

TAMWORTH (HIGH LEVEL) 23.58
11B : to Nuneaton
Tamworth Viaduct (River Anker) 24.16-05

Derby PSB (DY) 23.30
Saltley PSB (SY) LINE 23.55
TAMWORTH (LOW LEVEL) 110.01
WILNECOTE 25.47
M42 27.63

Kingsbury Branch Jn 28.35
-0.02 UP DERBY DOWN DERBY
28.40 SHUNTING
29.27 Kingsbury Jn
29.39
DERBY to BIRMINGHAM LINE
LMS : Mid DBP1 [MD 501]

LMS : Mid [MD 545] KJW
DERBY to BIRMINGHAM LINE

KINGSBURY to WATER ORTON LINE
Adam Dales Viaduct 30.64-62
HAMS HALL National Distribution Park
Associated British Ports
Hams Hall Control Centre (HH) 33.05
Loading Pad
TRANSFER LINE (OOU)
for future extn. 32
DEP R/R
W. ARR
UP SLOW DOWN SLOW
32.58
UP FAST
DOWN FAST
DBP2 [MD 501] LMS : Mid
32.37
River Tame Flood Arches
32.54 M6 (Toll) 32.40
OOU
Coleshill 33.05
32.26-22
River Blythe Viaduct 32.15 31.77
DBP3 [MD 555] LMS : Mid
33.17 33.00
31.69 Whitacre Jn
32.10
32.00
31.67
Controlled by Saltley (SY)

Daw Mill Colliery UK Coal
Reception/Departure
Loading Pad
Bunker
T & G Discharge Hopper
Daw Mill GF 2.37
T & G = Tare and Gross
15.65 NR limit
15.73

16 : to Nuneaton

UP NUNEATON
DOWN NUNEATON
2.04
Windridge (UWC) 3.03
[MD 555] NWO LMS : Mid

Miles from Dudley Junction
Anglesea Sidings
12.66 M6 (Toll)
12.64
12.34
Aldridge 44.73
12.15 19 : to Walsall
BROWNHILLS

Foss way (AHBC) 15.32
UP & DOWN BRANCH
Lichfield City 13.37
Lichfield City
Engineers' Sdg
STABLING
16.47 16.70
Controlled by Aston ASC (AN) located at Duddeston
LICHFIELD CITY
BJW3 [MD 350]
LMS : LNW [MD 340] BJW3
SOUTH STAFFORDSHIRE LINE

SUTTON COLDFIELD and LICHFIELD LINE
Miles from Aston North Jn
13.13 18.04
LICHFIELD TRENT VALLEY 18.05/116.19
Aston (AN) TV
12A : to Rugeley
LTV [MD 350]
LMS : Mid DBP1 [MD 501]
DERBY to BIRMINGHAM LINE

11.38 M6 (Toll)
10.75-11.00 Shenstone Viaduct
SHENSTONE 10.53
BLAKE STREET 8.15
BUTLERS LANE 7.27
FOUR OAKS 6.26
8.04
ALC2 [MD 340]
6.13 'XC'
Walsall PSB WL
Saltley PSB SY
DOWN SUTTON
UP SUTTON
DOWN SUTTON PARK
UP SUTTON PARK

SUTTON PARK 40.09
Sutton Park No. 1
Birmingham & Fazeley Canal
Park Lane Jn 0.00 36.04
WATER ORTON CURVE
Sutton Coldfield Tunnel (172 yards)
SUTTON COLDFIELD 4.74
16 : to Aston 7
40.14 5.14
39.78 5.12
5.04
Jaguar Terminal
Ramps
WATER ORTON, WALSALL and WOLVERHAMPTON LINE
Miles from Derby via Whitacre Jn
35.16 35.10 DN SLOW
Park Hall Water Orton Viaduct
Water Orton East Jn 34.43
[33.34] 34.54
WOP [MD 560]
WATER ORTON CURVE
35.43-40 36DN & UP SLOW
36DN & UP FAST
DOWN FAST UP FAST
DN SLOW UP SLOW
River Tame
34.43 DBP3 [MD 501] LMS : Mid
33.22 33.43
COM

CASTLE BROMWICH CURVE
0.52 CBR1
DOWN WALSALL
UP WALSALL
36.47 36.22
0.521 CBR1
CBR2 [MD 565] LMS : Mid
Castle Bromwich Jn 36.22
36.08
36.12
DOWN MAIN UP MAIN
DOWN GOODS UP GOODS
36.76 site of Castle Bromwich Station
37.38 37.88
Heartlands: Rolls-Royce Power Station
OIL DISCHARGE SDG
Jaguar Terminal
Ramps
DOWN & UP GOODS
CASTLE BROMWICH
[MD 501] DBP3 LMS : Mid
DERBY to BIRMINGHAM LINE
Miles from Derby via Whitacre 37

16 : to Saltley

March 2005

20C : to Stourbridge Junction

21B : to Perkridge

18 : to Water Orton

HANDSWORTH JN to STOURBRIDGE JN LINE

OXFORD, WORCESTER and WOLVERHAMPTON LINE

WATER ORTON, WALSALL and WOLVERHAMPTON LINE

THE 'CHASE' LINE

WALSALL and CANNOCK LINE

STOUR VALLEY LINE

MIDLAND METRO
There are no distance posts; mileages are based on BR to Priestfield and by extension to Wolverhampton (BR mileages are from Paddington via Oxford).

BIRMINGHAM and BUSHBURY LINE (Grand Junction)

PORTOBELLO and HEATH TOWN JN LINE

SOUTH STAFFORDSHIRE LINE (OOU)

OLDBURY BRANCH

SOUTH STAFFORDSHIRE LINE

BESCOT LOCAL DISTRIBUTION CENTRE

★ **BLACK COUNTRY LIVING MUSEUM**
3' 6" gauge tramway overhead electric 525 yards

Wolverhampton St. George's

WOLVERHAMPTON 12.75

WATER ORTON, WALSALL and WOLVERHAMPTON LINE

WOLVERHAMPTON STEEL TERMINAL EWS

Portobello Jn 12.64

CHASEWATER RAILWAY 1435mm

NORTON LAKESIDE

CHASEWATER HEATHS 1.38

CHASETOWN (CHURCH ST)

BROWNHILLS WEST 0.06

WALSALL 6.29

Park Street Tunnel (143 yards)

Priestfield 140.33

Bilston Central 139.23

Loxdale 138.58

Bradley Lane 138.20

Wednesbury Parkway 137.03

Wednesbury Great Western Street

Wednesbury Town 136.59

COSELEY 9.46

TIPTON 8.16

DUDLEY PORT

DUDLEY

SANDWELL & DUDLEY 5.28

SMETHWICK GALTON BRIDGE (High Level) 133.21

SMETHWICK WEST

ROOD END YARD

LANGLEY GREEN 134.49

West Bromwich Central 134.05

Dudley Street Guns Village 134.70

Lodge Road West Bromwich Town Hall 134.22

Dartmouth Street 134.44

Black Lake 135.26

Swan Village 135.55

Kenrick Park 133.05

THE HAWTHORNS 132.41

Trinity Way 133.49

BESCOT STADIUM

BESCOT Jn

Newton Jn 7.59

TAME BRIDGE PARKWAY 7.48

Pleck Jn

Darlaston Jn

Walsall North Jn

Walsall South Jn

Tasker Street

Bescot Traction Maintenance Depot

© Copyright TRACKmaps. No reproduction without permission

16 : to Birmingham Snow Hill

16 : to Aston

Controlled by Walsall PSB (WL)

A

BATTLEFIELD STEAM RAILWAY

Miles from Moira West Jn

Coalville

SHACKERSTONE 8.25
8.09
8.34
2 1
Loco Shed

Shackerstone Jn
8.18

9   10   11   12

former Ashby & Nuneaton Joint (LNW/Mid)

SHENTON 12.49
12.55

MARKET BOSWORTH 10.68
10.61

UP →

Nov 2004

FAIRBOURNE and BARMOUTH STEAM RAILWAY

12¼" gauge

BATHING BEACH

PASSING LOOP

LC

GORSAF NEWYDD (FAIRBOURNE)

NORTH WALES COAST LIGHT RAILWAY CO. LTD

Nov 2004

GORSAFAWDDACHAÏDRAIG-DDANHEDDOGLEDDOLON-PENRHYNAREURDRAETHCEREDIGION (GOLF HALT)

Jack Steele Tunnel
OOU

PENRHYN POINT (BARMOUTH FERRY)

LC

M = Moveable sectors
S = Sector plate
W = Workshop

Loco Shed
Traverser
M
M
W
S

B

SEVERN VALLEY RAILWAY

BRIDGNORTH 149.73
149.76
2 1
149.28-32
Oldbury Viaduct (87 yards)

Loco shed   Boiler shop   150.09
150

Knowlesands Tunnel (44 yards)
149.04-06

148.60

Bridgnorth Cliff Railway
3'8" gauge
201 ft long
1 in 1.8

Castle Hill

EARDINGTON 147.57

149
148
147

PENSNETT
London & Cambridge Properties Ltd

146.30

KINGSWINFORD BRANCH (OOU)

146

145.73

NR limit 145.60

KWD
GW [MD 455]

DOWN UP BRANCH

145

Kingswinford Jn GF 144.56

Brierley Hill Terminal: EWS
Steel Stock area
Stone Stockpile
RUN ROUND

Kingswinford Jn South (KJ)
144.33
(Brettell Lane)

HAMPTON LOADE 145.33
145.31
2 1
Stearns 145.72

COUNTRY PARK HALT 144.07

Miles from Paddington via Worcester & Stourport

145
144

SEVERN VALLEY RAILWAY Plc
Nov 2004

HIGHLEY 143.20

143
142.34
Borle Viaduct (43 yards) 142.28-30

ARLEY 140.74
141

Victoria Bridge (River Severn) 140.33-38

NORTHWOOD HALT 138.78

143
142
141
140
139
138

(AOCL) 138.75

Wribbenhall (Bewdley) Viaduct 137.33-38

Bewdley North 137.32
137.39

BEWDLEY 137.28
Bewdley South 137.14

Carriage shed

Sandbourne Viaduct 137.02-05

Bewdley Tunnel (486 yards) 136.69-137.11

P.W. Sidings

To Stourport & Hartlebury

SVB / BYK
SVB
BYK

Change of mileage
138.21/137.12 (Bewdley South Jn)
137 miles from Paddington via Worcester & Kidderminster (reverse)

Branch mileage reverses from Main Line at 135.21

Miles from Paddington via Didcot, Oxford & Worcester

C

to Walsall 19:

Stop blocks 146.13

146

Round Oak Steel Terminal
Innovate Log 146
DOWN & UP ROUND OAK No. 2
DOWN & UP ROUND OAK No. 1

145.51

Miles from Paddington via Oxford & B. (Snow Hill) 145

to Smethwick 19:

UP STOURBRIDGE
DOWN STOURBRIDGE
135.61-58
M5 136.09

ROWLEY REGIS 136.14
136.40
9
136
Old Hill (or Blackheath) Tunnel (896 yards) 137.30

OWW OXFORD, WORCESTER and WOLVERHAMPTON LINE
GW [MD 450]

Controlled by Stourbridge Jn (SJ)

Stourbridge Railway   Stourbridge Railway Extension

Miles from Paddington via Worcester

137.01

GSJ 2 [MD 435]
GW

OLD HILL 137.30
6

CRADLEY HEATH 138.70
7
River Stour

138
139.04
(CCTV) (SJ)
138.65

STOURBRIDGE TOWN 142.71
1

NMOD ←

Shed

Chiltern Railways LMD

Stourbridge North Jn 142.68-77

Stourbridge Viaduct (190 yards)

144.13

Stourbridge Middle Jn 142.21

141.06
142.51 *
UP MAIN
DN MAIN
DGL
DN LN

SJS
GW [MD 445]

Stourbridge Jn 142.25
Stourbridge (SJ) 142.24

LYE 140.14
5
140
141

OWW [MD 430]
OWW [MD 450]
GSJ 2 [MD 435]
142.51 *
141.06

STOURBRIDGE JUNCTION 142.16
7
7
[BN] (SJ)

140

OWW GW [MD 430]

HAGLEY 140.29
4

139

BLAKEDOWN 138.54
6
Blakedown (BN) 138.51
Blakedown (or Churchill) Viaduct (173 yards) 138.17-25

138

137

KIDDERMINSTER TOWN (SVR) 135.40
7

KIDDERMINSTER 135.46

Kidderminster Jn (KJ) 135.17

Diesel Depot (SVR) 135.28

C&W Shed 135.28

DOWN MAIN   UP MAIN
135.52

136
135
134

Kidderminster/Hoobrook Viaduct (371 yards) 134.36-53

Falling Sands (Kidderminster) Viaduct (132 yards) 135.77-136.03

(Foley Park) 136.32

River Stour & Canal

P.W. Sidings

132.15
former Hartlebury Jn
132

HARTLEBURY (HY) 131.72
3
131.68
(MCB)
(MCB)

OWW OXFORD, WORCESTER and WOLVERHAMPTON LINE
GW [MD 430]

To Stourport & Bewdley

Hartlebury Depot English Property Co.

Elmley Lovett GF
OOU

LNW Cuthall Green 130.40
W [GW 370]

DN MAIN   UP MAIN
132

131

130

3: 14A: to Droitwich Spa

(WALSALL) - CANNOCK - (RUGELEY) ● (WOLVERHAMPTON) - COSFORD - (TELFORD) ● IRONBRIDGE BRANCH

A

Miles from Ryecroft Junction

12A : to Rugeley
12A : to Rugeley 'B' Power Station

RRN 2 LMS : LNW [NW 1004]

Rugeley 'B' Power Stn Jn 14.00 13.69
[MD 345]
13.62 Trent & Mersey Canal

RUGELEY TOWN 13.27
Brereton Sidings 13.25

Moors Gorse (UWM) 11.23

CANNOCK and RUGELEY LINE

1 RRN 2 LMS : LNW [MD 345]
7.20 7.16
CANNOCK

HEDNESFORD 9.05 8.60

Bunkers
Mid Cannock GF 6.30
Mid Cannock Colliery GF 6.30
Mid Cannock Opencast Disposal Point : UK Coal
LMS : LNW 'THE CHASE LINE'

WYRLEY & CHESLYN HAY 5.67
LANDYWOOD 5.12

CANNOCK BRANCH

BLOXWICH NORTH 3.01
BLOXWICH 2.32 3.41
2.06 (BH) BLOXWICH GF
Friars Road 2.22
Trident Alloys 2.01
THOMAS' SDG

19 : to Walsall

B

Dunstall Pk 142.79
21C
Oxley (Stafford Road Jn)
Change of mileage 142.79 143.02

[MD 805] OXC [MD 301]
2 RBS 3 PBJ
Oxley (Oxley) Jn
Bushbury V. 14.43
Bushbury (Oxley) Jn
15.35 DOWN MIN 16.18
15.32 15.23
BR 14

OXLEY CHORD [MD 805] OXC

1 WSJ 2 (WN) (OY)
Wolverhampton North Jn 13.32
VICTORIA BASIN BRANCH 143.52
STOUR VALLEY LINE LMS : LNW
BR [MD 301]
RBS 2 PBJ [MD 805]

BIRMINGHAM and BUSHBURY LINE

* Miles from Paddington via Oxford & Birmingham Snow Hill, reversed at Stafford Road Jn

BUSHBURY to STAFFORD LINE (Grand Junction)

Controlled by Wolverhampton PSB (WN)

Miles from Birmingham (former Curzon Street) via Bescot

M54 17.32
Four Ashes 19.71 20.20
18.61 Stafford & Worcester Canal
Staffordshire No. 1
Trent Valley Jn No. 1 28.50
DOWN BIRMINGHAM 27.55 Rickerscote
M6 26.38
Penkridge Up HABD 25.20
Parrott's No. 2 (UWG) 25.45
Parrott's No. 1 (UWG) 25.57
Shelson's (UWG) 24.72 24.17
Penkridge Down HABD 24.01
Penkridge Viaduct (River Penk) 23.52 23.56
PENKRIDGE 23.32
23.30 Stafford No. 4 PSB (SD4)
Wolverhampton PSB (WN) [MD 301] [NW 1002]
RBS 3 LMS : LNW

19 : to Bescot

12B : to Stafford
12B : to Rugeley LEC

C

21C
Oxley (Stafford Road Jn)
Oxley Viaduct (188 yds) 143.02
143.03-13
142.79 143.02
Oxley (Oxley) 143.14
OXLEY CHORD [MD 805] OXO

1 WSJ 2 [MD 801]
Lift shed
Main Carriage shed
OXLEY T&RSMD (OY) Midland Traincare Centre Alstom UK
Down Sidings CW
WASHER ROAD
143.49
Stafford & Worcester Canal
143.65-67
Up Sidings
DOWN LOOP DOWN MAIN UP MAIN UP LOOP

DIDCOT and CHESTER LINE
GW : Shrewsbury & Birmingham

Miles from Paddington via Oxford & Birmingham Snow Hill

Stocking Farm (UWC) 147.32
BILBROOK 145.66
CODSALL 146.41
(CL) 146.26
ALBRIGHTON 149.38
COSFORD 151.07
150.69 150.75
151.23
Tamper Sdg
DOWN MAIN UP MAIN

21D
22A : to Telford
21D
12B : to Stafford

Madeley South Jn 156.51
Madeley Jn (MJ) 156.26
[MD 810]
DRS 156.19
MADELEY BRANCH MJI 1
SHIFNAL 154.24 154.28-154.38
Shifnal Viaduct (194 yds)
River Worfe 152.08-12
Ruckley Viaduct (90 yds)
156 155 154 153 152 151 150 149 148 147 146 145 144 143

D

Madeley South Jn 156.51
21C
Miles from Paddington via Oxford & Birmingham Snow Hill

MADELEY BRANCH
MADELEY 159.10
[MD 810] 1 MJI 2 160.15 162.25
Lightmoor Junction 162.21
TSR proposed
DOSELEY 163.00 (Proposed)

KETLEY BRANCH
161.37-161.25 Coalbrookdale Viaduct (275 yards)
Chimes (UWC) 160.59

Miles from Paddington via Oxford & Stourport (Severn Valley) and reversing at former Buildwas Jn Signal Box 160.03

End of running line 160.03 (COM)
NR Power Gen
Albert Edward Viaduct 160.34-160.29
IRONBRIDGE GORGE 160.20 (Seasonal, temporary)
Control Room Tare Gross
No. 2 RECEPTION WB HH WB
No. 1 RECEPTION
No. 2 DEPARTURE
No. 1 DEPARTURE CB
RUN ROUND (160.61)
OIL SDG SD (OY)

IRONBRIDGE POWER STATION Power Gen

HORSEHAY & DAWLEY 163.75
163.40 163.20
DOSELEY 163.00 (Proposed)
Heath Hill Tunnel (59 yds)
164.07
164.45 (2004) 164.30 164.35
Ketley 164.70
Lawley 164.70
passenger limit
SPRING VILLAGE
Steam Tramway 2' 0" gauge 18 chains
TELFORD STEAM RAILWAY Standard gauge Nov 2004
LC

162 161 160 159 158 157 164

(continued left)
(Continued right)

March 2005

© Copyright TRACKmaps. No reproduction without permission

Miles from Paddington via Oxford & Birmingham Snow Hill

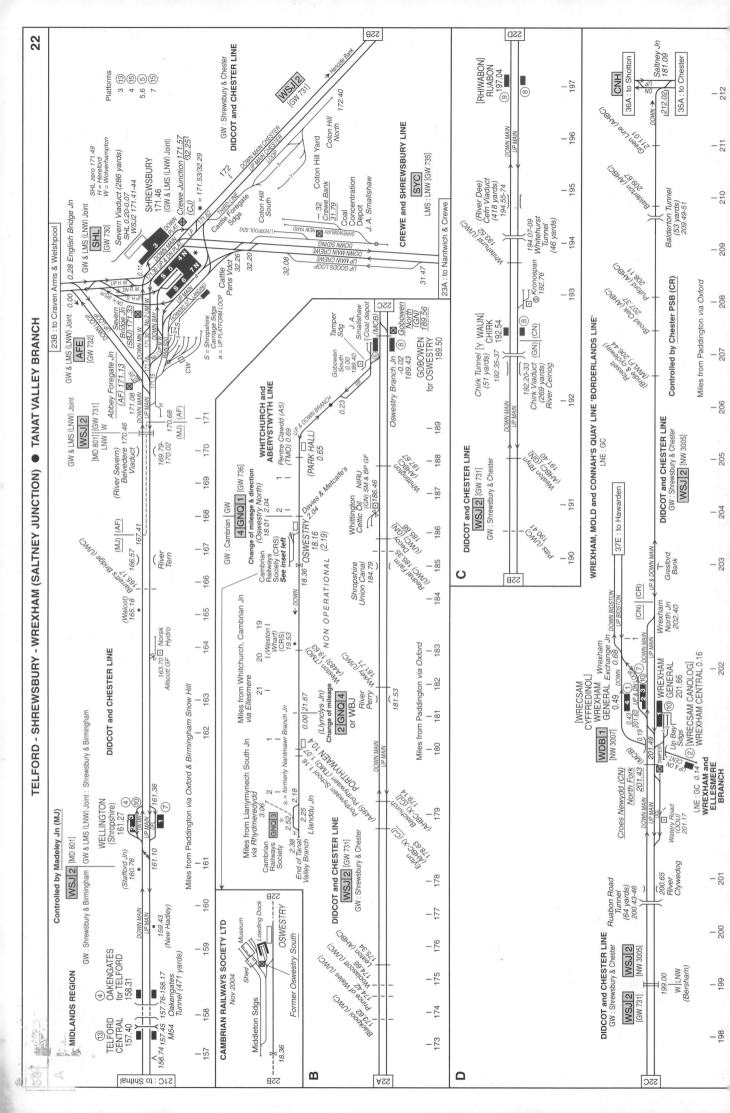

Row A — CREWE and SHREWSBURY LINE

13 : to Crewe

Gresty Green

Williamston (CCTV) (Gresty Lane)

Newcastle Rd (AHBC-X) 3.46 / 2.60

Nantwich Emergency GF 4.07

Nantwich 4.19

River Weaver 4.40

Shropshire Union Canal 5.30

Green Lane (UWC) 4.51

Fields Farm (UWC) 4.74

Reed's Farm (UWC) 6.51

[GW 735] W | LNW [NW 1007]

WRENBURY 8.48

Marley Green (UWC) 10.10

Marley Green Emergency Facing Crossover GF 10.14 (OOU)

Marley Green Emergency Trailing Crossover GF 10.1 (OOU)

Whitchurch 13.35

Kynaston (UWC) 12.30

Brick Kiln Lane (UWC) 12.30

WHITCHURCH 13.44

Durlington's (UWC) 14.32

[GW 735] SYC LMS : LNW

Prees 18.39 / PREES 18.36

New House Farm (UWC)

Mickelwood No. 2 (UWC) 8.45 / 7.67

WEM / Wem 21.55 / Wem 21.57

Wem Emergency Facing Crossover GF 21.72

Wem Emergency Trailing Crossover GF 21.76

Cambrian Farm (UWC) 20.05

YORTON 25.14

Lyons Wood Fm (UWC) 23.64 / 23.56

Harlescott Crossing 30.29

22A : to Shrewsbury

Shrewsbury

Row B — SHREWSBURY / SHREWSBURY to HEREFORD LINE

22A : to Shrewsbury

English Bridge Jn 0.28

Coleham Sidings

Abbey Foregate Viaduct

SHREWSBURY

[GW 733] SBA1 Joint: GW & LMS (LNW) Joint: 1 Shrewsbury & Welshpool

RR LOOP 0.58 / 0.65 (SB) Sutton Bridge Junction / 0.68 0.72

UP GOODS LOOP / UP MAIN / DOWN MAIN

1.31

SHREWSBURY to HEREFORD LINE

SHL [GW 730] GW : LMS (LNW) Joint : Shrewsbury & Hereford

2.77 Hopper GF Bayston Hill Tarmac (OOU)

Dorrington 6.25

CHURCH STRETTON 613 ft 12.63 / Church Stretton 12.54

Marsh Brook 15.29

Old Mill (UWC) 15.06

Woodlands (UWC) 14.66

3 : 27A : to Craven Arms

Row C — SHREWSBURY and WELSHPOOL LINE

2B — 22A : to Shrewsbury

Sutton Bridge Jn

(Hookagate) A5 2.03 / 2.10

(MH) Machynlleth

(SB) Sutton Bridge Jn

Miles from Sutton Bridge Junction

2.17 Hanesmans 1 (UWC)

8.76 Stretton Heath (AHBC)

10.23 Westbury (UWC)

Plas-y-Court (AHBC) 12.41

Miles from Whitchurch via Oswestry

15.21 Parry Green (UWC)

16.19 Buttington Jn

Buttington Crossing Flood Opening (38 yds) 32.30-32

Buttington Crossing Flood Opening (38 yds)

WELSHPOOL 33.70

GW : Cambrian [GW 733]

Glanhafon Viaduct (31 yds) 33.55

Cloddiau (UWC) 34.00

Rhydwhimen (R/G) 39.68

MONTGOMERY 40.18

Cherry Orchard (UWC) 41.18

Cemmes Road (R/G) 70.05

Miles from Whitchurch via Oswestry

Controlled by RETB from MH

Row D — WHITCHURCH and ABERYSTWYTH LINE

2C — (Hookagate)

Red House (UWC) 44.63 / Red House (UWC) 45.59

Panish House (UWC) 45.59

Pen-y-gaill (UWC) 46.34

3.73 Hanwood Road (UWC)

4.08 Hanwood (UWC)

NEWTOWN (Powys) 47.58 / 47.79

TROLLEY SDG / DN BAY SDG Newtown 47.65

Doughty's Viaduct (62 yds)

No. 1 Bed Ho Fm (UWC)

Mawr Fm (UWC) 51.18

51-1 Aberbechan Road (UWC) 50.35 / 50.12 49.42

CAERSWS 53.31 / 53.13

River Carno & River Severn (66 yds) 53.20-16 (Br. 171)

a = Weig La (AOCL) 54.26 / b = Bridge 172 (UWC) 54.10

54.90 Llwydiarth (UWC)

55.50 Needed (UWC)

Talerddig 56.57

Football Field (MG) 52.24 landrics Maw

57.15 Caemarth

57.15 Carreg Plas Newydd (UWC)

58.42 Village Viaduct (18 yds)

Sarn Pile Viaduct (19 yds) 59.46

River Severn 60-1

Cemmaes Road

Controlled by RETB from MH

Row E — WHITCHURCH and ABERYSTWYTH LINE / VALE OF RHEIDOL LIGHT RAILWAY

2D — WHITCHURCH and ABERYSTWYTH LINE

No. 2 (UWC) 74.05

Langley Fechan No. 4 74.74

MACHYNLLETH (MH) 75.04

AB = ABERYSTWYTH SIDING

Light Maintenance Depot

The Phyllis Rampton Narrow Gauge Railway Trust

75.11 / 75.2

Oil Sdgs

Dovey Jn 76.70 Rhosdyfe 77.70

DOVEY JUNCTION (CYFFORDD DYFI) 79.03

DJP [GW 734] 24A : to Tywyn

Dolgyfe (UWC) 77.13

RHIWFRON 10.69 c 590 ft

78.60

Track Circuit Block System

GW : Cambrian [GW 733] SBA2

Cottage Pie Viaduct (Bridge 243) (24 yds)

Tref'dol River Viaduct (Bridge 247)

x 82.48 Bridge 246 / 79.18 Bridge 242

DEVIL'S BRIDGE (PONTARFYNACH) 680 ft above sea level 11.65

ABERFFRWD 7.51

Leri Viaduct (Bridge 250) 85.32-85.31

Nantyronen (OC) 6.55

NANTYRONEN (197 ft) 6.58

CAPEL BANGOR 4.57

Borth Capel Soar (AOCL) 87.59

BORTH 87.27

Miles from Whitchurch via Oswestry

Ynyslas (UWC) 88.04

Llandre Vicarage (R/G) 90.02

Llandre (ABCL) 89.58

GLANYRAFON 2.26

Pant y Peron (UWC) 90.64

Caeneza (UWC) 63.13

New Glanyrafon (ABCL) 2.02

Llanbadarn (ABCL) 94.66

Llanbadarn Rheidol (AOCL) 1.18

LLANBADARN 1.15

Aberystwyth No.1 GF 95.30

Aberystwyth Oil Distributors

ABERYSTWYTH 95.60 / 0.16

No. 2 GF 95.56 UP & DOWN

Up Sdgs

14 ft

SDG1

Vale of Rheidol GF 0.25

Platforms 4 & 5 are OOU

VALE OF RHEIDOL LIGHT RAILWAY (1' 11½" gauge)
(Mileposts are on the north (up) side)

Jan 2005

Aberystwyth - Dovey Jn Controlled by RETB from MH

Controlled by RETB from MH

= Token Exchange Point

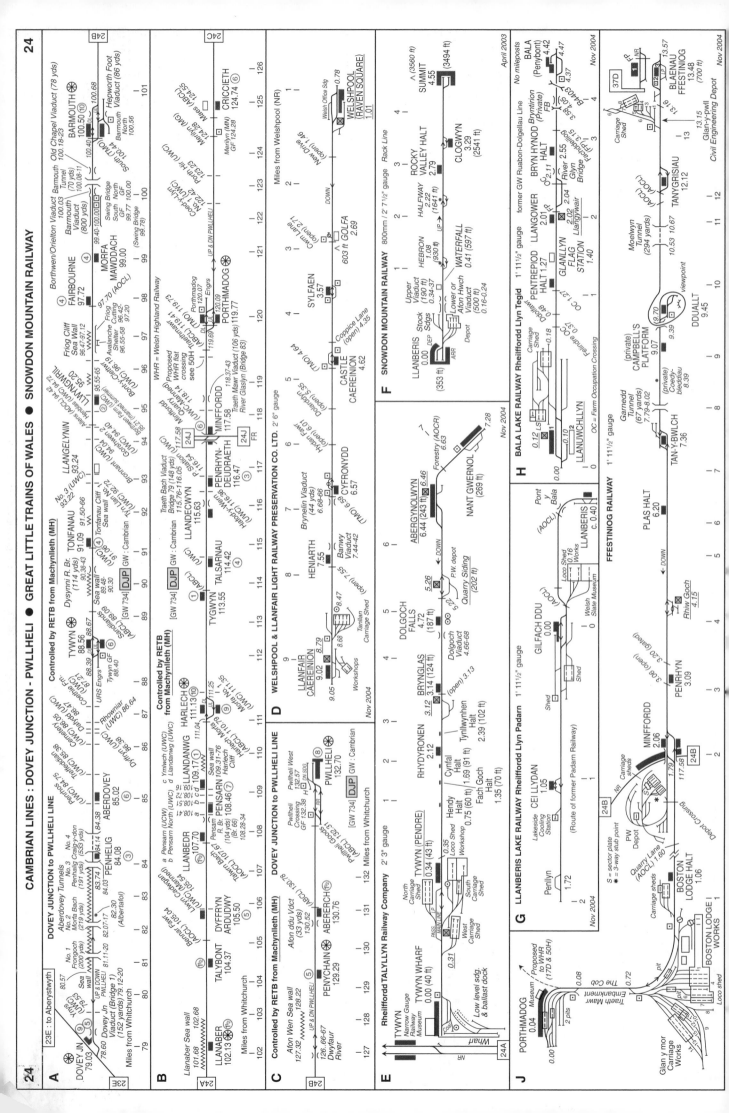

Panel A

CALDON LOW
Caldon Low GF 7.62
Caldon Low (open) 17.74
Lafarge/Tarmac
WB 8.01
DOWN →
Diesel Workshop
WATERHOUSES BRANCH
Non operational
[NW 5010] [SCQ] 3 LMS : NS
OAKAMOOR
WB 10.08
UP 10.40 WB 10.21
No passenger availability
Apesford (UWC) 3.20
2.17-2.19
Leek Brook Jn 17.49 CVR
Leek Brook Halt (OOU) 17.50
17.57 NR
6.65/0.00 NR
0.08
Birchall Tunnel 18.09-18.12 17.74
Leekbrook (open)
River Churnet 6.58/17.50
6.37
CVL
Cheddleton Tunnel 6.58/17.50 (OOU)
(531 yds)
Cheddleton (TMO) 16.45
CHEDDLETON 16.43 (Jan 2004)
Carriage Shed
DN 17.04 —17
LS 16
15
Diesel Shed
CVL
CONSALL 14.19
KINGSLEY & FROGHALL 12.17
12.00 Froghall Jn
RR Stock Sdg with road access
CHURNET VALLEY RAILWAY (1992) plc
[NW 5010] LMS : NS
NSS [MD 505] LMS : NS
Upper Leigh (T) (AHBC-X) (C) 9.57
13.27 Bakers (UWC)
14.50 Sharnams (UWC)
14.11 Loxley Lane (AHBC-X)
13.71 Messons (UWC)
13.55 Barnshall (AHBC-X)
13.32 (UWC)
DERBY LINE
Miles from Uttoxeter
Leigh (UWC) 9.04
Collies (UWC) 9.39

Panel B — FOXFIELD LIGHT RAILWAY SOCIETY LTD

BLYTHE BRIDGE (CAVERSWALL ROAD) 2.70
Hegarty's or Blakeley-bank Wood
DILHORNE PARK Near 0.50
FOXFIELD Bank 1/31, 1/25, 1/19, 1/28
FOXFIELD COLLIERY 0.00
Nov 2004
Loco Shed
Running Shed
Blythe Bridge West
BLYTHE BRIDGE 5.23
Creswell Ford 2.13
Cash Heath 2.61
Forsbrook Road 2.55
NIRU 1.67
0.72
2.72
3.27
3.32

LEEK LINE
Non operational
LMS : NS [NW 5010] [SCQ] 2
Stockton Brook Tunnel (72 yds)
2.09-2.12
0.40 (Milton)
Abbey (TMO) 3.20
Change of mileage
Eardon (AOCL) 3.11
River Trent
BIDDULPH VALLEY LINE
Non operational
Fenton Manor Tunnel (106 yds)
[NW 5010] LMS : NS [SCQ] 1
(Milton Jn) 0.00 / 3.51
(ELR origin at -0.22)
Controlled by (SOT)
MACCLESFIELD and COLWICH LINE
Miles from Macclesfield
Cockshute Sdgs
Cliff Vale Imerys
London North Western Yard
Newcastle & Mersey Canal
STOKE-ON-TRENT 19.78
Stoke-on-Trent (SOT) SC
LMS : NS [NW 5009]
CMD [NW 5009]
Stoke North Jn 19.61
19.60
Stoke/Seven Arches Viaduct 20.22-20.26
Glebe Street Jn
Stoke Jn 20.36
UP MAIN No.1 TGT 20.10
UP DERBY 20.33
DOWN DERBY
12D : to Wedgwood
LNW LINE [NW 5012] LMS : NS
NSS [MD 505] LMS : NS
LONGTON 1.71
Foley Crossing 450(T) 1.56
Longton Vdct 1.75-2.05
Meir Tunnel (814 yds) 4.13
3.12 3.49
Caverswall 4.20
Caverleigh Farm (UWC) 4.54
Stallington (CCTV) 5.19 (C) 5.19
Newton (farm) 7.61
Bostocks (UWC) 8.7
6.76 Cresswell (UWC)
5.74 Jacksons (UWC)
6.07 Bennetts (UWC)
7.04 (Cresswell Jn)
BLYTHE BRIDGE 5.23
25A
(CCTV) 5.23
4.59
[NW 5012] LNW LINE
All level crossings are "open"
ETRURIA 18.64
(CCTV) 5.19 NR
25B

Panel C — DERBY to BIRMINGHAM LINE

NSS [MD 505] LMS : NS
DERBY LINE
Miles from Stoke Jn
Egginton Jn (EN) 26.69
Hilton (MGH) 27.08
Egginton (AHBC) 27.50
Willington (AHBC) 29.19
Findern (AHBC) 29.49
Trent & M. Canal 30.10
Stenson Jn (UWC) 4.56
Stenson Raynos (UWC) 4.16
UP CHELLASTON ON CHELLASTON
SSJ 2 [MD 520]
6C: to Sheet Stores Jn
STENSON BRANCH
Willington North 5.14
Willington Down HABD 6.01
WILLINGTON 6.03
Controlled by Derby PSB (DY)
IDY] (EN) [DY]
Clay Mills (CCTV) 7.79-7.76
River Dove 7 8.4 Jn
8 13 Bromleys (UWC)
8 17 Wilsthams (UWC)
25 45 Marston-on-Dove
25 28 Hayside (UWC)
24 57 Rowes (UWC)
24 33 Rocks (UWC)
Wetmore Jn 9.60
9.51 9.42
9.46 9.51
NIRU
East Yard
West Yard
DEP ARR
Horninglow Sdgs Steel Terminal
Maurice Hill
Wetmore Sdgs
TUTBURY & HATTON 24.13
Tilbury Crossing (UWC)
22 73 Rocks (UWC) 23 23 Brivots Mill Ln (UWC)
22 41 Acres No.1 (UWC)
22 33 Scorpion (UWC)
22 5 (UWC)
23 28 Weir Lane (UWC)
MARCHINGTON 18.78
Marchington Old Stn 19.61 19.62
Sudbury Vdct 21.15-21.19
Horninglow Bridge Jn 10.33
10.67 10.25
New Wetmore Sdgs
BURTON ON TRENT 1 2
Mosley Street Sdgs
Cambridge Street
M. St GF 11.00
Leicester Jn 11.17
Burton Jn 12.15
Branston (OOU) 127.13 127.19
Branston Up HABD 13.44
Branston 13.31 (UWC)
Pinhoe (MCB) 16.00 GF
Bridge St Vdct 16.17
UTTOXETER 16.29
Pinfold (MCB) 16.00
Uttoxeter Racecourse (UWC) 16.33
Hockley (CCTV) 15.67
Uttoxeter 16.00
Dunsalls (UWC) 12.47
Tunbridge No.2 (UWC) 23.33
Leicester Jn 11.11
17.20 Tuncliffs No.1
17.75 Langdale (UWC)
Boulthns (UWC) 13.31
DERBY to BIRMINGHAM LINE [MD 501] DBP 1
BCJ [MD 535] LMS : Mid
LMS : Mid TSY [MD 525]
Birmingham Curve (OOU) 127.13
BIRMINGHAM CURVE
Birmingham Curve 126.40 (miles from St. Pancras)
7B: to Coalville
LEICESTER and BURTON LINE
18 : to Wichnor Jn & Tamworth
25B

Panel (top right) — DERBY to MELBOURNE LINE

4B : to Derby
25
March 2005
St. Andrews Sidings 1 & 2
OOU
PEARTREE 1.16
RAMSLINE HALT 0.51
DERBY to BIRMINGHAM LINE [MD 501] DBP 1 LMS : Mid
Melbourne Jn 1.31
Sinfin No.1 GF 1.02
SINFIN NORTH 1.44
DOWN MAIN WEST
ON MAIN WEST
UP MAIN WEST
UGL 1.31
2.08
Sunny Hill 2.34
DOWN GOODS
Sinfin No.3 GF 130.31
Sinfin North 130.73 (3)
Sinfin No.2 GF 130.56 130.69
L & NW
S & T Sdg GF 0.27
SINFIN CENTRAL 130.37
Rolls Royce Ltd
SDG
RR
—131
131
SINFIN BRANCH
LMS : Mid
130.20 (Oil Terminal)
DN
129.79 St. Pancras
130.37 (miles from St. Pancras)
MJS 1 [MD 515]

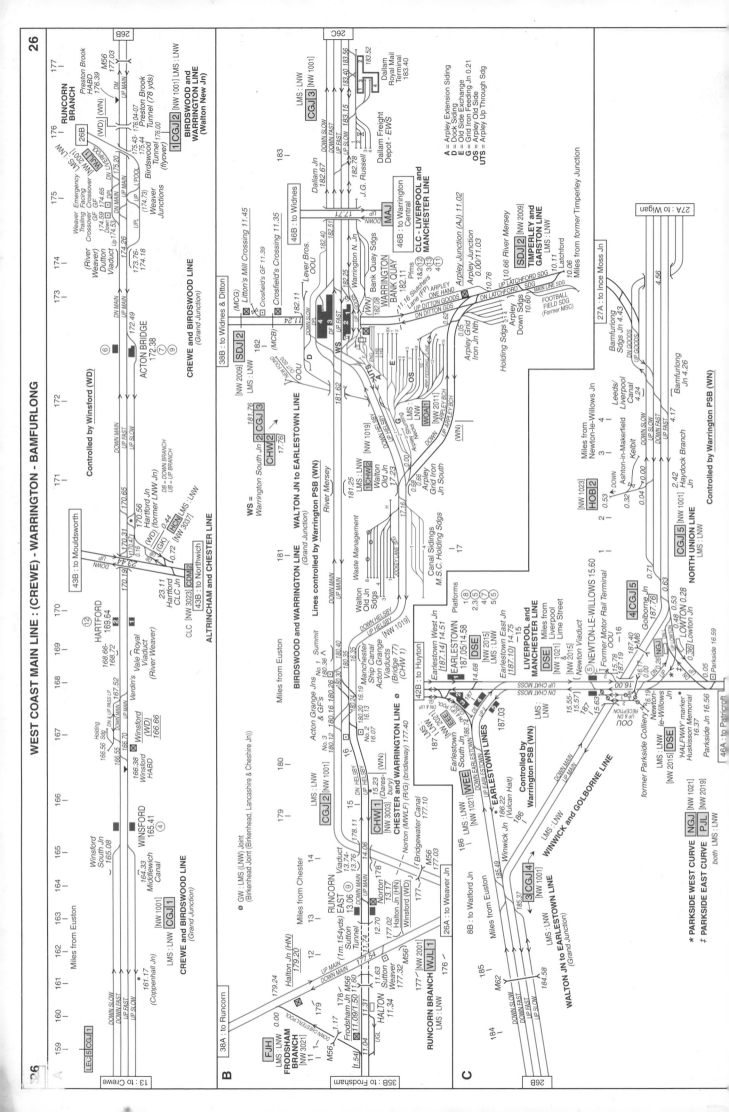

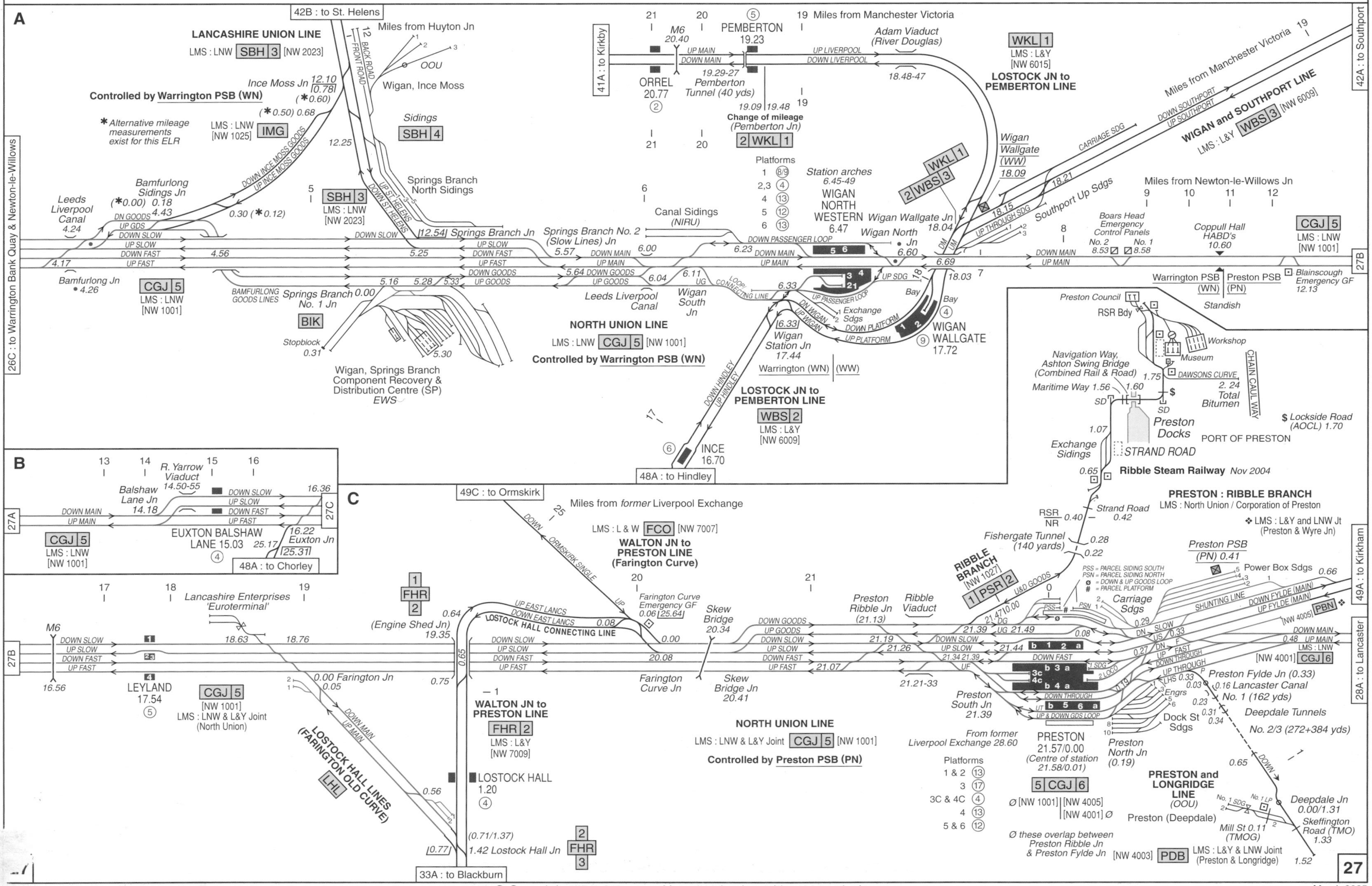
A
42B : to St. Helens
Miles from Huyton Jn
LANCASHIRE UNION LINE
LMS : LNW SBH 3 [NW 2023]
Ince Moss Jn 12.10 [0.78] (*0.60)
Controlled by Warrington PSB (WN)
(*0.50) 0.68
* Alternative mileage measurements exist for this ELR
LMS : LNW [NW 1025] IMG
Wigan, Ince Moss
OOU
Sidings SBH 4
BACK ROAD
FRONT ROAD
12.25
DOWN INCE MOSS GOODS
UP INCE MOSS GOODS
Bamfurlong Sidings Jn (*0.00) 0.18 4.43
Leeds Liverpool Canal 4.24
0.30 (*0.12)
SBH 3 LMS : LNW [NW 2023]
Springs Branch North Sidings
[12.54] Springs Branch Jn
Springs Branch No. 2 (Slow Lines) Jn 5.57
Canal Sidings (NIRU)
26C : to Warrington Bank Quay & Newton-le-Willows
4.17
Bamfurlong Jn 4.26
CGJ 5 LMS : LNW [NW 1001]
4.56
5.25
BAMFURLONG GOODS LINES
Springs Branch No. 1 Jn 0.00
5.16 5.28 5.33
BIK
Stopblock 0.31
5.30
Wigan, Springs Branch Component Recovery & Distribution Centre (SP) EWS
6.00
5.64
6.04
6.11
Leeds Liverpool Canal
Wigan South Jn
NORTH UNION LINE
LMS : LNW CGJ 5 [NW 1001]
Controlled by Warrington PSB (WN)
41A : to Kirkby
M6 20.40
ORREL 20.77 (2)
PEMBERTON 19.23 (5)
19 Miles from Manchester Victoria
19.29-27 Pemberton Tunnel (40 yds)
19.09 19.48
Change of mileage (Pemberton Jn)
2 WKL 1
Adam Viaduct (River Douglas)
18.48-47
WKL 1 LMS : L&Y [NW 6015]
LOSTOCK JN to PEMBERTON LINE
Platforms
1 (8/9)
2,3 (4)
4 (13)
5 (12)
6 (13)
Station arches 6.45-49
WIGAN NORTH WESTERN 6.47
Wigan Wallgate Jn 18.04
Wigan North Jn 6.60
6.23
6.33
6.69
18.03
WKL 1
2 WBS 3
Wigan Wallgate (WW) 18.09
18.15
18.21
Southport Up Sdgs
CARRIAGE SDG
Miles from Manchester Victoria
WIGAN and SOUTHPORT LINE
LMS : L&Y WBS 3 [NW 6009]
42A : to Southport
Miles from Newton-le-Willows Jn
Boars Head Emergency Control Panels No. 2 8.53 No. 1 8.58
Coppull Hall HABD's 10.60
CGJ 5 LMS : LNW [NW 1001]
27B
Warrington PSB (WN) Preston PSB (PN)
Blainscough Emergency GF 12.13
Standish
Bay
WIGAN WALLGATE 17.72 (4) (9)
Exchange Sdgs
[6.33] Wigan Station Jn 17.44
Warrington (WN) (WW)
LOSTOCK JN to PEMBERTON LINE
WBS 2 LMS : L&Y [NW 6009]
DOWN HINDLEY
UP HINDLEY
INCE 16.70 (6)
48A : to Hindley
Preston Council
RSR Bdy
Workshop
Museum
DAWSONS CURVE
CHAIN CAUL WAY
Navigation Way, Ashton Swing Bridge (Combined Rail & Road) 1.75
Maritime Way 1.56 1.60
2.24 Total Bitumen
$ Lockside Road (AOCL) 1.70
Preston Docks
PORT OF PRESTON
1.07
Exchange Sidings
STRAND ROAD
0.65
Ribble Steam Railway Nov 2004
B
Balshaw Lane Jn 14.18
R. Yarrow Viaduct 14.50-55
16.36
27A
27C
CGJ 5 LMS : LNW [NW 1001]
EUXTON BALSHAW LANE 15.03 (4)
25.17
16.22 Euxton Jn [25.31]
48A : to Chorley
C
49C : to Ormsksirk
Miles from former Liverpool Exchange
DOWN ORMSKIRK SINGLE
LMS : L & W FCO [NW 7007]
WALTON JN to PRESTON LINE (Farington Curve)
Farington Curve Emergency GF 0.06 [25.64]
0.08
0.00
20.08
Farington Curve Jn
Skew Bridge 20.34
Skew Bridge Jn 20.41
UP EAST LANCS
DOWN EAST LANCS
LOSTOCK HALL CONNECTING LINE
1 FHR 2
0.64
(Engine Shed Jn) 19.35
0.65
0.75
M6
16.56
27B
Lancashire Enterprises 'Euroterminal'
18.63
18.76
LEYLAND 17.54 (5)
CGJ 5 [NW 1001] LMS : LNW & L&Y Joint (North Union)
0.00 Farington Jn 0.05
LOSTOCK HALL LINES (FARINGTON OLD CURVE)
LHL
0.56
[0.77]
WALTON JN to PRESTON LINE
FHR 2 LMS : L&Y [NW 7009]
LOSTOCK HALL 1.20 (4)
(0.71/1.37)
1.42 Lostock Hall Jn
2 FHR 3
33A : to Blackburn
NORTH UNION LINE
LMS : LNW & L&Y Joint CGJ 5 [NW 1001]
Controlled by Preston PSB (PN)
Preston Ribble Jn (21.13)
Ribble Viaduct
21.19
21.26
21.07
21.21-33
21.39
21.49
21.44
21.34 21.39
RIBBLE BRANCH [NW 1027]
1 PSR 2
U&D GOODS
RSR NR 0.40
Strand Road 0.42
Fishergate Tunnel (140 yards)
0.28
0.22
PRESTON : RIBBLE BRANCH
LMS : North Union / Corporation of Preston
❖ LMS : L&Y and LNW Jt (Preston & Wyre Jn)
Preston PSB (PN) 0.41
PSS = PARCEL SIDING SOUTH
PSN = PARCEL SIDING NORTH
ø = DOWN & UP GOODS LOOP
= PARCEL PLATFORM
Carriage Sdgs
Power Box Sdgs 0.66
SHUNTING LINE
DOWN FYLDE (MAIN)
UP FYLDE (MAIN)
PBN ❖
49A : to Kirkham
[NW 4005]
DOWN MAIN
UP MAIN
0.48
LMS : LNW
[NW 4001] CGJ 6
28A : to Lancaster
0.29
0.33
0.27
0.08
Preston Fylde Jn (0.33)
0.16 Lancaster Canal No. 1 (162 yds)
Deepdale Tunnels No. 2/3 (272+384 yds)
Engrs
Dock St Sdgs
0.23 0.31 0.34
0.03
Preston South Jn 21.39
From former Liverpool Exchange 28.60
PRESTON 21.57/0.00 (Centre of station 21.58/0.01)
Preston North Jn (0.19)
Platforms
1 & 2 (13)
3 (17)
3C & 4C (4)
4 (13)
5 & 6 (12)
5 CGJ 6
Ø [NW 1001] [NW 4005]
[NW 4001] Ø
Ø these overlap between Preston Ribble Jn & Preston Fylde Jn
[NW 4003] PDB
LMS : L&Y & LNW Joint (Preston & Longridge)
PRESTON and LONGRIDGE LINE (OOU)
Preston (Deepdale)
0.65
Deepdale Jn 0.00/1.31
Mill St 0.11 (TMOG)
Skeffington Road (TMO) 1.33
1.52
27

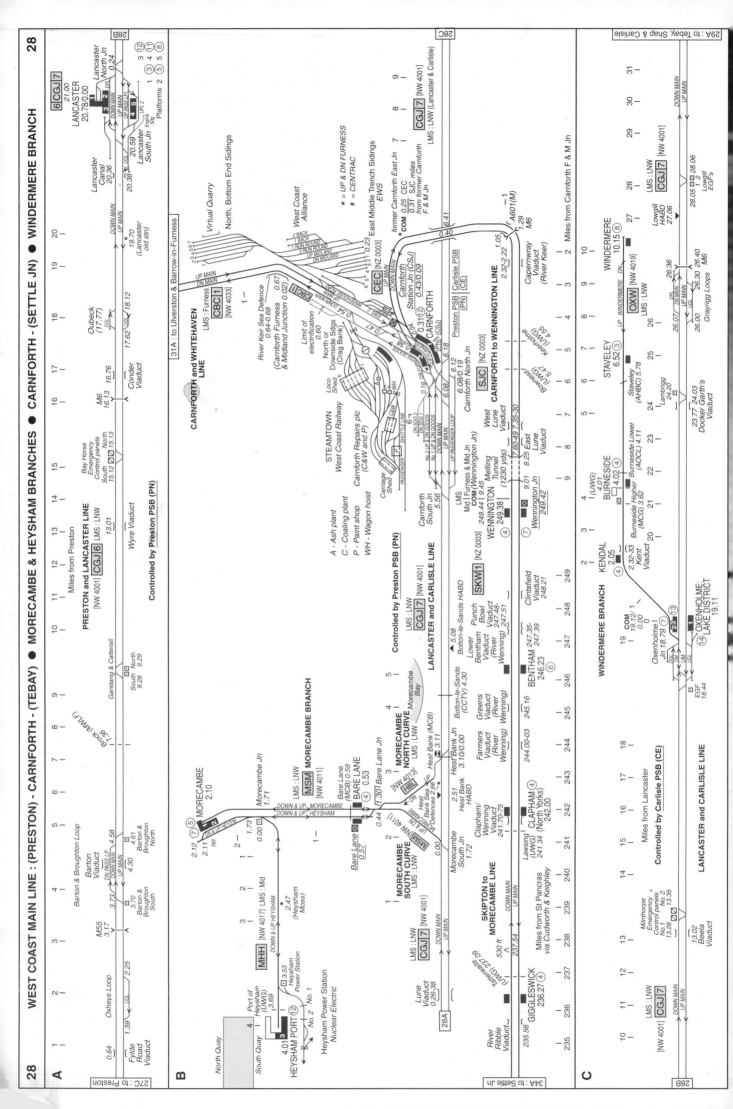

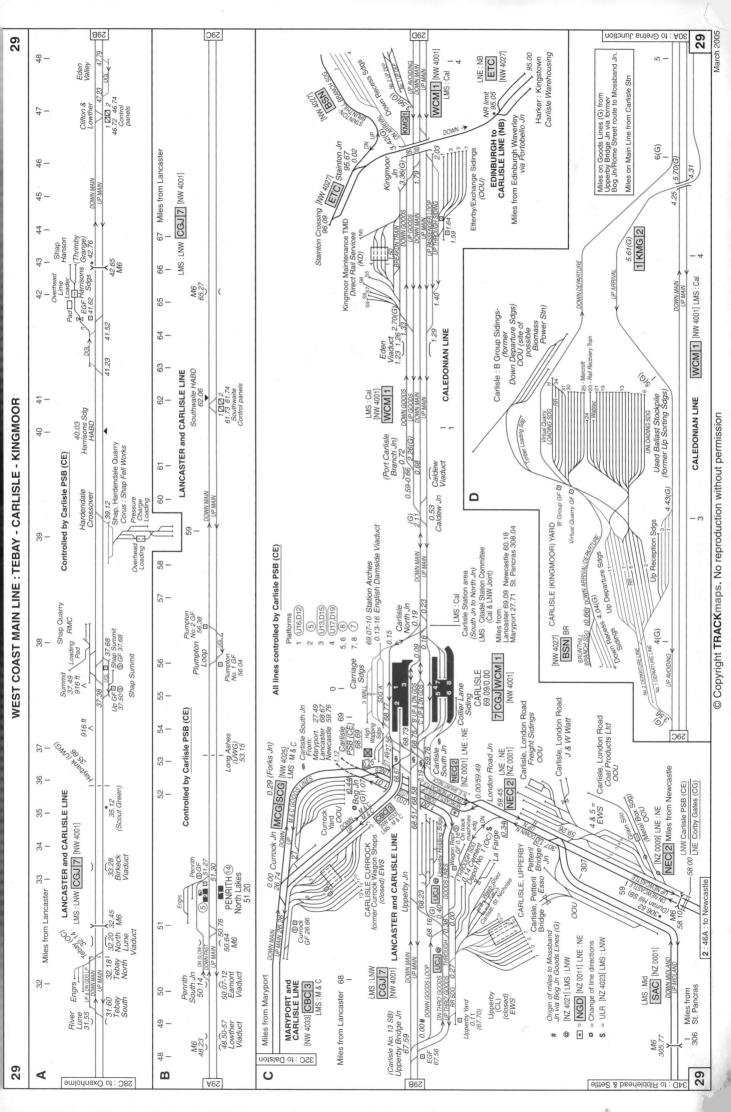

WEST COAST MAIN LINE : TEBAY - CARLISLE - KINGMOOR

March 2005

© Copyright TRACKmaps. No reproduction without permission

30

Nov 2004

B — EAST LANCASHIRE RAILWAY

EAST LANCASHIRE LIGHT RAILWAY CO. LTD.

The three single line sections named after intermediate points on each one:
"Up & Down Broadfield" (Bury-Heywood)
"Up & Down Summerseat" (Ramsbottom-Bury)
"Up & Down Irwell Vale" (Rawtenstall-Ramsbottom)

RAWTENSTALL 17.47
Rawtenstall West 17.27
Rawtenstall West GF 17.24
New Hall Hey Bridge (River Irwell) 17.00
Townsend Fold 16.79
16.21 (Ewood Bridge & Edenfield)
16.09 Lower Ashen Bottom Viaduct
15.75 Hardsough Weir Viaduct (River Irwell)
IRWELL VALE 15.55 15.62
15.09 (Alderbottom) Viaduct No. 2 (River Irwell)
(Stubbins) 14.32
former Stubbins Jn 14.23

BCP CTA 2

13.50 — 13.51
RAMSBOTTOM 13.46
Square River Bridge (River Irwell) 13.31
Nuttall Viaduct (River Irwell) 13.16
Nuttall Tunnel (115 yards) 12.73-12.78
Brooksbottom Tunnel (423 yards) 12.48-12.67
Brooksbottom Viaduct (River Irwell) 12.44-12.36
SUMMERSEAT 12.18
UP & DOWN SUMMERSEAT
Burrs Viaduct
Calrows Viaduct — River Irwell 10.70-72 / 10.60-65

Bury Transport Museum

Miles from Manchester Victoria via Whitefield

Bury EL Tunnel (80 yards) 9.55-9.58
BURY BOLTON STREET 9.48
Bury Steam Locomotive Co. Ltd. 9.21
Castlecroft Yard
Castlecroft Diesel/Shed
Bury South 9.42
Bury South 9.38
Buckley Wells 9.24

Metrolink Intersection Bridge
UP & DOWN BROADFIELD
Buckley Wells
Bury Steam Locomotive Co. Ltd.
Locomotive & Carriage Shed
Baron Street Locomotive Works

HEYWOOD 5.35
West GF 5.50 East GF 5.28
Hopwood 5.03 (F)
ELR | NR 5.02 | 5.04
Roch 8.36-31 M66
Miles from Manchester (Victoria) via Whitefield & Bury South Jn (reverse)

47A : to Castleton

—8.74
9.00 —

A — WEST COAST MAIN LINE : (KINGMOOR) - SCOTLAND ● BRUNTHILL, LONGTOWN & SMALMSTOWN BRANCHES

29C : to Carlisle

MAIN LINES WCM 1 LMS : Cal [NW 4001]
CALEDONIAN LINE
GOODS LINE KMG 2

Controlled by Carlisle PSB (CE)

Miles on Goods Lines (G) from Upperby Bridge Jn via former Bog Jn/Rome Street route to Mossband Jn

Miles From Carlisle Station

Esk Viaduct 6.51-6.58
7.47 (G) 6.03
6.07
6.04
Floriston 7.48 (G) (AHBC)
7.45 (G)
Floriston HABD's
7 (G)

Admiralty Sdgs Jn (7.23)
8.69 (G)
Mossband Jn 7.64
7.57
9.18 (G) 3.02 (G)
9 (G)

NIRU emergency connection

LONGTOWN SIDING
Depot
Ministry of Defence (Navy Dept)

NB : No up-to-date information available for the Longtown Branch area

LONGTOWN
Ministry of Defence (Defence Munitions)

'Circular Railway'

North No. 1 2.74
North No. 2 3.10
North No. 3 3.27
North No. 4 3.41
North No. 5 3.57
North No. 6 3.74
North No. 7 4.10

South No. 1 2.07
South No. 2 2.01
South No. 3 1.65
South No. 4 1.50
South No. 5 1.34
South No. 6 1.16
South No. 7 1.38

Loco shed 4.22
Exchange Sidings 0.67 / 0.24

MOD (Navy)
Solway No. 1
Solway No. 2
Solway No. 3

Bush-on-Esk No. 4 (OC) 1.79
Bush-on-Esk No. 2 (AOCL) 1.07
West Jn NR Bdy 1.06
Bush-on-Esk
Bush-on-Esk No. 1
East Jn 0.69
Zero at former Longtown Branch Jn 88.46 (Edinburgh)
0.65 0.55 0.24
0.00½
Qy

Smalmstown
Ministry of Defence (Army Department)

S1 S2 S3 S4 S5 S6 S7 S9 S10
T5 T10
U1 U2 U3 U4 U5 U6 U7 U8 U9 U10

Shed
LC / LC / LC
Maintenance shed
MOD : Defence Munitions

[NW 4031][SC 031] GSW LMS : GSW UP & DOWN DUMFRIES

Kirtle Water Viaduct 113.47
Rigghead (UWG) 113.10
Stanfield Farm (UWG) 111.05
Muirho Fm (UWG) 110.73
Riggmoor (UWG) 110.75
Eastrigs 109.75
109.00 — 109
1 : 1C : to Annan, Dumfries & Glasgow
Annan (AN) SC 031

[NW 4031][SC 031]
LNW Carlisle PSB (CE)

116 — 116.09
115.20
GRETNA GREEN 115.12
UP & DOWN DUMFRIES
DPL 10.30
DN 10.36
UP 10.33
UPL
GSP 10.19
Old box 10.13
Quintinshill 9.72

Miles from former Bridge Street Station via Dairy & Kilmarnock

1 : 10A to Lockerbie & Glasgow
Carlisle PSB (CE) LTD NW 4001 SC
Motherwell SC (MO) SC 001

WCM 1 LMS : Cal

Sark Viaduct (England/Scotland border)
8.55 8.57 8.00
Gretna Jn 16.13
former regional boundary LMR / Sc (1948-92)

DOWN / UP
9.26 (G)
DOWN MAIN
UP MAIN
UP GOODS
9 (G)

DN DEP / DN GDS
DOWN MAIN
UP MAIN
UP ARRIVAL

CUMBRIAN COAST LINE : (CARNFORTH) - BARROW - BRAYSTONES ● LAKESIDE AND HAVERTHWAITE RAILWAY

A

28B : to Carnforth

Miles from Carnforth

SILVERDALE 3.55

Silverdale (AHBC) 3.11
Leaming (UWG) 4.11
Waterslack Quarry (UWG) 4.74
Black Dyke 5.12

ARNSIDE 6.21
Kent/Arnside Viaduct 6.49-72
6.29

Sea Defence Works

Crook Wheel (UWG) 14.24

CARK & CARTMEL 13.59

Waysholme (AOCL) 12.42

KENTS BANK 11.27
(UWB) 11.30
Cart Lane (UWB) 10.59

Bathing Pool (UWG) 10.20

GRANGE-OVER-SANDS 9.31 9.43

CBC 1 [NW 4033]
DOWN MAIN / UP MAIN

Sea Defence Works

CARNFORTH and WHITEHAVEN LINE
LMS : Furness CBC 1 [NW 4033]

ULVERSTON 19.28 19.47
Ulverston Canal Viaduct 18.38-43
Fuel Services (Cumbria)
(NIRU)

17.62 (Plumpton Jn)

Leven/Plumpton Viaduct 16.57-17.01

Sea Defence Works

DALTON 23.67
Lindal Tunnel (439 yards) 22.53-22.73
Dalton Tunnel (225 yards) 24.01-11

31B

SEA DEFENCE WORKS
E = Embankment

1.34-1.67	Warton Sands E.
2.04-2.50	Warton Sands E.
2.68-2.70	Quicksands Pool Bridge
6.28-6.33	Arnside Station E.
6.33-6.49	Kent Viaduct Approach E.
6.47-7.66	Meathop March E.
7.66-8.09	Meathop Fell E.
8.09-9.18	Meathop E.
9.18-9.34	Grange Goods Yard
9.34-9.66	Grange Station

9.77-10.19	Pitching & Prom.
10.32-10.66	Cart Lane E.
10.66-11.27	Kents Bank Pitching
11.27-11.51	Kents Bank E.
11.67-11.78	Kirk Head E.
14.21-16.49	Capes Head E.
16.49-16.57	Leven March E.
17.01-17.05	Approaches
17.05-17.24	Threadlow Point E.

B

PORT OF BARROW

DEVONSHIRE DOCK

BUCCLEUCH DOCK

British Nuclear Fuels
RAMSDEN DOCK

CAVENDISH DOCK

(Buccleuch Jn) 28.10

28.03 28.10
RDK1

LC 28.19
SIDING No. 2
SIDING No. 1
27.57

NR
ABP
LC

Salthouse Jn 27.59
Salthouse Viaduct

ROOSE 27.13

CARNFORTH and WHITEHAVEN LINE
LMS : Furness CBC 1 [NW 4033]

Fuel Point
Dukes Sdgs
Carriage Sdgs (BW)
29.28
29.05

BARROW-IN-FURNESS 28.76
28.58 28.10
DOWN MAIN / UP MAIN

(a) "Barrow-in-Furness North Box"

Goldmire Quarry (UWG) 0.61

Cistercian/British (AOCL) 31.44

Park House Farm (MWLO)
26.08

Furness Abbey Tunnel (76 yards)
25.41 25.44
25.20 (Furness Abbey)

Park South (PS)
Park South Jn 33.06
Park North (UWG)
Dunnerholme (UWG) 36.21
32.77

DOWN BRANCH / UP BRANCH
DOWN MAIN / UP MAIN

DALTON LOOP
[NW 4041]
LMS : Furness DAP
Dalton Jn 24.38/0.00
Dalton Jn 24.37

Miles from Carnforth via Barrow

31A

THE LAKESIDE and HAVERTHWAITE RAILWAY CO. LTD.

Nov 2004

D

LAKESIDE 7.72
7.61

6.69 (path)

NEWBY BRIDGE 6.66

Miles from Plumpton Jn 5

HAVERTHWAITE 4.71
4.67
4.59 4.67
4.56
4.04 5.08
5.04 5.08

Haverthwaite East Tunnel (87 yards)
Stock shed
Haverthwaite Works
Haverthwaite West Tunnel (165 yards)

DOWN

C

32A : to Whitehaven

Miles from Carnforth

MILLOM 45.01 45.07
Salthouse No. 1 (UWG) 44.46
DOWN SDG
Hesham Hall (UWG) 45.27
Moor Farm 1 (UWG) 45.32
Haverigg (AHBC) 46.05
Kirksanton (MCB) 47.06

SILECROFT 48.12 48.16
Limestone Hall (MCB) 47.43

Whitbeck (AOCL) 49.55

BOOTLE 53.34 53.37
Bootle Beck Viaduct 51.70

Middleton Place (UWG) 55.15

ESKMEALS 56.41
Eskmeals Viaduct 56.43-58

RAVENGLASS for ESKDALE 57.79
Saltcoats (MCG) 58.49
58.10-14 (River Mite)
Hall Carleton (UWG) 59.25
Barfield (UWG) 59.52
34F : to Ravenglass & Eskdale Railway

DRIGG 60.02
Drigg Viaduct (River Irt) 60.42
Drigg : British Nuclear Fuels
No. 2
59.79 (D)

SEASCALE 62.12

Sellafield/Calder Viaduct 63.34
SELLAFIELD 63.72 63.76
Sellafield British Nuclear Fuels
63.32
64.02 (S)
Up Sdgs
Eden Viaduct 64.20
North SDG

GREEN ROAD 42.37
Green Road Viaduct
Wateman Nurseries (UWG) 42.34
Underhill (UWG) 43.12

FOXFIELD 40.37
Duddon/Foxfield Viaduct 40.40
Foxfield (Approaches) 40.70-41.06 41.11-41.27
41.06-11 42.20
41.00-41.41

Sleiry Crag (MCG) 40.24 (UWG) 40.41

KIRKBY-IN-FURNESS 38.19 38.40
Kirkby Viaduct

ASKAM 35.06
35.03
Askam (MCB) 35.46

CARNFORTH and WHITEHAVEN LINE
LMS : Furness CBC 1 [NW 4033]

SEA DEFENCE WORKS
E = Embankment

35.59-36.00	Dunnerholme E.
36.48-36.53	Souter Gate
36.65-37.41	Souter Gate Marsh E.
37.41-37.57	Lidge Gate Wall
37.57-36.18	Sandside Marsh E.
38.18-38.50	Head Cragg Marsh E.
40.00-40.17	Angerton Marsh E.
40.25-40.41	Foxfield Marsh E.

SEA DEFENCE WORKS
E = Embankment

56.59-56.73	River Esk Pitching
57.24-57.37	Walls Bridge E.
58.18-58.23	River Mite Pitching
62.06-63.02	Seascale Foreshore
63.33-63.67	Sellafield Pitching
65.14-67.07	Braystones E.

Sea Defence Works

CARNFORTH and WHITEHAVEN LINE
LMS : Furness CBC 1 [NW 4033]

Sea Defence Works

BRAYSTONES 65.76

31B

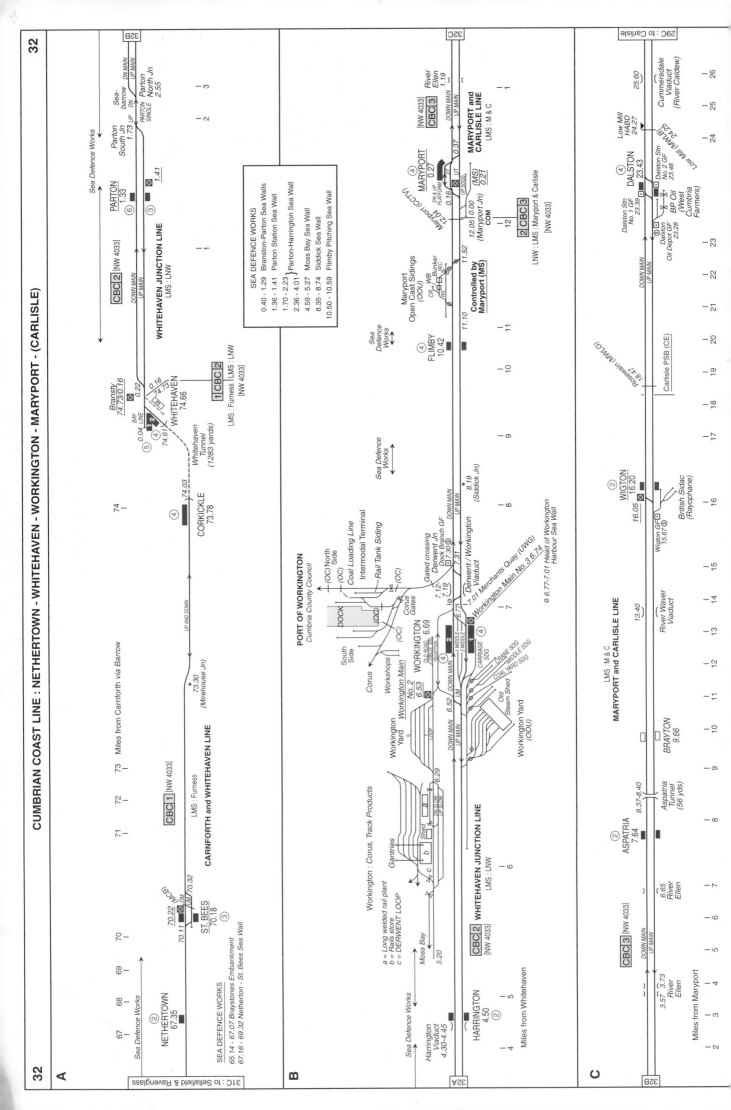

CUMBRIAN COAST LINE : NETHERTOWN - WHITEHAVEN - WORKINGTON - MARYPORT - (CARLISLE)

A

PRESTON to BLACKBURN LINE
LMS : L&Y
FHR 3 [NW 7009]

Miles from Farington Curve Junction

27C : to Preston

Bamber Bridge
Engineers Holding
Sidings : EWS
OOU
BBS

Bamber Bridge Station
CE's Sdgs GF 2.10
Bamber Bridge GF 2.25
BAMBER BRIDGE 2.29
(Bamber Bridge Jn)
Bamber Bridge W. H. Bowker

Whittle International 1.70
Bamber Bridge 1.73

3 FHR 4

Hospital (CCTV) 3.24
Bankhead (CCTV) 3.40
Orams No.1 (UWG) 3.77
M61 3.40
M6 2.61

Orams No.3 (UWG) 4.14
Greyson Lane (UWG) 4.21
Minthorne (CCTV) 4.49

Hoghton Tower Viaduct 6.51-6.56
Hoghton GFs West 5.32, 5.33
Hoghton GF's East 5.27
Pleasington Golf Club (UWG) 5.17
River Darwen N°4

PLEASINGTON 7.43
Pleasington Viaduct (River Darwen) 7.71-7.74

CHERRY TREE 8.50 ③

MILL HILL (Lancs) 9.24 ④

BLACKBURN 10.42
Platforms 1, 2 ①, 3, 4, 5

Blackburn East
DN EAST LANCS
UP EAST LANCS
10.50
4 FHR 5 LMS : L&Y [NW 7009]

Blackburn Tunnel (435 yards) 10.75
Station Holding Sdgs
(E. Lancs Sdgs)
BBS1 1

Blackburn West 10.28
10.17
Blackburn Bolton Rd 10.11/24.08
10.07
Blackburn, Bolton Road P & G Fogarty
BBS 3

Taylor Street 10 9.60
Blackburn, King Street Scottish Coal Co OOU 9.55
BBS 4

Goods Shed Blackburn, Bolton Road
23.60
Blackburn, Bolton Branch Jn
BBB [NW 60-11]

BOLTON to BLACKBURN LINE
LMS : L&Y
48A : to Darwen and Bolton

Controlled by Preston PSB (PN)

B

BLACKBURN to COLNE LINE
LMS : L&Y
FHR 5 [NW 7009]

33A

Miles from Farington Curve Jn

Cobwall Viaduct 11.09
Daisyfield (DS) 11.30
Daisyfield Jn 10.75
Blackburn Victoria Viaduct

RAMSGREAVE & WILPSHIRE 13.20
Wilpshire Tunnel (324 yds) 13.71-14.06
Shore House Farm (UWG) 13.26

RISHTON 13.26
Rishton Tunnel (68 yds)

CHURCH & OSWALDTWISTLE 14.76
Church Viaduct 14.64-14.70

ACCRINGTON 15.64
Accrington EGF 15.56
Accrington 15.72-16.08
5 15.41

HUNCOAT 17.41
Huncoat SB (MCB) 17.36

LANGHO 15.51
M65

WHALLEY 17.60
Whalley Viaduct No. 41 17.27-17.58
DOWN MAIN
UP MAIN

CLITHEROE 21.60
21.26
Primrose Viaduct 20.21-28
Low Moor (AL-GF) (CCTV) 20.17
PRG [NW 7015]
HOK
Horrocksford Jn
Horrocksford Castle Cement (Chatburn) 23.23

DJH [NW 7013] LMS : L&Y
Swan Side Viaduct

Gisburn Tunnel (157 yds)
Stockbeck Viaduct 29.12-19

BLACKBURN to HELLIFIELD LINE (NORTH LANCASHIRE LINE)

33C : to Hellifield

2 : 41A : to Hebden Bridge

NELSON 25.35
25.44 Nelson Vdct
Marsden/ 25.43 25.37-
GJC [NW 7017] 27.29
COLNE 27.37
27.41
Colne Viaduct

BRIERFIELD 24.20
Brierfield Tnl (73 yds) 24.37-24.40

BURNLEY BARRACKS 21.38
Burnley Viaduct 21.60-21.75
River Calder Viaduct #1.53-1.56

BURNLEY CENTRAL 22.05 ②

Gannow Jn 21.03
DN E L
UP E L

ROSE GROVE 20.32
Rose Grove West Jn 20.05
20.15
20.17 M65
DOWN GOODS 20.50

BURNLEY MANCHESTER ROAD 21.67
5 FHR 6
GJC

HAPTON 18.73 ④
19.1

Padiham 1.76
Padiham Power Station (closed) National Power 1.58
1.56
0.17 M65
0.00

BURNLEY BRANCH
FHR 6 [NW 7009] LMS : L&Y

Miles from Manchester Victoria [NW 7001] MVN 2 LMS : L&Y

y = Whitley Viaduct 22.55
z = Lobb Mill Viaduct Hebden Bdge(HB) 20.29-20.35
MANCHESTER LINE (Eastwood) (PN) 22.62
LNW LINE

Hall Royd Jn 19.49
30.54 19.61
19.63 Millwood Tnl (225 yds)
19.73 Millwood Tnl (274 yds)
Horsfall Tnl. (274 yds)
Castle Hill Tnl. (194 yds)
Cockden Viaduct 21.34
21.22
21.21

Towneley Tunnel (398 yards)
Towneley 22.46
23.06-23.25

Copy Pit 26.20
Holme Tunnel (265 yards)
25.52-25.65 749 ft
Portsmouth (MWB) 25.90
Kitson Wood Tunnel (290 yards)
Lydgate Viaduct 28.65-28.73
28.76-29.10

30.17 30.24
Stansfield Hall Loco
Stansfield Hall Spur
(OOU) DN L&Y

47B : to Todmorden & Rochdale
30.49 MANCHESTER and NORMANTON LINE

Controlled by Preston PSB (PN)

C

BLACKBURN to HELLIFIELD LINE
33B

HELLIFIELD 231.14 (H)
231.09
231.20
SKW1 [NZ 0001] LMS : Mid (N. Western)

West Coast Railway Co Ltd
Down Recess Sdgs
UP GOODS CRIPPLE
DOWN BRANCH
UP BRANCH
Haw Lane (UWG)
Switches Farm (UWC) 230.06
(34.68) DN SDG
230.68
[NW 7013] LMS : L&Y
[LN 922] LMS : Mid (N. Western)

34A : to Settle

SKW1 [NZ 0001] LMS : Mid (N. Western)
231.50
231.39

GARGRAVE 224.79 ④
225.04
225.63 226.59
226.82
River Aire 227.44
Bell Busk Viaduct
RYLSTONE Tilcon (P.W. Spencer Lime)
7.09
6.78
6.50 NR Limit

LONDON NORTH EAST ZONE
LMS : Mid (North Western)

York (L) 225.72
Nlfirby (UWG) 222.50
223.04 River Aire
Marshalls (UWC) 222.18

SKIPTON to MORECAMBE LINE
SKIPTON to MORECAMBE LINE

(former Skipton North Jn) for Colne 221.68
3 TJC SKW1 [LN 922] 221.60
Skipton North Jn

SKIPTON 221.21
Skipton Middle Jn 221.21
221.33
DOWN SHIPLEY SLOW
DOWN SHIPLEY FAST
UP SHIPLEY MAIN
Broughton Road CS
Up Sdgs
CW
SS

UP BAY ⑤

Skipton South Jn 221.00
STABLING SDG
DN MAIN
SKS 1 TJC
1 SKS 2 [LN 930]

34E : to Embsay & Bolton Abbey Steam Railway (Yorkshire Dales Railway)

Haw Bank Tunnel (220 yds) 221.07-77
220.64 0.00

Keighley Road Viaduct 222.27
222.24 220.71
222.71

River Aire 219.76

LEEDS and BRADFORD EXTENSION LINE
LMS : Mid
DOWN SHIPLEY MAIN
UP SHIPLEY MAIN

Controlled by York (North West Work Station) (L)

Miles from St. Pancras via Cudworth & Keighley
* Miles from St. Pancras via Ilkley

Rylstone (TMO) 5.17

GRASSINGTON or SWINDEN BRANCH
LMS : Mid (Yorkshire Dales)
SKS 2
(Details Unverified)

2 : 44A : to Keighley

B

SKIPTON and MORECAMBE LINE

LONG PRESTON 232.41 ④

SKW 1 [NZ 0001]

LMS : Mid (North Western)

Settle Jn 234.44

(SJ) 234.35

234.42

28B : to Carnforth

SAC

Settle or Church Viaduct 236.50-52

Marshfield Viaduct 236.60-62

(510 ft)

⑤ SETTLE 236.40 LMS : Mid

Ribble Viaduct 238.54-59

Stainforth Tunnel (120 yards)

Ribble or Sheriel Brow Viaduct 239.51

Little Viaduct 239.67

HORTON IN RIBBLESDALE 242.43 ④

Craig Hill Frm (UWG) 241.31

SETTLE and CARLISLE LINE

Miles from St Pancras via Cudworth & Keighley

DOWN MAIN / UP MAIN

232 233 234 235 236 237 238 239 240 241 242 243 244 245 246 247 248 249 250 251 252 253 254 255 256

Dent Head Viaduct 251.12-22

Risehill Tunnel (1213 yards) 254.11 254.66

⑤ DENT 253.32 (1156 ft)

Artengill Viaduct 252.07-17

Blea Moor Tunnel (1 mile, 869 yards) 249.25, 250.65 ↕1151 ft

Batty Moss Viaduct 249.16, 250.65

Ribblehead/BleaMoor/ Batty Moss Viaduct 247.22, (440 yards) 247.50-70

⑤ RIBBLEHEAD Down 247.13/247.20 Up 248.39 Blea Moor (BM) 248.39

248.28 248.24 248.40 UGL

Virtual Quarry 247.22

(Selside SB) 244.68

34B

Shotlock Hill Tunnel (106 yards) 258.38-43

Moorcock Tunnel (98 yards) 257.39-44

⑥ GARSDALE 256.53 (Formerly Hawes Jn)

256.55 (G)

Ais Gill Summit 1169 ft (site of former SB) 259.57

Grisedale (UWG) 257.70

Miles from St Pancras via Cudworth & Keighley

Y = Garsdale, Dandy Mire (or Moorcock) Viaduct 257.01-12
z = Lunds Viaduct 257.54-59

SETTLE and CARLISLE LINE

LMS : Mid SAC [NZ 0001]

257 258 259 260 261 262 263 264 265 266 267 268 269 270 271 272 273 274 275 276 277 278

Ais Gill Viaduct 260.53-56

Birkett Tunnel (424 yards) 264.23-42

263.21 (Mallerstang SB)

④ KIRKBY STEPHEN 266.47 266.40 (KS)

266.27 DRS

Smardale Viaduct 268.49-59

Crosby Garrett Tunnel (181 yards) 269.00-08

Crosby Garrett Viaduct 269.35-40 269.61

Griseburn Viaduct 271.53-59

Helm Tunnel (571 yards) 273.13-39

Griseburn (UWG) 271.3

Ormside Viaduct 275.20-29

274.64 (Ormside)

⑧ APPLEBY 277.22 (525 ft)

Appleby North 277.27 North Jn 277.34

EDE

11.46 NE SDSS

Appleby West Jn 278 11.36

EDE [NZ 0007]

LINE : NE

APPLEBY EAST 10.78 (TMOG) 11.03 NR

WAR

RR 277.56

⑩ WARCOP 5.56

Miles from Kirkby Stephen 6 5.53 5.21

Retained out of use
EDEN VALLEY LINE

Coupland Viaduct

Ø = DOWN & UP THROUGH SDG

34A

C

z = Wagon Maintenance Sdg
New Biggin British Gypsum Discharge Pad

Kirkby Thore (KT) 282.02

New Biggin 283.28

New Biggin or Crowdundle Viaduct 283.64-68

NEW BIGGIN 283.28

LONG MARTON 280.15 280.7

Long Marton Viaduct 279.67-72

Miles from St Pancras via Cudworth & Keighley

SETTLE and CARLISLE LINE

LMS : Mid SAC [NZ 0001]

279 280 281 282 283 284 285 286 287 288 289 290 291 292 293 294 295 296 297 298 299 300 301 302 303

Culgaith Tunnel (661 yards) 284.78-85.28

CULGAITH 284.55 (MCB)

Waste Bank Tunnel (164 yards) 285.48-55

LANGWATHBY 288.23 ⑤

Little Salkeld Viaduct 289.35-41

LITTLE SALKELD 289.56

290.63 (Long Meg SB)

Long Meg (or Eden Lacy) Viaduct 291.06-12

④ LAZONBY AND KIRKOSWALD 292.50

Lazonby Tunnel (99 yards) 292.25-30

Baron Wood Tunnels No. 1 (207 yds) 295.42-51 No. 2 (252 yds) 295.55-67

Armathwaite Tunnel (325 yards) 296.51-66

Armathwaite Viaduct 297.23-30

④ ARMATHWAITE 298.09

Drybeck Viaduct 299.06-12

(MCB)

Low House Crossing (LH) 299.55

Cotehill/ High Stand Gill Viaduct

301.02-05

302.68 303.13

Howe & Co's Sdg (HS) 302.77 D & UGL

Hornicks (UWG) 300.5 Ske Pool 301.18

Miles from St Pancras via Cudworth & Keighley

34B

D

EMBSAY & BOLTON ABBEY STEAM RAILWAY
Yorkshire Dales Railway Museum Trust
(Details Unverified)

CUMWHINTON 304.12

SETTLE and CARLISLE LINE

LMS : Mid SAC [NZ 0001]

29C : to Carlisle

(CE) Carlisle PSB 303.40

M6 305.77

DOWN MIDLAND / UP MIDLAND

304 305 306

to Rylstone

Bow Bridge Loop 220.58

220.65

(Embsay Jn)

33C : to Skipton

Embsay Jn

SETTLE and CARLISLE LINE

LMS : Mid SAC [NZ 0001]

Miles from St Pancras via Ilkley

Dock metre gauge

Workshop

EMBSAY 220.25

1 2

LANGWATHBY

287 288 289 290 291 292 293 294

LITTLE SALKELD 289.56

Embsay Station

HOLYWELL HALT 219.01

Skibeden P.W. Sdg

Stoneacre Loop 218.45 Stoneacre

DOWN

BOLTON ABBEY 216.66

216.56

THE DUKES SDG 1 2 3 D & UGL

Coal & water

to be constructed

Draughton (Priors Lane) c 217.65

Engineers'

217 218 219 220

303 302 301 300 299 298 297 296 295 217

34C

F

RAVENGLASS AND ESKDALE RAILWAY 15" gauge

RAVENGLASS (NR) for Eskdale 0.00

31C

2 3 1

Railway Museum

Workshop

Joinery and paint shop

Loco Shed

Diesel Shed

Carriage Shed

0.03 0.05

MUNCASTER MILL 1.06

MITESIDE HALT 1.49

(MURTHWAITE HALT) 2.55

Murthwaite Sdg (Per. Way Store) 2.43

Miteside Loop 1.67

IRTON ROAD 4.08

THE GREEN 4.59

Fisherground Loop 5.28

Gilbert's Cutting 5.68, 5.73

FISHERGROUND HALT 5.35

BECKFOOT 6.30

DALEGARTH 6.68

6.70

1 2 3 4 5 6

Control is by 'Radio-controlled Train Order' except at Ravenglass

SETTLE AND CARLISLE LINE ● EMBSAY & BOLTON ABBEY STEAM RLY ● RAVENGLASS & ESKDALE RAILWAY

33C : to Hellifield

CHESTER - HELSBY/MOULDSWORTH ● HELSBY - ELLSMERE PORT

Kemira Fertilisers (OOU)

Warehouse (OOU)

HELSBY
8.60 8.66 7.40
Helsby (HY)
8.61 7.34
Helsby Junction (HY)
7.34

Helsby West Cheshire Jn
8.19 8.52 M56
8.12 8.10
Helsby (OOU)
LC (OOU)

Engrs' RS

DOWN HOOTON
UP HOOTON

Miles from Chester "Zero"
3 3.52

DOWN MAIN
UP MAIN

MOULDSWORTH
31.02
Mouldsworth (MH)
31.13 Jn 31.05

DOWN & UP MANCHESTER
Farnell (UWG) 34.06 CLC
Plantsnall (UWG) 34.45
34.5

River Gowy

INCE & ELTON
6.66

MML (MWL) 6.69

Mickle Trafford Jn 2.59

ML CR

35.35 35.24
35.41
Miles from former Manchester Central via Altrincham

MANCHESTER SHIP CANAL
Ellesmere Port East

Shell No. 2 Entrance (OOU)

STANLOW & THORNTON
5.67
Stanlow & Thornton (OOU)
6.04 6.21

OUTWARD
INWARD
REC RR
SHUNT NK

Wagon Repairs
Central Workshops
Filling Racks (OOU)
Middle Yard
Reception
Departure

THORNTON SOUTH SIDINGS
Shell (UK) Ltd (OOU)
Stanlow Refinery

LPG
LC
H-F

RUNNING ROAD

Shell Sidings (OOU)
5.15 5.17

River Gowy
5.15

Shropshire Union Canal

Associated Octel Ltd (OOU)

Stanlow Sdgs (OOU)

Shell (UK) Ltd (OOU) Propylene Import Site (OOU)

Wagon Rep (OOU)
Wagon Rep Sdgs (OOU)

4.71
4.30

HOOTON AND HELSBY LINE
HHJ [NW 3013]

GW and LMS (LNW) Joint: Birkenhead Joint (Birkenhead, Lancashire and Cheshire Junction Railway)

Ellesmere Port: East Yard Sdgs

MSC
NR

MSC NECK
NR NECK
3.60 3.44
B.D GF
3.78 M53

ELLESMERE PORT
3.70
DOWN HELSBY
UP HELSBY
Ellesmere Port (7)

38C : to Hooton
38C : to Hooton

Mollington Viaduct 2.42-47

BACHE
0.79 (7)

(Mollington)
2.74

Miles from Chester "Zero"

Controlled by Chester PSB (CR)

WSJ [NW 3005]
GW : Didcot & Chester Line

CHESTER AND HOLYHEAD LINE
[NW 3001] CNH3
LMS : LNW
UP DOWN
Saltney Jn
181.28 181.09
181.02

River Dee
Roodee Viaduct 180.47-23
180.18 179.77 180

Roodee Jn 179.67
179.61
179.56

Chester South Jn
0.00 or 0.13/179.48
(former Tunnel Jn)

Chester North Jn 0.38
(former Brook Lane Jn) (0.25)

Engineers' Sidings

CHESTER CURVE

Windmill Lane Tunnel (104 yards)
Northgate Street Up and Down Tunnels (218 yards)

CRR1 [NW 3013]
CHESTER AND BIRKENHEAD LINE
GW and LMS (LNW) Joint: Birkenhead Joint (Chester and Birkenhead Railway)

CHESTER TRAIN CARE CENTRE (CH)

Undercarriage Wash
Maintenance Shed
OTM Shed

CVS
CRR1 [NW 3009]
3CNH2
3CNH1

Chester West Jn (former Holyhead Jn) (179.30)

CRR1 CNH2
179.22/0.09
179.30/0.17
179.39/0.24
179.29
179.26

Former Joint Lines zero at 179.14

CNH1 CNH2
0.09/179.22

CHESTER
179.11
CNH2 [NW 3001]

Platforms
1 6
2 6
3 18
4 15
5 5
6 5
7 15

7b 7a 6
4b 4a 5
2 3 PARCELS

UP FAST
DN FAST
UP SLOW
DN SLOW
UP MAIN
DN MAIN
DN THROUGH
DN UP GOODS

REC
SDG
Station Yd
WAREHOUSE

Chester PSB (CR)
179.00

SHUNT NECK

Chester East Jn (178.66/0.24)
178.56
178.67/0.27
178.70/0.24
178.72/0.21
178.75

(a) 178.67/0.27
(b) 178.70/0.24
(c) 178.72/0.21
(d) 178.75

2CNH1 [NW 3001]

CNH1 [NW 3001] LMS : LNW
CREWE AND CHESTER LINE

Miles from Euston

Tattenhall Emergency GF 174.50

Christleton Tunnel (160 yards) 177.59-52

CHESTER AND WARRINGTON LINE

DOWN WARRINGTON
UP WARRINGTON

DN WARRINGTON
UP WARRINGTON

LNW Joint : Birkenhead (Birkenhead, Lancashire & Cheshire Jn Railway)
[NW 3003]

CHW1 [NW 3023]

B Miles from Chester "Zero"

35A

FRODSHAM
9.68
Frodsham Tunnel (87 yards) 10.07-11

Weaver or Frodsham Viaduct 10.48-65

Weston Viaduct 10.76-11.03

Beeston Castle & Tarporley 168.60 168.46
168.51
(BC)

CNH1 [NW 3001] LMS : LNW
CREWE AND CHESTER LINE

GW and LMS (LNW) Joint etc.
CHW1

CALVELEY 166.11

Dairy Worleston Viaduct 161.12-05
House Farm (UWG)
161.42

CNH1 [NW 3001]
LMS : LNW
UP MAIN
DOWN MAIN
CREWE AND CHESTER LINE
Miles from Euston

C

35B

43B : to Northwich

MOULDSWORTH

26B : to Runcorn East

35C
13 : to Crewe

CDM2

LNW1

CHW1

35 March 2005

© Copyright TRACKmaps. No reproduction without permission

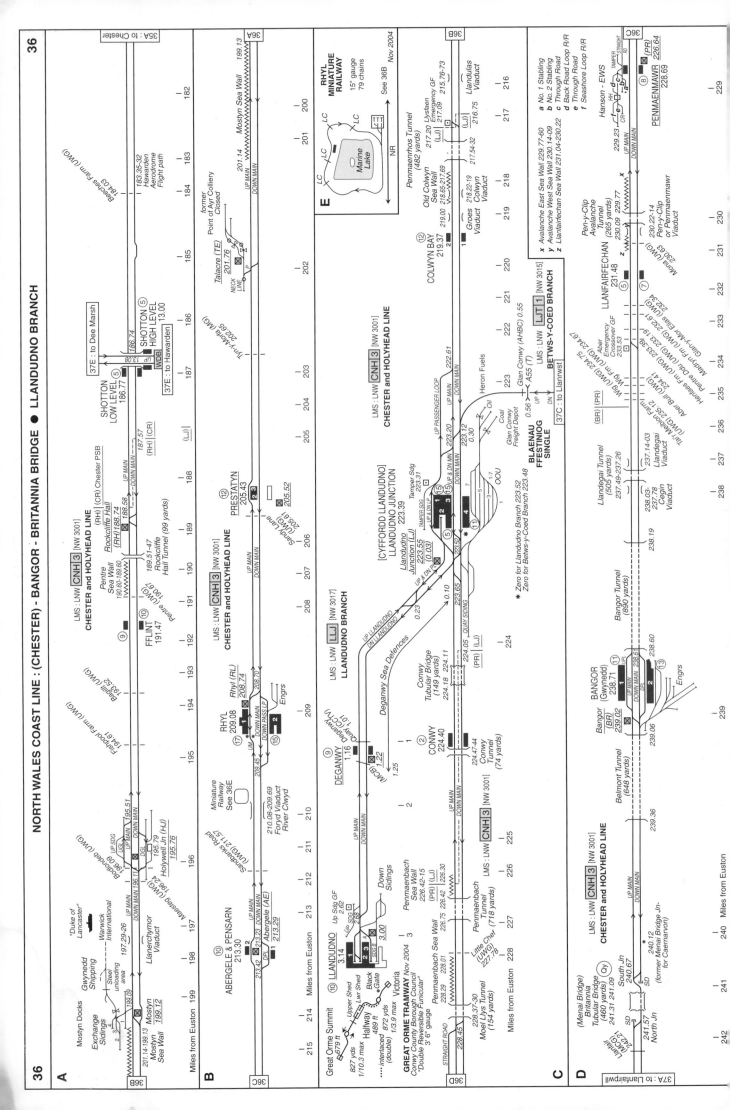

NORTH WALES COAST LINE : (CHESTER) - BANGOR - BRITANNIA BRIDGE ● LLANDUDNO BRANCH

A — AMLWCH BRANCH

Workshop
Chlorine Plant
Cefni (Uchaf) 260.57 (UWG)
Level crossings O = open, G = gates
AMLWCH
Stanley Embankment 261.29-260.59
VALLEY (Y DYFFRYN) 260.09 (MCB)
Former (AMLWCH) Station
Direct Rail Services
Rhosgoch Anglesey Borough Council RHOSGOCH 15.51 / 14.06
Shell Oil depot c.0.54
RHOSNEIGR 256.04
Trewin Sands Viaduct 256.19- / 256.17
TY CROES 254.31 (Up) / 254.27 (Up) / 254.34 (Down)
LLANERCH-Y-MEDD 11.06
LLANGWYLLOG 7.10
BODORGAN 251.52
Bodorgan No. 1 Tunnel (413 yds) 250.78- / 250.59
Bodorgan No. 2 Tunnel (115 yds) 251.06-01
Bodorgan Viaduct 249.74- / 249.65
LLANGEFNI 4.41
River Cefni
OOU
LLANFAIRPWLL 242.29
Llanfair (MCG) 242.21
Bangor (BR)
Star (UWG) 243.27 / 243.75
Llanddaniel (UWG) 243.75
Gaerwen GF 245.09
Gaerwen Jn (MCB) 0.00 / 245.15
Line Closed
"ISLE OF ANGLESEY RAILWAY CO." (Anglesey County Council)
GLA [NW 3019] LMS : LNW
CNH 3 [NW 3001]
36D : to Bangor
UP MAIN / DOWN MAIN
Miles from Euston

ANGLESEY CENTRAL LINE

CHESTER and HOLYHEAD LINE
LMS : LNW

B — HOLYHEAD

Holyhead Anglesey Aluminium Metal Ltd. (Rio Tinto)
Fuel and inspection point
HOLYHEAD (CAERGYBI) 263.52 / 263.49 / 263.57 / 263.56
Platform 1 GF / Platform 3 GF 263.26
Holyhead (HD) 263.26
CNH 3 [NW 3001] LMS : LNW
INNER HARBOUR
Miles from Euston 263.07
ENGINE RELEASE / CARRIAGE SDG / RUN ROUND / NECK / MAIL LINE
261.56

C — CONWY VALLEY LINE
Miles from Llandudno Junction
LJT 1 [NW 3015] LMS : LNW
GLAN CONWY 1.39
TAL-Y-CAFN 5.05
DOLGARROG 8.12
(GOGLEDD LLANRWST) NORTH LLANRWST 11.17
Tan Dōl 9.17 / 10.31 (UWG) 9.73
Tan Lan (UWG)
LLANRWST 11.57 / 11.08 / 11.03 / 11.22
Llanrwst Tunnel (85 yards)
36C : to Llandudno Jn

BETWS-Y-COED BRANCH - BETWS-Y-COED & FESTINIOG LINE
See 37F
Conwy Electric Valley 15" gauge Tram 500 yds
BETWS-Y-COED 15.02
Flood Opening 12.64- / 12.67
R. Conwy Viaduct 13.07- / 13.11
Cethin's Bridge / Lledr Viaduct 17.35- / 17.51
Beaverpool Tunnel (110 yards) 16.14-19
Lledr Viaduct
Bryn-yr-Odyn Viaduct 14.49- / 14.54
Lugwy Viaduct 21.17-15 (61 yards)
Cwmbowydd (TMO) 25.15 / 25.25
Gelli (Vct) (TMO) 23.04-24.18 (108 yds)
Fronllas 24.07
Miles from Bala Junction

D
Miles from Llandudno Junction
PONT-Y-PANT 19.29
Pont-y-Pant Lower Tunnel (144 yds) 19.10- / 19.17
Pont-y-Pant Upper Tunnel (66 yds) 19.56- / 19.59
DOLWYDDELAN 20.62
(PONT RUFEINIG) ROMAN BRIDGE 22.48
Bertheos Tunnel (46 yds) 22.19- / 22.57 / 22.22
Roman Bridge Tunnel (43 yds) 22.55- / 22.57
Ffestiniog Tunnel (2 miles, 333 yds) 24.33
BLAENAU FFESTINIOG 790 ft
Old Station
Festiniog Railway
LMS : LNW LJT 1 [NW 3015]
BLAENAU FFESTINIOG SINGLE / UP SINGLE DN
COM LMS : GW 27.53 25.25 / 27.53 27.51 / 27.33 27.51
No. 1 GF / No. 2 GF 27.33
FP Stop Block 27.53
FP 13.57- 50 13.48
24J : to Porthmadog
37C / 37D / 37A

BLAENAU FFESTINIOG BRANCH
Trawsfynydd 19.04 / 18.78 / 18.77
MAENTWROG ROAD 20.02 / 20.60
Closed
LJT 2 GW

E — WREXHAM, MOLD AND CONNAH'S QUAY LINE
Miles from Wrexham Central
Croes Newydd North Fork (CN) 0.68
Wrexham Exchange Jn
GWERSYLLT 2.29
CEFN-Y-BEDD 4.20 / 4.13
Cefn-y-Bedd Viaduct 4.09-
CAERGWRLE 4.73
HOPE (Flintshire) (Y HOB) 5.44
Penyffordd Castle Cement (Padeswood Hall Works)
PENYFFORD 7.39 / 7.41 (UWG)
HOPE EXCHANGE 7.64
BUCKLEY (BUCLE) 8.68
(PENARLÂG) HAWARDEN 10.64
HAWARDEN BRIDGE 14.12 / 13.33 14.15
SHOTTON HIGH LEVEL 13.00
SHOTTON LOW LEVEL 186.77 / 186.74
River Dee 13.24- / 13.37 / 13.08
Change of mileage (mileage meet) 13.33 14.15
WDB1 [NW 3007] LNE : GC
MDH 1
1WDB2 / 2WDB3
CNH
36A : to Flint / 36A : to Chester
22D : to Wrexham
DOWN MAIN / UP MAIN

NORTH WALES and LIVERPOOL LINE
DEE MARSH
Shotton Steel Works (Summers)
Corus Coated Products Division
Government Sdgs
Birkenhead Sidings
WB
Dee Marsh North Jn 13.11 / 13.40
Dee Marsh Jn (DM) 13.77 (formerly Dee Marsh Jn West or Wrexham Jn)
(formerly Birkenhead Jn)
WDB 3 / WDB3
DOWN WREXHAM / UP WREXHAM
Shotwick / Shotton Paper Co. Ltd. GF 11.74
BURTON POINT 10.64
Shotwick GF 11.74
WDB 3 [NW 3007]
39A : to Bidston

F — CONWY VALLEY RAILWAY
Nov 2004
Pond / Museum / DEP / ARR
7¼" gauge 950 yards
CONWY VALLEY TRAM 110v DC
LC
37C
Miles from Bidston

HALTON JUNCTION - RUNCORN - (SPEKE JUNCTION) ● DITTON - (WARRINGTON) ● (CHESTER)/ELLESMERE PORT - ROCK FERRY

A

Widnes, Tanhouse Lane, La Farge
Tarmac
Widnes, Tanhouse Jn
Widnes, Carterhouse Jn 'ZENECA'
Sullivan Wks
Former GC & Mid Joint
Widnes, Carterhouse Jn (UWE)
Tarmac (mothballed)
16.27
Sullivan Sdg GF 16.00
SDJ 2 [NW 2009] LMS : LNW
3BB
17 Miles from former Timperley Jn

limit NR
RECAR Lane (UWE)
UP A GOODS
DN ARPLEY GDS
OOU
16.75 16.60

WIDNES SOUTH
Viaduct 17.18 17.15
WIDNES LOOP
LMS : LNW
17.50 (West Deviation Jn)
Ditton Viaduct
Runcorn Viaduct North (River Mersey: Spans 1-5)
16 Spans
3 Spans
49 Spans
181.69
181.33
181.11
181.25
Runcorn Viaduct South
180.77 Runcorn Viaduct South
915 yards
180.52 Bridgewater Canal
Manchester Ship Canal
The Queen Aethelfreda Viaduct

TIMPERLEY and GARSTON LINE
LMS : LNW [WJL] 2 [MD 2001]

UP DITTON FAST
DOWN DITTON FAST
UP DITTON SLOW
DN DITTON SLOW

Ditton East Jn 18.55
182.67 182.60
182.53
182.52
Emergency Crossover
UP LOW LEVEL
DOWN LOW LEVEL
BOC SDG
AMC
Foundry Lane
Widnes Intermodal Rail Depot O'Connor
182.57 182.53 [MD 2009] SDJ 2
RUNCORN BRIDGE River Mersey 915 yards
181

DITTON 182.79
182.69
182.74
CR
3
Ditton West Jn 183.22
Reception Sdgs
Ditton (DN) 183.00
183.30
183.22

RUNCORN BRANCH
[MD 2001] WJL 1 LMS : LNW
a = UP DITTON
b = DOWN DITTON

RUNCORN 180.40
Runcorn Jn 180.22
1 b a
180.48
16
180.29
15
180.33
A533(T)
0.25 (RN) 180.33
UP 0.00
UP MAIN
DOWN MAIN
DN CHESTER
Halton Jn (HN) 179.20
179.24
26B : to Frodsham/Acton Bridge

RUNCORN DOCK BRANCH
FOLLY LANE SINGLE
RDB [MD 2003]
FOLLY LANE
Ineos Chlor Chemicals
0.69 NR boundary
Loading facility
180

TIMPERLEY and GARSTON LINE
LMS : LNW [WJL] 2 [MD 2001]

Speke Jn (SE) (DN) Ditton
185.58
Halewood East Jn 184.64
184.45 (Halebank)
184.01 (Halebank)
E. NECK
Halewood
Jaguar
4
3
1 Car Ramps
5
Exchange Sdgs
Ford Motor Co.
W. NECK
UP ONE
Halewood West Jn 185.16
185.16
W NECK

3 WJL 2
186.72 (22.59)
186.57
Speke Jn GF 186.72 (22.59)
186.56
(Speke) 186.21
Garston Car Terminal
Ansa Logistics
Ramps
Sullivan Sdg GF 16.00

186
185
184 Miles from Euston

40 : to Garston & Liverpool Lime Street

B

FIDDLERS FERRY POWER STATION
Scottish & Southern Energy
Control Building
Coal Track Hoppers
0.00
0.33
HOPPER APPROACH
WB
CR
RD.2
FLY/ASH SDG
RD.1
WB
(WB Down)
(WB Up)
A
B
Fiddlers Ferry Power Station 14.46

TIMPERLEY and GARSTON LINE
[NW 2009] SDJ 2 LMS : LNW

Litton's Mill Crossing 11.45
Monks Sdg 11.70
St Helens Canal
Marsh House (CCTV) 14.09
Fiddlers Ferry Hall (UWE) 13.83 13.37
Penketh Hall (UWE)
26B : to Arpley Jn

Sullivan Sdg GF 16.00
UP ARPLEY GOODS
DOWN ARPLEY GOODS

16
15
14
13
12 Miles from former Timperley Jn

38A

C

CHESTER and BIRKENHEAD LINE
[NW 8013] CRR 2 GW & LMS (LNW) Joint : Birkenhead Joint
Wirral Line

Controlled by Merseyrail (ML)
Located at Sandhills

Rock Ferry South Jn 13.30
BEBINGTON 12.36
PORT SUNLIGHT 11.61
DOWN SDG
SPITAL 11.16
11.42
Merseyrail (ML)
BROMBOROUGH RAKE 10.38
BROMBOROUGH 9.71
EASTHAM RAKE 8.68
EASTHAM M53 8.53
6

HOOTON and HELSBY LINE
[NW 3013] HHJ GW & LMS (LNW) Joint : (Birkenhead, Lancashire & Cheshire Jn Railway)
UP HELSBY
DOWN HELSBY

HHJ 2 CRR 1
HOOTON South Jn 8.08
8.17
Hooton North Jn 7.72
7.68
Hooton (HN) 7.72
HOOTON 8.08
BAY
SIDING
DOWN CHESTER
UP CHESTER
6 1 2 3
[NW 3011] CRR 1 GW & LMS (LNW) Joint : (Chester & Birkenhead Railway)

CHESTER and BIRKENHEAD LINE
CAPENHURST 5.11
(CR) Chester PSB
(HN) Chester PSB
UP BIRKENHEAD
DOWN BIRKENHEAD
35A : to Chester
35A : to Chester

LITTLE SUTTON 1.47
OVERPOOL 2.28
CAPENHURST 5.11
Chester PSB

MANCHESTER SHIP CANAL
Ellesmere Port : West End Sidings
(approx. distances from Ellesmere Port, NR)

Ellesmere Port Docks (1 mile) (OOU)
LS (OOU)
Dock Rd (OOU)
MSC
NR
West End Sdgs
Richaw Lawson Transport
Ramps
3
e limit
35A : to Helsby
ELLESMERE PORT 3.44
3.37

Gulf Oil (1½ miles)
GATX 3½ miles
Panocean Storage & Transport Eastham
3½ miles
Manisty Wharf 1¾ miles

DOWN MAIN
UP MAIN
180

1
2

8
7
6
5
4 Miles from Chester

39A : to Birkenhead

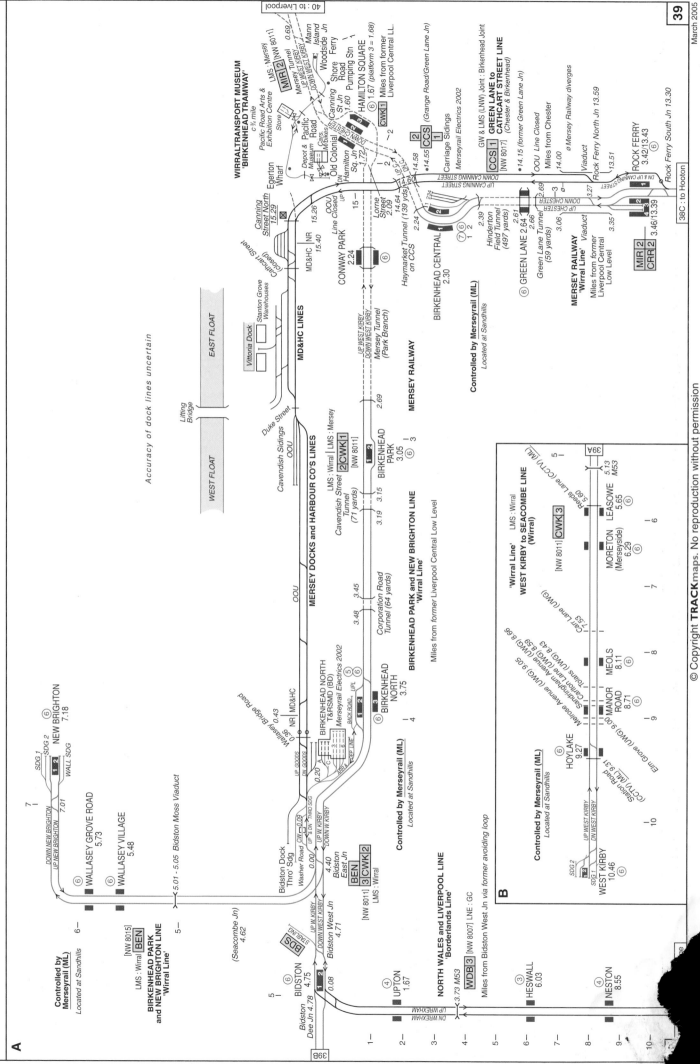

March 2005

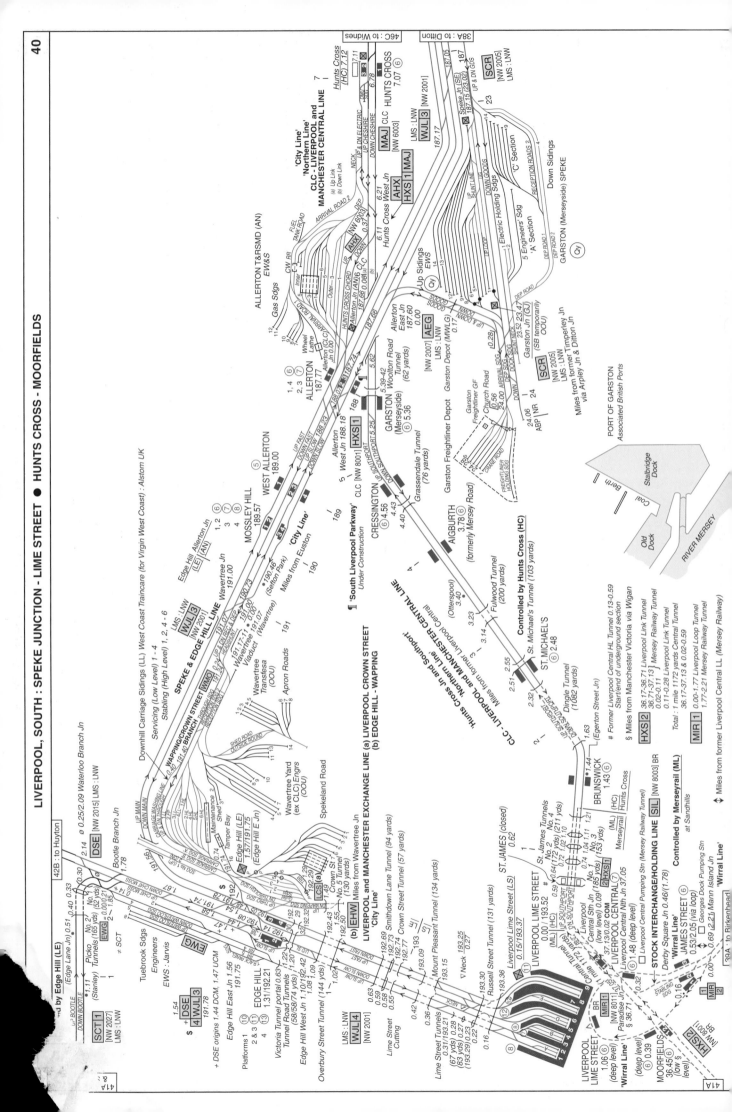

LIVERPOOL, NORTH : (MOORFIELDS) - BIRKDALE, AUGHTON PARK & ORRELL ● BOOTLE BRANCH

A

Controlled by Merseyrail (ML) at Sandhills

Miles from Manchester Victoria via Wigan

Upholland Tunnel (959 yards)

M6

ORRELL 20.40 20.77
UPHOLLAND 22.01 22.24 21.37
Dykes Wood (UWG) 23.11
RAINFORD 24.30 24.39
Rainford Jn 24.35
TOWN GREEN 10.08

'Northern Line'

AUGHTON PARK 10.78

ORMSKIRK 12.01 12.13 12.15
UP ORMSKIRK 9.79
DOWN ORMSKIRK

SJO 2 [NW 8005]

HXS 3 [NW 8001]

'Northern Line'

MAGHULL 7.29
7.13 (ML)
6.49 6.12 M58 M57
OLD ROAN 5.62

LMS : L&Y

PEMBERTON to LIVERPOOL LINE

UP & DOWN SINGLE
1 mile
Container area
Knowsley Freight Terminal
Potter Group 29
Warehouse
GSP @ Dale

KIRKBY 29.40 29.41
30.06 30.10
DN & UP KIRKBY

WKL 2 LMS : L&Y

M57

FAZAKERLEY 31.31
Fazakerley (UWG) 31.16
30.72

WJK 2 LMS : L&Y [NW 8009]
SJO 2 [NW 8005]

RICE LANE 32.60
Walton Junction 33.16
WJK 2 / SJO 1

Kirkdale No. 1 Tunnel (497 yards)
Kirkdale No. 2 Tunnel (210 yards)
33.33 33.56 33.60 33.71
34.03 Kirkdale North Jn
34

WALTON (Merseyside) 3.45
ORRELL PARK 3.75
AINTREE 0.33
Aintree Station Jn 0.40 0.62
EGF (ML) (Sefton Jn) 32.43 32.42
Aintree West (UWG) 32.65

AFL [NW 8007]
NMB

LMS : L&Y
WALTON JN to PRESTON LINE

NORTH MERSEY BRANCH
LMS : L&Y

DOWN & UP GOODS ON AINTREE
LINE CLOSED

Miles from Manchester Victoria via Wigan

B

LIVERPOOL, CROSBY AND SOUTHPORT LINE
(Hunts Cross and Southport)

LMS : L&Y

Controlled by Merseyrail (ML) at Sandhills

HIGHTOWN 9.09
River Alt 10.25
Hoscar (UWG) 9.61
FORMBY 11.14
Eccles (ML) 11.79
11.25
Fisherman's Path (UWG) 12.46
FRESHFIELD 12.03
AINSDALE 14.62
Crescent Road (ML) 14.67
HILLSIDE 16.26
BIRKDALE 17.22
Crescent Road (UWG) 16.76
Aughton Road (CCTV) 18.00
Portland Street (CCTV) 17.65
Duke Street (ML) 17.26
South Jn 18.13

HXS 3 [NW 8001]

SPELLOW 3.74 (closed)
WALTON & ANFIELD 3.41 (closed)
Spellow No. 1 Tunnel (339 yards)
4.04 4.19
Spellow No. 1 Tunnel (62 yards)
Westminster Tunnel (288 yards)

Miles from Bootle Branch Jn, Edge Hill
LMS : LNW

BOOTLE BRANCH
SCT 1 [NW 2027] LMS : LNW
1.67 (Tue Brook)

Controlled by Edge Hill (LE)

KIRKDALE 34.14 34.17
4.30 4.33 4.35

Merseyside Electrics 2002

Controlled by Merseyrail (ML)

LMS : L&Y [NW 8005]
SJO 1

(KK) Kirkdale Servicing Depot
Kirkdale South Jn
Carriage Shed
OTM
Atlantic Dock Jn (to Canada Dock) 4.55
4.49 Former
Oriel Road Tunnel (288 yards)
2.04 Canada Dock Tunnel Under
BANK HALL 2.06

SCT 1 / 2 [NW 2027] LMS : LNW

BSJ xover only

BOOTLE ORIEL ROAD 2.61
4.79 4.68 2.39 Bootle Jn
2.31 2.54 Alexandra Dock Tunnel (283 yds)
5.25 5.38
Regent Road (AOCL) 5.53
5.43 Stop board

BOOTLE EXTENSION LINE
LMS : LNW
SCT 2 [NW 2027]

BOOTLE NEW STRAND 3.15
(North Mersey Jn) Marsh Lane 3.52
NMM / NMB
3.77 Marsh Lane Crossover
34.02 34.12 Viaduct
34.23 34.40 / 3.52 Change of mileage
NMM / HXS

SEAFORTH & LITHERLAND 4.14
WATERLOO (Merseyside) 5.20
Waterloo (ML) 5.38
Brook Hall Road (CCTV) 5.69
BLUNDELLSANDS AND CROSBY 6.28
HALL ROAD 7.10 7.14
Wallside Sdg
Hall Road Depot Network Rail

LMS : L&Y
LIVERPOOL, CROSBY and SOUTHPORT LINE

UP SOUTHPORT
DOWN SOUTHPORT
HXS 3 [NW 8001]

'Northern Line'

Miles from former Liverpool Exchange

Liverpool Bulk Terminal : PowerGen
Alexandra Dock Sidings
European Metal Recycling Ltd.

Coal Loading Bunker
Bootle Bunker
Strand Rd 5.72
MD&HC NR
5.53 5.52

Allied Mills Grain Terminal
LIVERPOOL FREEPORT (OOU)
Loading Bank
Regent Road

LIVERPOOL BULK TERMINAL

Seaforth Container Terminal : Cawoods
Dock 7.22

Royal Seaforth Dock
Gladstone Docks

No. 1 Bch
No. 2 Bch
No. 3 Bch
Alexandra Docks

40 : to Liverpool Central
40 : to Edge Hill

'Northern Line'

ø Start/End of Underground Section

Miles from Manchester Victoria via Wigan
36.17
Leeds Street Portal
Central Tunnel (1 mile 1172 yds)
Leeds St Jn 35.72
SANDHILLS 35.03 35.14
HXS 2 [NW 8001] LMS : L&Y
Merseyrail (IECC)
ASC (ML) 35.00
34.75
Sandhills 1.41
SJO 1 35.03
HXS 2

Controlled by Merseyrail (ML) at Sandhills

35.14 - 35.62
Spans 1 - 68B
Liverpool Exchange Viaduct
35.62 - 36.10
Spans 69 - 100
Great Howard Street Viaduct
36.08 - 36.12
Great Howard Street Incline

41A
27A : to Wigan Wallgate
42A : to Southport
41B
49B

March 2005

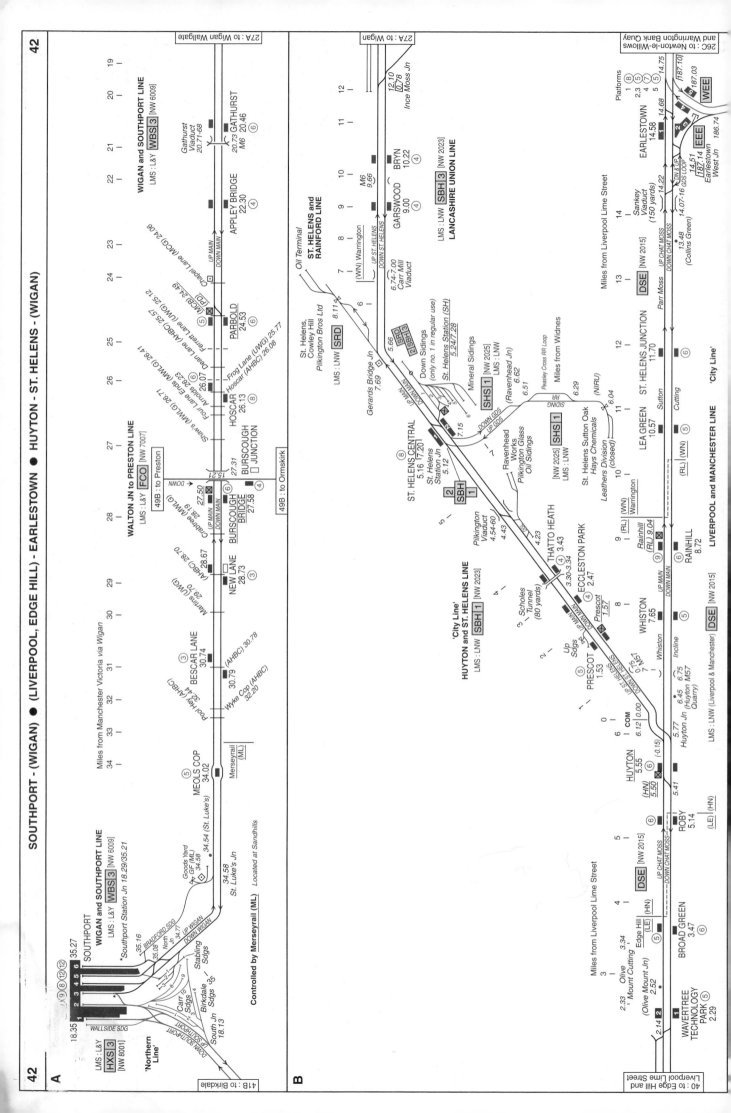

43

ETRURIA - CHEADLE HULME ● (CREWE) - CHEADLE HULME ● MOULDSWORTH - KNUTSFORD ● SANDBACH - NORTHWICH ● WILMSLOW - HEALD GREEN

43

A

25B : to Stoke-on-Trent

West Coast Main Line Project

Granville Sidings

former Shelton : Corus (Closed)

ORE FULLS / ORE EMPTIES

ETRURIA 18.64

Grange Jn 18.16

18.54 UP GDS

18.30

MACCLESFIELD and COLWICH LINE [NW 5009]
LMS : NS CMD2

Miles from Macclesfield Hibel Road

18

Controlled by Stoke-on-Trent SC (SOT)

Up Sidings
EWS International

FREIGHT DEPOT

LONGPORT 17.03

Down Sidings
EWS International

LOCO RELEASE

16.71

Longport Jn

16.63

16.57

Pinnox Branch Sdgs (OOU)

Bradwell Jn
16.16

Esso (LPG)

16.31 UP GOODS LOOP
16.24

16.20 DOWN SDG

Carless Solvents Sdg (closed)

Chatterley Valley UK Coal
Disposal Point
(Chesterton Branch)

16 (old)

CMD3
was Old Harecastle
Tunnel Line
13.70-16.20

16.00 | 15.65

16 (new)

1CMD2

Harecastle Tunnel (310 yards)

Trent & Mersey Canal
13.69
13.68

Kidsgrove Jn
14.13-21
14 15

Trent & Mersey Canal
13.60 13.52
KIDSGROVE
13.60 0.05

(SOT) Stoke-on-Trent SC

(CE) Crewe

Coopers (UWG)
1.35

CREWE BRANCH

LMS : NS KCS1 [NW 1005]

Mow Cop (CCTV) 11.30

MACCLESFIELD and COLWICH LINE [NW 5009]
LMS : NS CMD1

Ackers HABD 10.58

ALSAGER 2.33
2.27

RADWAY GREEN 4.03

Home Farm (UWG) 3.01

13 : to Crewe

43B

B

46A : to Altrincham

46A : to Gatley

44A : to Stockport

44A : to Stockport

(Manchester Airport) trip wires both sides approx. ¾ to 1 mile post

*

Controlled by (MP)

KNUTSFORD 14.40

MANCHESTER AIRPORT 0.00

HEALD GREEN 3.37

ALTRINCHAM and CHESTER LINE
[NW 3023] CLC (Cheshire Midland)

Woods Tenement Farm

Stone 16 'a' end ct.27
'b' end

NR limit 10.43

Heald Gn. W. Jn 1.10
1.48

STYAL 1.79

Heald Gn, S. Jn Gn. N. Jn 1.51
2.50 3.13

180 [NW 5001]

CMP1

LMS : LNW (Man & B'ham)

MANCHESTER AIRPORT BRANCH

PLUMLEY 17.17

Field House Farm (UWG)

Octel Plumley (PY)
18.43 & Sdg West (PY)
18.07
18.43
18

CHORD SMA

AIRPORT MIA

FRT BRANCH - Nil

Dean Viaduct 179

Manchester Sth
178.52

HANDFORTH 178.24
178

LOSTOCK GRALAM 19.15

Greenbank (GK) [NW 5005] BR [NW 5007] BR

WILMSLOW 176.71
176.65

Wilmslow Platforms

177

176.53

176.52 0.00

WILMSLOW MCH

x Wilmslow Viaduct (R. Bollin) 0.26-35
y Wilmslow Old Viaduct 176.79-177.05
z Handforth Viaduct 178.05-11

POYNTON 2.79

BRAMHALL 1.49

Shop Sdgs

Brunner Mond
Lostock
East

Wade Works
Brunner Mond

Wilmslow Jn

19.48
19.77

Northwich East Jn

Dn Gp Sdgs

Underline discharge

20

ADLINGTON (Cheshire) 5.15

MACCLESFIELD BRANCH [NW 5009] MCH

NORTHWICH 20.47
20.56

Northwich Station Jn 20.52

Northwich West Jn 20.74
21.16

20.79

West Goods Line [NW 3035] CLC

East Goods Line [NW 3033] CLC

[NW 3029] LNW

HWG WEST GOODS LINE

HEG EAST GOODS LINE

NSN [NW 3029] LNW

Northwich South Jn 8.37

NORTHWICH BRANCH LMS : LNW

SNJ [NW 3029]

Alderley Edge North Jn 175.34
South Jn 175.12

ALDERLEY EDGE 175.21

175

CREWE and STOCKPORT LINE
LMS : LNW (Manchester & Birmingham)

174

PRESTBURY 7.10

Prestbury Tunnel (273 yards)

173

Macclesfield Hibel Road

9.27-12
9.37

LMS : LNW

Hartford North Jn 21.57
21.67

Northwich (or Leftwich) Jn

R. Weaver R. Dane

21.60

21.12 Hartford West Jn
22.28

Hartford CLC Jn 23.11

172

MIDDLEWICH LOOP 3.46
River Dane 4.07

CHELFORD 172.17

Chelford Loops 172.20

MACCLESFIELD 0.37
0.25
0.20

171.21

170.20-27
Peover Viaduct

171

WINNINGTON BRANCH

Concrete Pad Wagon Repairs

Northwich Oakleigh Sidings 1.03

Winnington Brunner Mond 0.56

HNO [NW 3035] CLC

GREENBANK 22.12

Hartford 22.18

22.21

(GK) 22.10

GOOSTREY 168.35 (SH)
168.52

166.78-167.24
Dane or Holmes Chapel Viaduct

HOLMES CHAPEL 166.37/166.52

170

170.59

British Salt

Middlewich 166

WEST COAST MAIN LINE

26A : to Warrington

Discharge Hopper

Vale Royal

0.44 (limit of elect.)

[WD] (GK)

[WSF]

Hartford LNW Jn 170.47
170.56

UP FAST
DN MAIN

CGJ1

26A : to Crewe

23.44

23.11

170.19

British Salt GF 1

165.01

North Rode Viaduct 5.54-35

R. Dane 4.69
(North Rode Jn)

2.28

166

167

165

164

Higher Delacre (UWG) 1.27

CUDDINGTON 25.15

ALTRINCHAM and CHESTER LINE
CLC CDM2 [NW 3023]

Mouldsworth 30.60

Miles from former Manchester Central

DELAMERE 28.11

Elworth Works

Hays Process Chemicals

Forest House Farm (UWG)

26.74

SANDBACH 162.50
162.61

Sandbach North Jn 162.69

Sandbach South Jn

162.23

Trent & Mersey Canal 161.05 161.52

160 161 162

Miles from Euston

CMP1 [NW 5001]
LMS : LNW (Manchester & Birmingham)

Elton Wheelock Viaduct 162.28

CONGLETON 8.12

Congleton Viaduct 7.68-58

8.16

SOT (MD)

13 : to Crewe

43A

© Copyright **TRACK**maps. No reproduction without permission

March 2005

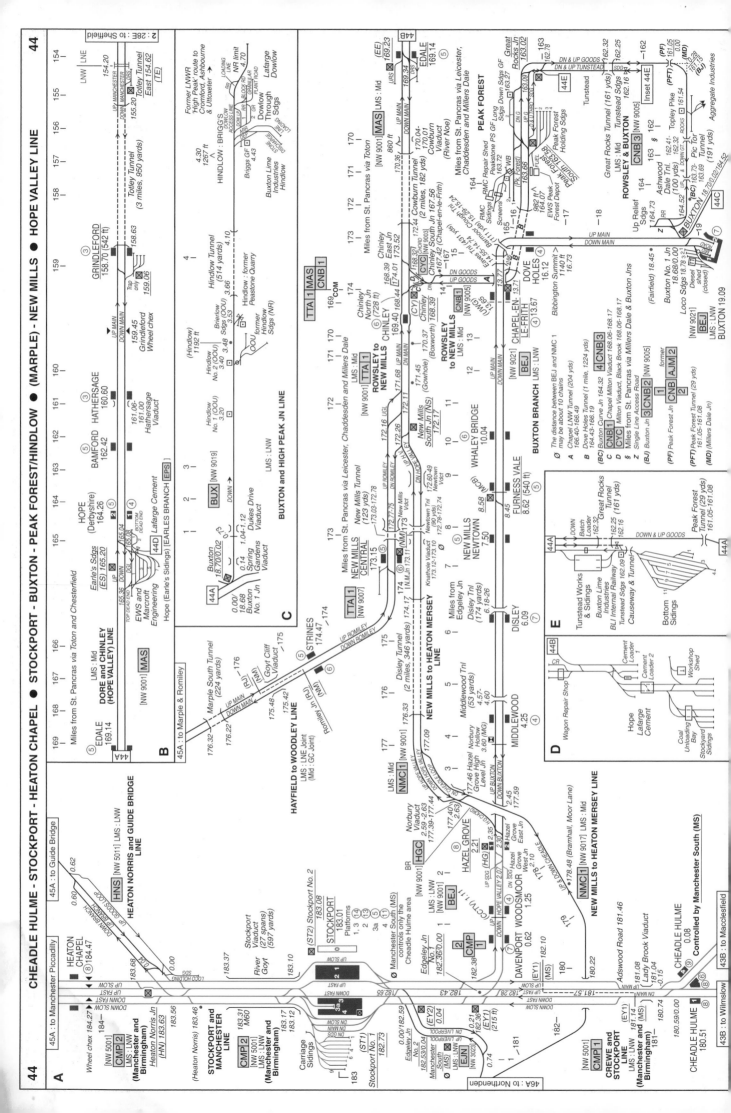

45   45

MANCHESTER, SOUTH-EAST : PICCADILLY - LEVENSHULME, MARPLE, GLOSSOP, HADFIELD & STANDEDGE ● STALYBRIDGE - PARK & HEATON NORRIS

A

Manchester Piccadilly (MP)
Signalling Centre in station building

MANCHESTER PICCADILLY 188.70   -0.05
Manchester Piccadilly East Jn 188.48   188.56

formerly 'London Road' GC Terminus (188.64)

Piccadilly platforms

ASHTON BRANCH
STALYBRIDGE   7.46   7.63
Stalybridge Viaduct
Stalybridge Jn   7.46
Stalybridge Tunnel (92 yards)
Katherine Street Tunnel (92 yards)

Miles from Manchester Victoria
LNE : GC   [NW 7021]   LMS : LNW

B   HUDDERSFIELD and MANCHESTER LINE
GREENFIELD   12.54
MOSSLEY (Greater Manchester)   10.39
Diggle Jn   14.61   14.59
Standedge Tnl. (3m. 66 yards)
Scout Tunnel (202 yards)
Uppermill Vdct. (Saddleworth)

C   2 : 41A : to Huddersfield

ASHTON-UNDER-LYNE   6.33
Dukinfield East Vdct.
Dukinfield West Vdct. (Stockport Canal)
Avenue Sidings
East Curve Viaduct (River Tame)
Guide Bridge North Jn   0.00
GUIDE BRIDGE   4.76
DENTON   3.39
HYDE NORTH   6.33
HYDE CENTRAL   7.27
Hyde Viaducts
NEWTON for Hyde   7.27
FLOWERY FIELD   6.56
GODLEY   7.72
HATTERSLEY   8.58
GODLEY EAST

D   MANCHESTER and SHEFFIELD LINE   LNE : GC
HADFIELD   12.61
DINTING   11.72
Dinting Vale Viaduct
GLOSSOP   0.01
BROADBOTTOM   9.60
MOTTRAM STAFF HALT   10.71
HADFIELD

Manchester Arr   9.72-10.02
Mottram Viaduct 10.07-15

LEVENSHULME   186.01
MAULDETH ROAD   8.07
LONGSIGHT
TRACTION MAINTENANCE DEPOT
ALSTOM UK   Manchester Traincare Centre
Diesel TMD (LO)
ARDWICK   0.64
PARK   2.18
PARKS FORK
Philips Park South Jn
Philips Park West Jn   1.59

ASHTON MOSS CURVE
Ashton Moss North Jn   5.52
Baguley Fold Jn
Clayton Bridge Viaduct
Caxton Bridge Jn

OLDHAM, ASHTON and GUIDE BRIDGE LINE
FAIRFIELD   3.52
GORTON   2.54
ASHBURYS   1.42
BELLE VUE
RYDER BROW   45.00
REDDISH NORTH   44.09
REDDISH SOUTH   1.50

REDDISH BRANCH
ARDWICK BRANCH

BRINNINGTON
BREDBURY   179.34
ROMILEY   178.27
MARPLE   176.57
ROSE HILL MARPLE   10.04

REDDISH JN to ROMILEY JN LINE
40 Miles from Liverpool Central (CLC)

HEATON NORRIS and GUIDE BRIDGE LINE   [HNS]   LMS : LNW

GLAZEBROOK and GODLEY LINE

HAYFIELD to WOODLEY LINE
WOODLEY   8.72
MACCLESFIELD, BOLLINGTON and MARPLE LINE
LNE (GE) & LMS (Mid) Joint

STOCKPORT and MANCHESTER LINE
[CMP 2]   [NW 5001]   LMS : LNW

Slade Lane Jn   186.46
Longsight South Jn   186.77

44A : to Stockport
44A : to Heaton Norris Jn & Stockport
44A : to New Mills
46A : to Burnage
47A : to Miles Platting

March 2005
© Copyright TRACKmaps. No reproduction without permission

45   45

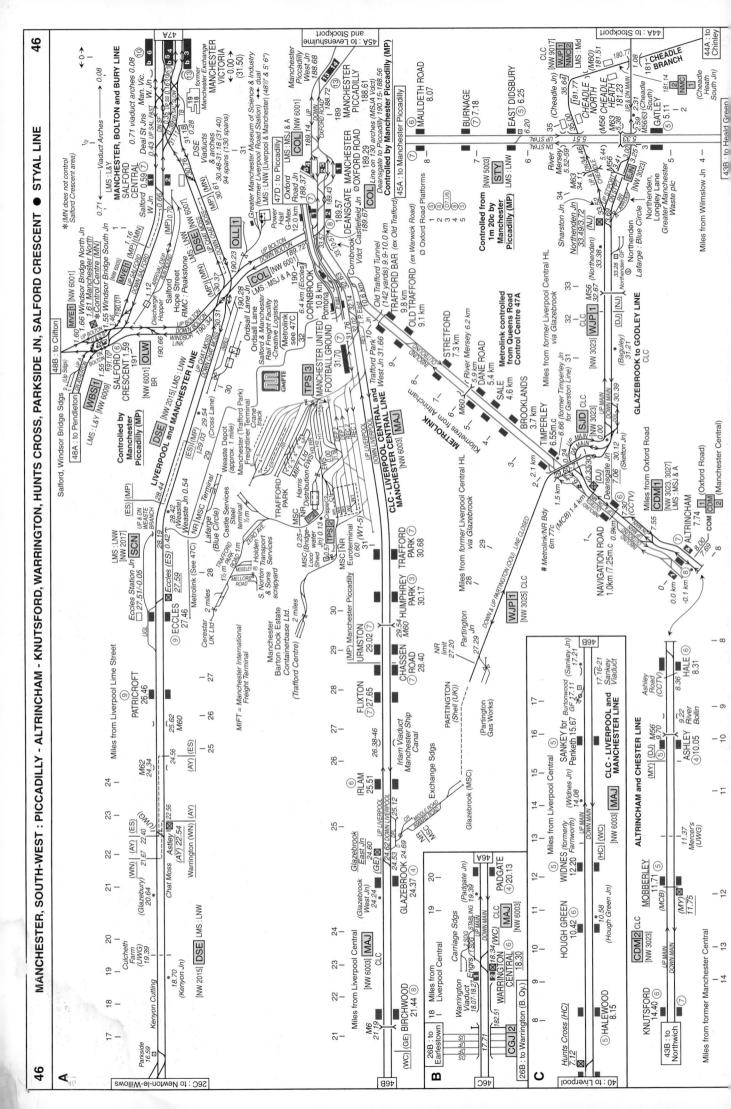

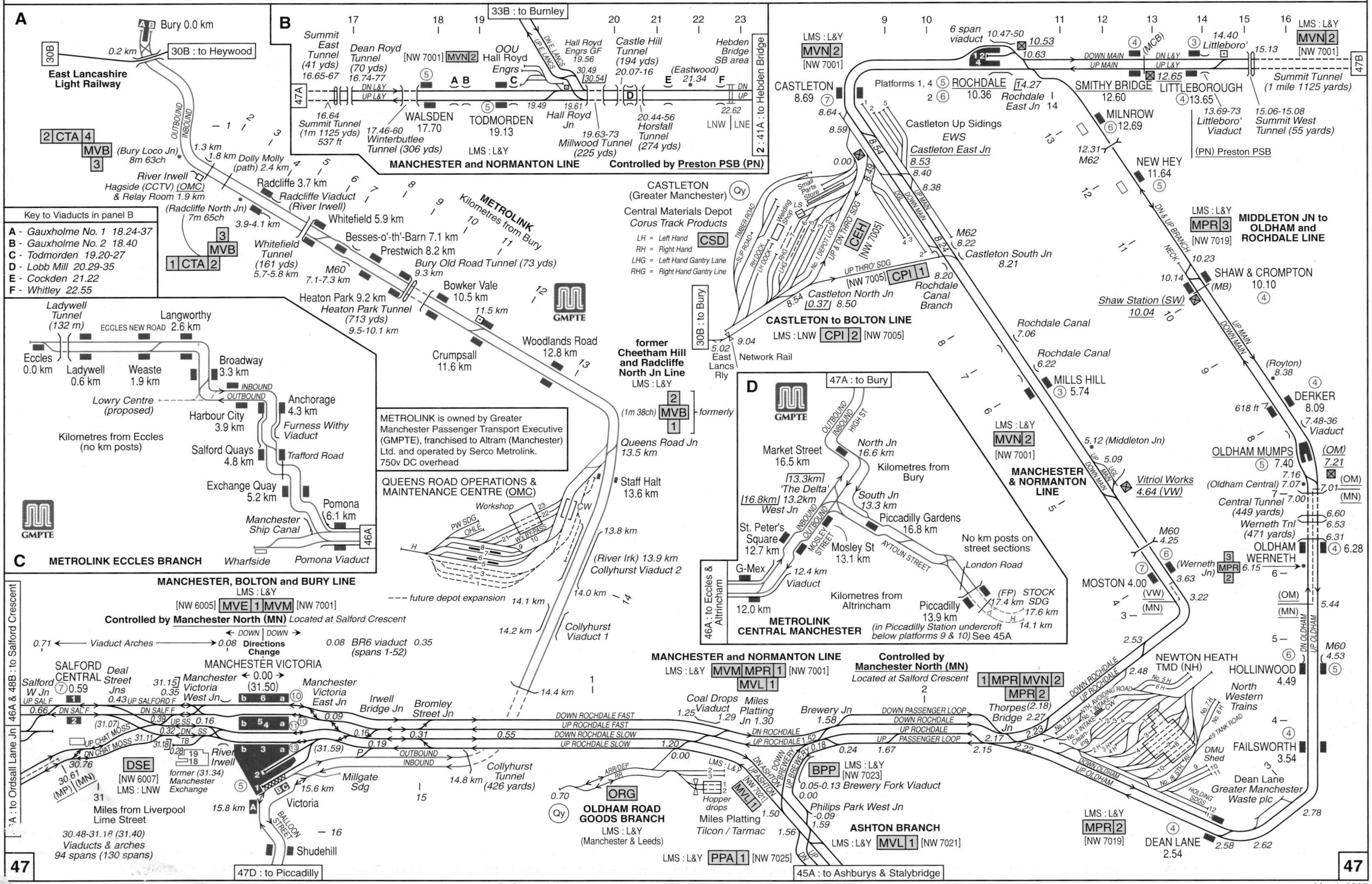

MIDDLETON JN to OLDHAM and ROCHDALE LINE

CASTLETON to BOLTON LINE

CASTLETON (Greater Manchester)
Central Materials Depot
Corus Track Products

CSD

LH = Left Hand
RH = Right Hand
LHG = Left Hand Gantry Line
RHG = Right Hand Gantry Line

former Cheetham Hill and Radcliffe North Jn Line

METROLINK is owned by Greater Manchester Passenger Transport Executive (GMPTE), franchised to Altram (Manchester) Ltd. and operated by Serco Metrolink. 750v DC overhead

QUEENS ROAD OPERATIONS & MAINTENANCE CENTRE (OMC)

MANCHESTER, BOLTON and BURY LINE

METROLINK ECCLES BRANCH

MANCHESTER and NORMANTON LINE

Key to Viaducts in panel B
A - Gauxholme No. 1 18.24-37
B - Gauxholme No. 2 18.40
C - Todmorden 19.20-27
D - Lobb Mill 20.29-35
E - Cockden 21.22
F - Whitley 22.55

East Lancashire Light Railway

MANCHESTER & NORMANTON LINE

MANCHESTER and NORMANTON LINE
Controlled by Manchester North (MN)
Located at Salford Crescent

METROLINK CENTRAL MANCHESTER

ASHTON BRANCH

OLDHAM ROAD GOODS BRANCH

48

MANCHESTER, NORTH-WEST : SALFORD CRESCENT - BOLTON - EUXTON JN ● LOSTOCK - HINDLEY ● BOLTON - (BLACKBURN) ● PENDLETON - INCE

48

A

48B : to Clifton

LMS : L&Y
BOLTON to BLACKBURN LINE

Mileposts north of Manchester may be either side or both sides (unless missing)

§ Bolton ELR changes
BBB - BBB
BBB 10.55 10.40 10.31
MVE2 2MVE1 MVE1

WEST COAST MAIN LINE
LMS : LNW & L&Y Joint (North Union)
27B-C : to Preston, then Blackpool (49A)

Miles from Manchester Victoria (Mileposts on both sides)

33A : to Blackburn

Leeds-Liverpool Canal
Blackburn, Bolton Branch Jn 23.60
Raikes Viaduct 22.25-22
M65 21.17
Hoddlesden Jn 21.55

DARWEN 20.27
Sough Tunnel (1 mile, 255 yds) 18.73
Turton (UCCL) 15.19
ENTWISTLE 16.47 737 ft
BROMLEY CROSS 13.45 / 13.47 (FP)
The Oaks (UWG) 12.72
HALL I'TH' WOOD (12.39)
Astley Bridge Jn
Bradshawgate Tunnel (88 yds) 11.05-13
Tonge Viaduct (72 spans)
Croal Viaduct 11.30
Bolton West Jn 10.55

CHORLEY 22.20 Yarrow Viaduct
Chorley Tunnel (124 yds)
Euxton ROF GF 24.18
Euxton Jn 25.31
CGJ5 [NW 1001]
CHORLEY ROF HALT 24.46
25.17

BOLTON to EUXTON JUNCTION LINE
LMS : L&Y [NW 6001] MVE2

ADLINGTON (Lancashire) 19.15
Huyton Viaduct, River Douglas 18.60
HORWICH PARKWAY 15.50
BLACKROD 17.14
Blackrod Jn (BJ) 17.27
M61 Link [MP]
Lostock Jn 13.39
LOSTOCK 13.52
Bullfields or Moor Lane Tunnels (77 yds) 11.05-11.01

MVE2 [NW 6001]

MOSES GATE 9.06
FARNWORTH 8.31
Farnworth Tunnels (295 yds) 8.24-8.10
KEARSLEY 7.57
MVE1 [NW 6001]
Moses Gate Jn 9.28
Manchester Road Sdgs EWS
UP BOLTON / DOWN BOLTON
Burnden Jn 10.04
Bolton East Jn 10.31
BOLTON 10.50 BBB
Platforms 1 2 3 4

MANCHESTER, BOLTON and BURY LINE
Controlled by Manchester Piccadilly (MP)

B

48A : to Kearsley

MANCHESTER, BOLTON and BURY LINE
Controlled by Manchester Piccadilly (MP)

CLIFTON 4.57 (Clifton Jn) 4.51
MVE1 [NW 6001]
Agecroft North Jn 3.33
Pendleton Tarmac/Tilcon Roadstone
Agecroft South Jn (Pendleton) 2.70
Pendleton, Brindle Heath Greater Manchester Waste plc
SALFORD CRESCENT 1.59
OLW [NW 6001] BR
WBS1 [NW 6009]
Windsor Bridge North Jn 1.66
Windsor Bridge South Jn
46A : to Ordsall Lane Jn & Manchester Piccadilly
Salford Hope St RMC : Peakstone
SALFORD CENTRAL 0.59
Salford West Jn 0.43
Deal St Jn 0.31
River Irwell Manchester Victoria West Jn
Viaduct Arches
MANCHESTER VICTORIA 0.00
MVE1 MVM [NW 7001]
Directions change
47A

C

WEST LANCASHIRE LIGHT RAILWAY 2' 0" gauge
BECCONSALL
WILLOW TREE HALT 3
DELPH 14
wagon storage
Dec 2004
N

D

HEATON PARK TRAMWAY, Prestwich
810 yards. Standard gauge. Electrified 500v DC
Middleton Road
Lake Road
Boating Lake
Depot (crossover)

PENDLETON to HINDLEY LINE
LMS : L&Y

MOORSIDE 5.61
SWINTON 5.04
Pendlebury Tunnels (201 yds)
Pendleton PENDLETON 2.21
Pendleton Tunnels (52 yds) 2.27-25
WALKDEN 7.42
Walkden (WN) 7.33
ATHERTON 11.18
Atherton Goods Yard
HAG FOLD 11.59
DAISY HILL 12.57
WESTHOUGHTON 15.25
Crow Nest Jn (CN) 14.62
HINDLEY 15.17
INCE 16.70
27A : to Wigan
LOSTOCK JN to PEMBERTON LINE
Warrington PSB
Miles from Manchester Victoria via Walkden
Distances in chains

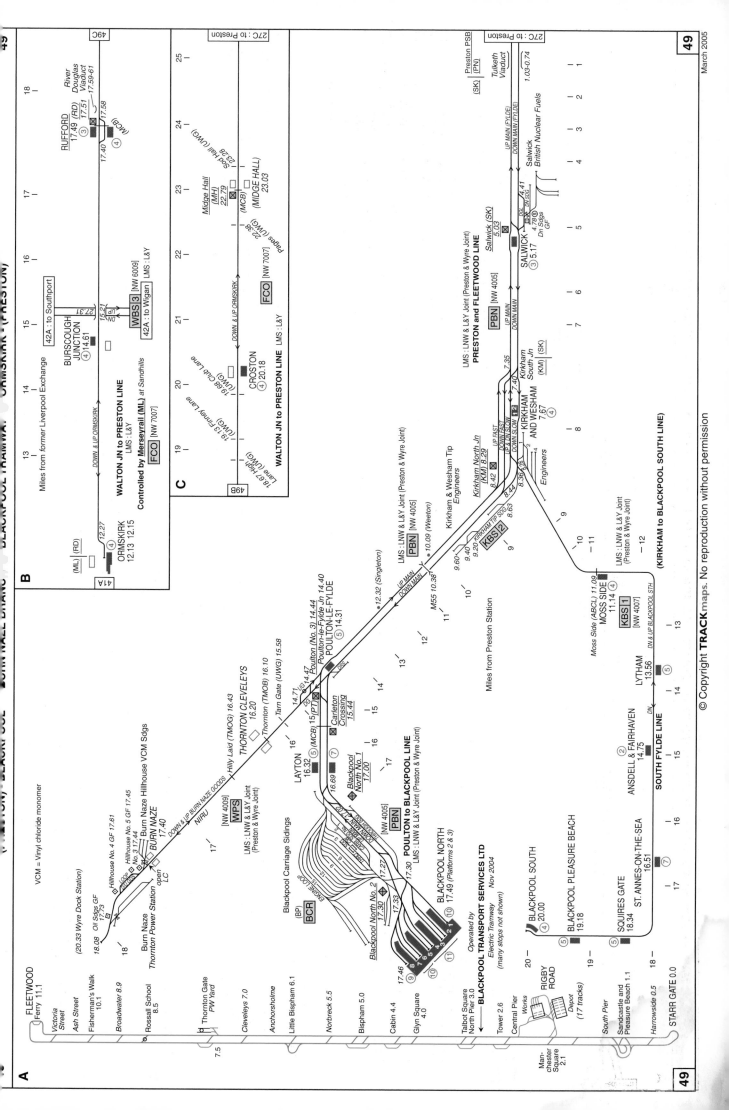

© Copyright TRACKmaps. No reproduction without permission

March 2005

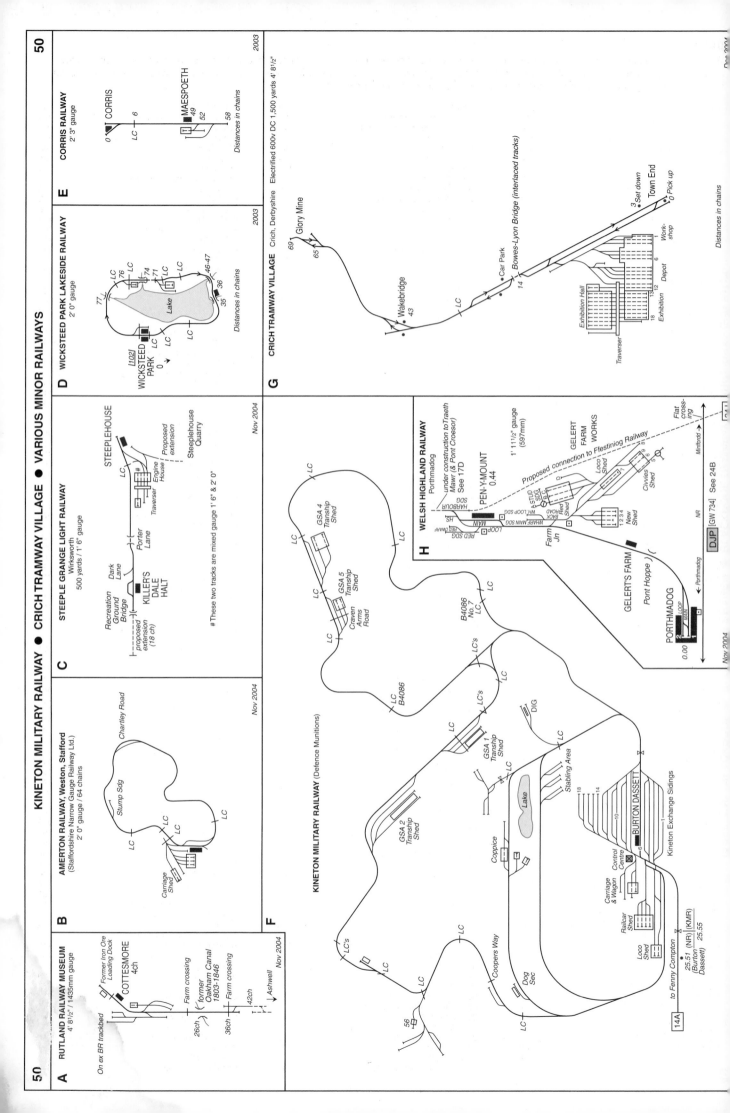

KINETON MILITARY RAILWAY ● CRICH TRAMWAY VILLAGE ● VARIOUS MINOR RAILWAYS

A RUTLAND RAILWAY MUSEUM 4' 8½" / 1435mm gauge
On ex BR trackbed
Former Iron Ore Loading Dock
COTTESMORE 4ch
former Oakham Canal 1803–1846
Farm crossing
Farm crossing
26ch 36ch 42ch →Ashwell
Nov 2004

B AMERTON RAILWAY, Weston, Stafford 2' 0" gauge / 64 chains
(Staffordshire Narrow Gauge Railway Ltd.)
Chartley Road
Stump Sdg
Carriage Shed
LC LC LC LC
Nov 2004

C STEEPLE GRANGE LIGHT RAILWAY Wirksworth 500 yards / 1' 6" gauge
Recreation Ground Bridge
Dark Lane
Porter Lane
KILLER'S DALE HALT
proposed extension (18 ch)
STEEPLEHOUSE
Traverser
Engine House
Proposed extension
Steeplehouse Quarry
LC #
These two tracks are mixed gauge 1' 6" & 2' 0"
Nov 2004

D WICKSTEED PARK LAKESIDE RAILWAY 2' 0" gauge
WICKSTEED PARK [102]
Lake
77 76 74 71 46-47 35 36
LC LC LC LC LC LC
Distances in chains
2003

E CORRIS RAILWAY 2' 3" gauge
CORRIS
0 6 LC
MAESPOETH
49 52 58
Distances in chains
2003

F KINETON MILITARY RAILWAY (Defence Munitions)
GSA 4 Tranship Shed
GSA 5 Tranship Shed
Craven Arms Road
GSA 2 Tranship Shed
GSA 1 Tranship Shed
Coppice
Lake
Stabling Area
DIG
B4086
B4086 No. 7
Control Centre
Carriage & Wagon
BURTON DASSETT
Kineton Exchange Sidings
Railcar Shed
Loco Shed
Dog Sec
Coopers Way
LC LC's LC LC LC's LC LC LC
18 14 10 6
56
to Fenny Compton 25.51 (NR)
(Burton Dassett) 25.55 (KMR)
14A

G CRICH TRAMWAY VILLAGE Crich, Derbyshire Electrified 600v DC 1,500 yards 4' 8½"
Glory Mine
Wakebridge
Car Park
Bowes-Lyon Bridge (interlaced tracks)
Set down Town End Pick up
Workshop
Exhibition Hall
Exhibition Depot
Traverser
69 65 43 14 3 0
18 12 6
LC
Distances in chains
Dec 2004

H WELSH HIGHLAND RAILWAY Porthmadog 1' 11½" gauge (597mm)
under construction to Traeth Mawr (& Pont Croesor)
See 17D
PEN-Y-MOUNT 0.44
GELERT FARM WORKS
Proposed connection to Ffestiniog Railway
HARBOUR
Loco Shed
Civvies Shed
New Shed
Red Shed
RED SDG RED DWARF SDG
BACK ROAD
WHARF MAIN SDG WH LOOP SDG
MAIN LOOP HS STUD SDG
Farm Jn
GELERT'S FARM
Pont Hoppe
PORTHMADOG
MAIN LOOP
→Porthmadog Minffordd→
Flat crossing
0.00 DJP [GW 734] See 24B NR
Nov 2004

Index

To create an index of reasonable size, a number of rules have been applied. In principle, all named locations on the Maps are represented in the Index. Where a number of assets share a name and a map page, the generic name only will appear. Where a name is unique, a fuller description appears. Generally, preserved lines appear by name but individual locations are not listed.

Abbey Foregate	22A, 23B
Abbey Jn, Nuneaton	11B
Abbey LC (TMO)	25B
Aber Bull LC (UWG)	36D
Aber Emergency Crossover GF	36D
ABERDOVEY	24A
ABERERCH	24C
ABERFFRWD	23E
ABERGELE & PENSARN	36B
Aberglaslyn Tunnels	17D
Aberleri LC (AHBC)	23E
Abermule LC (AHBC)	23C
ABERYSTWYTH	23E
ACCRINGTON	33B
Ackers HABD	43A
ACOCKS GREEN	15A
ACTON BRIDGE	26A
Acton Canal Wharf	1L
ACTON CENTRAL	1L
Acton Grange	26B
Acton Wells	1L
Adam Dales Viaduct	18
Adam Viaduct	27A
ADDERLEY PARK	14C
ADLINGTON (Cheshire)	43B
ADLINGTON (Lancashire)	48A
Admiralty Sidings Jn	30A
Adswood Road	44A
Afon ddu Viaduct	24C
Agecroft Jns	48B
AIGBURTH (formerly Mersey Road)	40
AINSDALE	41B
AINTREE	41A
Ais Gill Viaduct	34B
Albert Edward Viaduct, Ironbridge	21D
ALBRIGHTON	21C
Alderbottom Viaduct No. 2	30B
ALDERLEY EDGE	43B
Alders LC FP (R/G)	12A
Aldridge	18
Aldwinkle LC (UWC)	3B
Alexandra Dock Tunnel	41A
ALFRETON	5
All Stretton No. 1 LC (UWC)	23B
Allens LC (AOCL)	24A
ALLERTON	40
Allerton T&RSMD	40
Allscott	22A
Allsopps LC (UWW)	4A
Alrewas	18
ALSAGER	43A
Althorp Park GF	10B
ALTRINCHAM	46A
ALVECHURCH	17C
AMBERGATE	5
AMERTON RAILWAY	50B
Ampthill Tunnels	2C
Anchorage (Metrolink)	47C
Ancoats Viaduct	45A
Anglesea Sidings	18
ANSDELL & FAIRHAVEN	49A
Apesford LC (MG)	25B
Apethorne Jn	45A
APPLEBY	34B
APPLEBY EAST (Disused)	34B
APPLEY BRIDGE	42A
APSLEY	8B
Arblasters LC (UWC)	18
Archers No. 1 LC (UWC)	25C
ARDWICK	45A
Arena Tunnel, Birmingham	16
ARLEY	20C
ARMATHWAITE	34C
Armitage Jn	12A
Arnolds Flood Bridge	6B
Arnolds LC	42A
ARNSIDE	31A
Arpley Jn & Sidings	26B
Artengill Viaduct	34A
Asfordby	4C
Asfordby LC (AHBC)	3B
ASHBURYS	45A
Ashby Jn, Nuneaton	11B
ASHLEY	46A
Ashton Moss Jns	45A
Ashton-in-Makerfield	26C
ASHTON-UNDER-LYNE	45A
Ashwell	3B
Ashwood Dale Tunnel	44A
ASKAM	31B
ASLOCKTON	6B
ASPATRIA	32C
ASPLEY GUISE	9C
Astley	46A
Astley Bridge Jn	48A

ASTON	16
Aston-by-Stone LC (AHBC)	12B
Astrall (Shuttlewoods) LC (UWC)	4A
ATHERSTONE	11B
ATHERTON	48A
ATTENBOROUGH	6A
Attleborough Jn	11B
AUGHTON PARK	41A
Avenue Sidings GF	5
Avenue Sidings, Guide Bridge	45A
Averham Weir Viaduct	6B
Avon Viaduct	11A
Aylestone Viaduct	7B
'B' Group GF, Kingmoor	29D
BACHE	35A
Back Lane LC (UWCM) (R/G)	6C
Bagillt LC (UWG)	36A
Baguley Fold Jns	45A
Bagworth Jn	7B
Bakers LC (UWC)	25B
BALA LAKE RAILWAY	24H
Balderton LC (AHBC)	22D
Balshaw Lane Jn	27B
BAMBER BRIDGE	33A
BAMFORD	44B
Bamfurlong Jn	6C, 27A
Banbury Lane LC (CCTV)	10A
BANGOR (Gwynedd)	36D
BANK HALL	41A
Bankhead LC (UWG)	33A
BARBICAN	1R
Bardon Hill	7B
BARE LANE	28B
BARLASTON	12D
Barmoor Clough Tunnel	44A
BARMOUTH	24A
Barnsbury Jn	1R
Barnstone or East Leake Tunnel	4A
BARNT GREEN	17C
Baron Wood Tunnels	34C
Barrett's Bridge LC (UWC)	22A
BARROW-IN-FURNESS	31B
BARROW-UPON-SOAR	4A
Barthomley	13
Barton & Broughton GFs	28A
Barton Lane LC (AHBC)	6A
Barton Viaduct	28A
Bartons Jns	18
Baschurch LC (AHBC-X)	22B
Basford (NET)	6D
Basford Chemicals LC (UWC)	6D
Basford Hall Jn	13
Basford Wood GF	13
Baswich Viaduct	12B
Bath Row Tunnel	17C
Bathing Pool LC (UWG)	31A
BATTLEFIELD STEAM RAILWAY	20A
Bay Horse	28A
Bayles & Wylies LC (FPW)	6D
Bayston Hill	23B
Beaconsfield Street (NET)	6D
BEARLEY	15A
Beaumont Hill LC (UWC)	15A
Beaverpool Tunnel	37C
BEBINGTON	38C
BEDFORD	2C
BEDFORD ST. JOHNS	2C
BEDWORTH	11B
Beeches Farm LC (UWG)	36A
Beechwood Tunnel	14C
Beela Viaduct	28C
BEESTON	6A
Beeston Castle & Tarporley	35A
Beeston LC (UWC)	23B
Bell Busk Viaduct	33C
Bell Lane, Leicester	3B
BELLE VUE	45A
Belmont Tunnel	36D
BELPER	5
Belsize Tunnels	1R
Belvedere Viaduct	22A
Bennar Fawr LC (AOCL)	24B
Bennerley HABD	7A
Bennerley Viaduct	7A
Bennetts LC (UWC)	25B
BENTHAM	28B
Bentinck Colliery (closed)	5
Bentley Heath Crossing LC (MCB)	15A
BERKHAMSTED	9A
BERKSWELL	14C
Berry Lane LC (UWW)	9C
Bertheos Tunnel	37D
BESCAR LANE	42A
Bescot Local Distribution Centre	19

BESCOT STADIUM	19
Besses-o'-th'-Barn (Metrolink)	47A
Bestwood Park Jn	6D
BETWS-Y-COED	37C
BEWDLEY	20C
BIDSTON	39A
BILBROOK	21C
Bilston Central (Midland Metro)	19
Bilton GFs	11A
BINGHAM	6B
Birchall Tunnel	25B
BIRCHWOOD	46A
Birdswood Tunnel (flyover)	26A
BIRKDALE	41B
Birkeck Viaduct	29A
BIRKENHEAD CENTRAL	39A
BIRKENHEAD NORTH	39A
BIRKENHEAD PARK	39A
BIRKENHEAD TRAMWAY	39A
Birkett Tunnel	34B
Birmingham Curve Jn, Burton	25C
Birmingham Freightliner Terminal	16
BIRMINGHAM INTERNATIONAL	14C
BIRMINGHAM MOOR STREET	15B, 16
BIRMINGHAM NEW STREET	16
BIRMINGHAM SNOW HILL	15B, 16
Birmingham Snow Hill (Midland Metro)	15B, 16
BLACK COUNTRY LIVING MUSEUM	19
Black Dyke LC (AHBC)	31A
Black Lake (Midland Metro)	19
BLACKBURN	33A
BLACKPOOL Electric Tramway	49A
Blackpool LC (UWC)	22B
BLACKPOOL NORTH	49A
BLACKPOOL PLEASURE BEACH	49A
BLACKPOOL SOUTH	49A
BLACKROD	48A
(Blackwell)	17C
Blackwell South Jn	5
BLAENAU FFESTINIOG	37D
Blainscough Emergency GF	27A
BLAKE STREET	18
BLAKEDOWN	20C
Blea Moor	34A
BLEASBY	6B
BLETCHLEY	9B
BLOXWICH	21A
BLOXWICH NORTH	21A
BLUNDELLSANDS AND CROSBY	41A
BLYTHE BRIDGE	25B
Blythe or Hampton-in-Arden Viaduct	14C
Boars Head Emergency Control Panels	27A
Boathouse Bridge Road	5
Bodlondeb LC (UWG)	36A
BODORGAN	37A
Bog Jn	29C
Bollo Lane	1L
BOLTON	48A
Bolton-le-Sands	28B
Bont-y-Clettwr LC (UWC)	24A
BOOTLE	31C
Bootle Branch Jn	40
Bootle Jn	41A
BOOTLE NEW STRAND	41A
BOOTLE ORIEL ROAD	41A
BORDESLEY	15B
Bordesley Jns	15B, 17C
Borle Viaduct LC	20C
BORTH	23E
Borthwen Farm LC (UWC)	24A
Bostocks LC (UWC)	25B
BOTTESFORD	6B
Boultons LC (UWC)	25C
Bourne End Jn	9A
BOURNVILLE	17C
BOW BRICKHILL	9C
Bowker Vale (Metrolink)	47A
Bowness LC (UWG)	8B
Boxmoor Sidings, Hemel Hempstead	9A
Boxmoor Yard GF	9A
Brackmills	10A
Bradley Lane (Midland Metro)	19
Bradnocks Marsh HABD	14C
Bradshaw Brook Viaduct	48A
Bradshawgate Tunnel	48A
Bradwell Jn	43A
BRAMHALL	3B
Bramshall LC (AHBC-X)	25B
Brandon Viaduct	14C
Brandons LC (UWC)	2
Branston in, Burton	
Bransty SB, Whitehaven	
Brassey LC	
BRAYSTONES	31
BRAYTON (Disused)	32

Name	Ref	Name	Ref	Name	Ref
Breadsall	5	Caldew Jn, Carlisle	29C	CLC Viaduct, Bredbury	45A
Break Hills Hermitage Mill Viaduct	5	Caldon Low GF	25B	Cleifiog Uchaf LC (UWG)	37A
BREDBURY	45A	Caledonia Yard	15B	Clerkenwell Tunnels	1R
Brent Curve Jn & Viaducts	1L	CALEDONIAN ROAD & BARNSBURY	1R	Cliffe Hill GFs	7B
Brent Jns	8A	Calor Gas Sidings GF	11B	Cliffe Vale, Stoke	25B
Brentingby LC (UWW)	3B	Calrows Viaduct	30B	CLIFTON	48B
Brent Viaduct/Welsh Harp	2A	CALVELEY (Disused)	35C	Clifton & Lowther	29A
Brereton Sidings SB	21A	Calverleigh Farm LC (UWS) (CCTV)	25B	Clifton Road Jn	11A
Brettles LC (UWC)	6B	Calverton	6C	Clintsfield Viaduct	28B
Bretts LC (UWC)	3B	CAMBRIAN RAILWAYS SOCIETY	22B	CLITHEROE	33B
Brewery Jn	47A	Cambridge Single Line Jn	9B	Club Lane LC (UWG)	49C
Brewery Fork Viaduct	47A	Cambridge Street LC (UWC)	25C	Clunes LC (UWC)	21D
Brick Kiln Lane LC (UWC)	23A	Camden Jns	1R	Coal Drops Viaduct, Miles Platting	47A
BRICKET WOOD	8B	CAMDEN ROAD	1R	Coalbrookdale Viaduct	21D
Brickyard & Lane LC (private) (ABCL)	6D	Camp Hill Through Siding	16	Coalville Station	7B
Brickyard No. 3 LC (UWC)	23E	CANLEY	14B	Cobwall Viaduct	33B
Bridge 172 LC (UWC)	23D	Canning Street North LC	39A	Cockden Viaduct, Hall Royd	33B
Bridge Street Jn, Northampton	10A	CANNOCK	21A	Cockshute Sidings, Stoke	25B
Bridge Street Viaduct	25C	CAPEL BANGOR	23E	Codnor Park	5
Bridgeway LC (UWC)	23A	CAPENHURST	38C	CODSALL	21C
BRIDGNORTH	20C	Capernwray Viaduct	28B	Coed Cae No. 1 LC (UWC)	23D
BRIERFIELD	33B	CARK & CARTMEL	31A	Coed y Dinas LC (UWC)	23C
Brierley Hill	20C	Carleton Crossing LC (MCB)	49A	Coed-y-Llyn No. 1 LC (UWC)	24B
Brierlow Sidings GF (OOU)	44C	CARLISLE	29C	Coethie Farm LC (UWC)	24A
Briggs GF	44C	CARLTON	6B	Cofton	17C
Brindle Heath	49A	Carlton Lane LC (UWG)	39B	Coleham Sidings	23B
Brinklow	11A	Carlton Road Jn	1R	Coleshill	18
BRINNINGTON	45A	CARNFORTH	28B	Collier Lane Siding, Carlisle	29C
British Salt GF, Middlewich	43B	Carno LC (AHBC)	23D	Collier's LC (UWC)	25B
BROAD GREEN	42B	CARPENDERS PARK	8B	Collyhurst Tunnel/Viaduct	47A
Broad Oak LC (AHBC)	22D	Carr Lane LC (UWG)	39B	COLNE	33B
BROADBOTTOM	45D	Carr Mill Viaduct	42B	Colne Viaduct, Watford	8B
Broadholme	5	Carriage Shed Middle SF, Wembley	8A	Colwich SB (CH)	12A
Broadmarsh (NET) (proposed)	6A	Cart Lane LC (UWB)	31A	Colwick LC (CCTV)	6B
Broadway (Metrolink)	47C	Carterhouse Jn SB	38A	COLWYN BAY	36C
Brock LC (MWLF)	28A	Castle Bromwich Jn	18	Conder Viaduct	28A
BROMBOROUGH	38C	Castle Donnington	6C	Coney Green Jn	5
BROMBOROUGH RAKE	38C	Castle Foregate Sidings, Shrewsbury	22A	CONGLETON	43B
Bromford Bridge	16	Castle Hill Tunnel	47B	CONSALL	25B
Bromham Viaducts	2C	Castle Yard, Northampton	10A	CONWAY PARK	39A
BROMLEY CROSS	48A	Castlefield Jn	46A	CONWY	36C
Bromley Street Jn	47A	Castlethorpe (Disused)	9B	CONWY VALLEY RAILWAY	37F
Bromleys LC (UWC)	25C	Castlethorpe North HABD	10A	Cooks Lane LC (UWW)	3B
BRONDESBURY	1L	CASTLETON	47A	Coopers LC (UWG)	43A
BRONDESBURY PARK	1L	Cattle Pens Viaduct	22A	Copenhagen	1R
Bronnant LC (UWC)	24A	Cauldwell Depot, Bedford	2C	Coppull Hall HABDs	27A
Brook Carriage Sidings, Crewe	13	Cavendish Sidings	39A	CORBY (Disused)	3A
Brook Hall Road LC (CCTV)	41A	Cavendish Street Tunnel	39A	CORKICKLE	32A
Brooke Road LC (AHBC)	3B	Caverswall LC (MCB)	25B	Corks Farm No. 2 LC	18
Brookhay LC (AHBC)	18	Cefn Viaduct	22C	CORNBROOK	46A
BROOKLANDS	46A	CEFN-Y-BEDD	37E	Corporation Road Tunnel	39A
Brook's River Viaduct	3B	Cegin Viaduct	36D	CORRIS RAILWAY	50E
Brooksbottom Tunnel	30B	Cemetery LC (UWC)	24A	COSELEY	19
Brooksby LC (AHBC)	3B	Cemetery Viaduct	16	COSFORD	21C
Brookside Sidings, Guide Bridge	45A	Cemmes Road LC (R/G)	23D	Cotehill/ High Stand Gill Viaduct	34C
Broom Lane LC (AHBC)	3B	Central Rivers Depot	18	Cotgrave Colliery	6B
Brownhills	18	Central Tunnel, Liverpool	40, 41A	Coton Hill Yard, Shrewsbury	22A
BRUNSWICK	40	Central Tunnel, Oldham	47A	Cottage Pie Viaduct (Bridge 243)	23E
BRYN	42B	Cethin's Bridge Lledr Viaduct	37C	Coundon Road LC (MCB)	14B
Bryn-yr-Odyn Viaduct	37D	Chaddesden	4B	COUNTRY PARK HALT	20C
Buccleuch Jn	31D	Chaffers LC (TMOB)	33B	Coupland Viaduct	34B
BUCKLEY	37E	Chapel Lane LC, Parbold	42A	Court Farm LC (UWC)	23C
Buckley Wells LC	30B	Chapel LNW Tunnel, Chapel-en-le-Frith	44A	COVENTRY	14B
Bugbrooke	15A	Chapel Milton Viaduct, Chinley	44A	Covered way, Junction Rd Jn	1R
Bulcote LC (AHBC-X)	6B	CHAPEL-EN-LE-FRITH	44A	Cowburn	44A
Bullfields or Moor Lane Tunnels	48A	Charlmont Road LC (footpath) (R/G)	16	Cowley Hill, St. Helens	42
Bulwell (NET)	6D	CHASEWATER RAILWAY	19A	Coxbench LC (TMO)	5
BULWELL	6D	CHASSEN ROAD	46A	Crabtree LC (MWLG)	42A
Bulwell Forest (NET)	6D	Chatterley Valley Disposal Point	43A	CRADLEY HEATH	20C
Burley Viaduct	5	CHEADLE HEATH (Disused)	44A	Crag Hill Farm LC (UWG)	34A
BURN NAZE (Disused)	49A	CHEADLE HULME	3B, 44A	Craigfryn LC (UWC)	23D
BURNAGE	46A	CHEADLE NORTH (Disused)	46A	Crane Street, Wolverhampton	19
Burnden Jn	48A	CHEDDINGTON	9A	Creamore Farm LC (UWC)	23A
BURNESIDE	28C	CHEDDLETON	25B	Crescent Road LC (AHBC)	41B
Burnham Bros LC (UWC)	15A	CHELFORD	43B	Crescent Road Yard, Luton	2B
BURNLEY BARRACKS	33B	Cherry Orchard LC (UWC)	23C	CRESSINGTON	40
BURNLEY CENTRAL	33B	CHERRY TREE	33A	Cresswell LC (AHBC)	25B
BURNLEY MANCHESTER ROAD	33B	CHESTER	35A	Creswell Ford LC	25A
Burrs Viaduct	30B	CHESTER ROAD	16	Creswell Viaduct	12C
BURSCOUGH BRIDGE	42A	Chiltern Green HABD	2B	CREWE	13
BURSCOUGH JUNCTION	42A, 49B	CHINLEY	44A	Crewe Bank SB, Shrewsbury	22A
Burton Farm LCs	15A	CHIRK	22C	Crewe Local Distribution Centre	13
BURTON JOYCE	6B	Chivers Coton Viaduct	11B	CRICCIETH	24B
BURTON ON TRENT	25C	CHORLEY	48A	CRICH TRAMWAY VILLAGE	50G
BURTON POINT (Disused)	37E	Christleton Tunnel	35A	Crick Tunnel	10B
Burtonwood	46C	CHURCH & OSWALDTWISTLE	33B	CRICKLEWOOD	1L
Bury (Metrolink)	47A	Church Lane LC (CCTV)	12B	Croal Viaduct	48B
BURY BOLTON STREET	30B	Church Road Tunnel	17C	Croes Newydd North Fork	22D
Bury Old Road Tunnel	47A	Church Street LC's	9B	Croft Sidings	3B
Bushbury (Oxley) Jn	21B	CHURCH STRETTON	23B	CROMFORD	5
BUSHEY	8B	Church Viaduct, Church	33B	Crook Wheel LC (UWC)	31A
Bush-on-Esk	30A	Churchyard Terminal, St. Pancras	1R	Crosby Garrett Tunnel/ Viaduct	34B
Butler's Hill (NET)	6D	CHURNET VALLEY RAILWAY	25B	Crosfield's Crossing LC (MCB)	26B
BUTLERS LANE	18	Cilgwrgan LC (Manned, R/G)	23D	CROSTON	49C
BUTTERLEY	5	Cinderhill (NET)	6D	CROUCH HILL	1R
Buttington LCs	23C	CLAPHAM (North Yorks)	28B	Crown Street Tunnel, Liverpool	40
BUXTON	44A, 44C	Clapham Viaducts, Bedford	2C	Crow Nest Jn	48A
		Clapham/Wenning Viaduct	28B	Crowthorne Jn	45A
CADEBY LIGHT RAILWAY	3B	CLAVERDON	15A	CROXLEY GREEN	8B
CAERGWRLE	37E	Clay Cross	5	Crumpsall (Metrolink)	47A
CAERSWS	23D	Clay Mills Jn	25C	CUDDINGTON	43B
Caetwpa	23D	Clayton Bridge	45A	Culcheth Farm LC (UWG)	46A

Culgaith 34C, 34D
Cumberford Hall Farm LC (R/G) 12A
Cummersdale Viaduct 32C
CUMWHINTON (Disused) 34D
Currock, Carlisle 29C
Curzon Street Jn 16
Cutnall Green 20C
Cwmbowydd LC (TMO) 37D

Dafydd LC (UWC) 24A
Dairy House Farm LC (UWG) 35C
DAISY HILL 48A
Daisyfield Jn 33B
Dallam Freight Depot 26B
DALSTON 32C
DALTON 31A
Dane or Holmes Chapel Viaduct 43B
DANE ROAD 46A
DANZEY 15A
Darlaston Jn 19
Darlington's LC (UWC) 23A
Dartmouth Street (Midland Metro) 19
DARWEN 48A
DAVENPORT 44A
Daventry International Freight Terminal 10B
Daventry Jns 10B
David Lane (NET) 6D
Davies & Metcalfe's LC 22B
Daw Mill GF 18
Deal Street Jns 46A, 47A, 48B
DEAN LANE 47A
Dean Lane LC (AHBC) 42A
Dean Royd Tunnel 47B
Dean Viaduct 43B
Deans Brook/Stoneyfield Viaduct 2A
DEANSGATE 46A
Decoy LC (UWC) 22B
Dee Marsh Jn SB 37E
DEE MARSH Shotton Works 37E
Deepdale 27C
DEGANWY 36C
DELAMERE 43B
Denbigh Hall North Jn 9B
Denby Street Lane LC (TMO) 5
DENT 34A
Dent Head Viaduct 34A
DENTON 45A
Depot Jn, Longsight 45A
DERBY 4B
Derby Square Jn 40
DERKER 47A
Derwent Jn, Wolverhampton 32B
Derwent/Workington Viaduct 32B
Desborough Summit 3A
Desford LC (AHBC) 7B
Diggle Jn 45C
Dingle Tunnel 40
Dinham Sidings, Stafford 12B
DINTING 45D
DISLEY 44A
DITTON (Disused) 38A
Dock Jns, Kentish Town 1R
Dock Street Sidings, Preston 27C
Docker Garth's Viaduct 28C
Docks Branch GF, Workington 32B
Doe Hill 5
Doldyfi LC (UWC) 23E
DOLGARROG 37C
Dolly Molly LC (path) 47A
DOLWYDDELAN 37D
DORRIDGE 15A
Dorrington SB 23B
Doughty's Viaduct 23D
DOVE HOLES 44A
Dovefields LC (R/G) 25C
DOVEY 23E, 24A
Down Sidings GF 44A
Doxey Jn 12B
Drakelow 7C
Draughton (Priors Lane) GF 34E
Draycott GF 4B
DRIGG 31C
Drybeck Viaduct 34C
DUDDESTON 16
Duddeston Jn 16
Dudding Hill Jn 1L
Duddon/Foxfield Viaduct 31B
DUDLEY PORT 19
Dudley Street Guns Village (Midland Metro) 19
Dudley Tunnel 19
DUFFIELD 5
Duke Street LC (CCTV) 41B
Duke Street LC 39A
Dukes Drive Viaduct 44C
Dukes Wood LC (UWG) 41A
Dukinfield 45A
Dunnerholme LC (UWG) 31B
Dunstall Park 21B
Dunstalls LC (UWC) 25C
Durhams LC (UWC) 3B
Durn LC (UWC) 23D
Dutton Viaduct 26A

DYFFRYN ARDUDWY 24B
Dysynni River Bridge 24A

Eagle Crossing LC 19
Eamont Viaduct 29B
EARDINGTON (Disused) 20C
Earle's Sidings 44B
EARLESTOWN 26C, 42B
EARLSWOOD 15A
East Curve Viaduct, Guide Bridge 45A
EAST DIDSBURY 46A
EAST LANCASHIRE LIGHT RAILWAY 30B
East Langton HABD 3A
East Leake or Barnstone Tunnel 4A
East Lune Viaduct 28B
Eastcroft Depot 6A
EASTHAM RAKE 38C
Eastriggs GF 30A
ECCLES 46A
Eccles (Metrolink) 47C
Eccles LC (CCTV) 41B
ECCLESTON PARK 42B
EDALE 44A
Eden Viaduct 29C, 31C
EDGE HILL 40
Edgeley Jns 44A
Edstone Hall No. 1 LC (UWW) 15A
Egerton Road (Birkenhead Tramway) 39A
Egginton LC (AHBC) 25C
Egleton LC (UWB) 3B
ELLESMERE PORT 35A, 38C
Elliots LC (UWC) 6C
Elm Grove LC (UWG) 39B
Elmley Lovett GF 20C
Elstow 2C
ELSTREE & BOREHAMWOOD 2A
ELTON & ORSTON 6B
Elton Wheelock Viaduct 43B
EMBSAY & BOLTON ABBEY STEAM RAILWAY 34E
Endon LC (AOCL) 25B
English Bridge Jn, Shrewsbury 22A, 23B
English Damside Viaduct 29C
ENTWISTLE 48A
ERDINGTON 16
Esk Viaduct 30A
ESKMEALS (Disused) 31C
Etches Park, Derby 4B
ETRURIA 25B, 43A
Etterby 29C
EUXTON BALSHAW LANE 27B
Euxton Jn 48A
Exchange Quay (Metrolink) 47C
Eyton LC (AHBC-X) 22B

'F' Sidings Jn (Willesden No. 9) 8A
FAILSWORTH 47A
FAIRBOURNE 24A
FAIRBOURNE and BARMOUTH RAILWAY 20B
FAIRFIELD 45A
Falling Sands (Kidderminster) Viaduct 20C
Far Cotton Yard, Northampton 10A
Farington Jns 27C
Farmer Johnson's LC (UWG) 35A
Farmers Viaduct 28B
FARNWORTH 48A
FARRINGDON 1R
FAZAKERLEY 41A
Fechan No. 2 LC (UWC) 23E
Fenny Compton Jn 14A
FENNY STRATFORD 9C
Fenton Manor Tunnel 25B
Ferrett Lane LC (UWG) 42A
FFESTINIOG RAILWAY 24J
Ffestiniog Tunnel 37D
FFLINT 36A
Fford Jn 17A
FIDDLERS FERRY POWER STATION 38B
Field House Farm 43B
Field Sidings, Leamington Spa 14A
Fields Farm LC (UWC) 23A
FINCHLEY ROAD & FROGNAL 1L
Findern LC (AHBC) 25C
Fine Lane LC (MGH) 18
Finney Lane LC (UWG) 49C
Fishergate Tunnel 27C
Fishermans Path LC (UWG) 41B
Fishpool Farm LC (UWG) 36A
FISKERTON 6B
FIVE WAYS 17C
FLEETWOOD 49A
FLIMBY 32B
FLITWICK 2B
FLIXTON 46A
Floriston 30A
FLOWERY FIELD 45A
Flyover Jn (summit), Bletchley 9B
Foley Crossing SB (FY) 25B
FOLLY LANE 38A
Football Field LC (UWC) 23D
Forden LC (AOCL) 23C

Forders Sidings 9C
Forest House Farm LC (UWG) 43B
FORMBY 41B
Forsbrook Rd LC 25A
Foryd Viaduct 36B
Fosseway LC (AHBC) 18
Foundry Lane, Ditton 38A
Four Ashes Loop 21B
Four Lane Ends LC (MWLG) 42A
FOUR OAKS 16, 18
FOXFIELD 31B
FOXFIELD LIGHT RAILWAY 25A
Freeby LC (UWW) 3B
FRESHFIELD 41B
Friars Road LC 21A
Friday Street GF 48A
Frisby LC (MCB) 3B
FRODSHAM 35B
Frodsham Jn SB 26B
Frog Lane LC (UWG) 42A
Froghall Jn 25B
Fron LC (UWC) 23C
Fronlas LC 37D
Fulwood Tunnel 40
Furness Abbey Tunnel 31B
FURNESS VALE 44A
Furness Withy Viaduct 47C
Fylde Road Viaduct 28A

Gade Valley Viaduct (M25) 8B
Gaerwen 37A
Galton Jn 16, 19
Gannow Jn 33B
GARGRAVE 33C
GARSDALE (Formerly Hawes Jn) 34B
Garstang & Catterall South GFs 28A
GARSTON (Herts) 8B
GARSTON (Merseyside) 40
Garston Car Terminal 38A
Garston Freightliner Depot 40
GARSWOOD 42B
GATHURST 42A
GATLEY 46A
Gauxholme Viaducts 47B
Geddington HABD 3A
Geddington/Harpers Brook Viaduct 3A
Gedling Colliery 6B
Gelly Viaduct 37D
Gerards Bridge Jn 42B
GIGGLESWICK 28B
Gillets LC (UWG) 48A
Gisburn Tunnel 33B
GLAN CONWY 37C
Glanhafron LC (UWC) 23C
Glan-y-Mor Elias LC (UWG) 36D
GLANYRAFON 23E
Glaston Tunnel 3A
GLAZEBROOK 46A
Glebe Street Jn 25B
Glen Parva Jn 3B
Glendon Viaduct 3A
GLOSSOP 45D
G-Mex (Metrolink) 47D
GOBOWEN for OSWESTRY 22B
GODLEY 45A
GODLEY EAST (Disused) 45A
Golborne Jn 26C
GOLDEN VALLEY LIGHT RAILWAY 5
Goldmire Quarry LC (UWG) 31B
Gonalston LC (AHBC) 6B
GOOSTREY 43B
Gorsey Bank LC (AOCL) 5
Gorsey Lane LC (UWC) 6B
Gorshwen 2 LC (UWC) 24A
GORTON 45A
GOSPEL OAK 1R
Goyt Cliff Viaduct 44A
Grammers LC (UWC) 6C
Grand Jn Canal Viaduct 10A
Grand Jns 16
Grange Farm LC (UWG) 15A
Grange Jn 43A
GRANGE-OVER-SANDS 31A
Granville Sidings 43A
Granville Street Tunnel 17C
Grassendale Tunnel 40
GRAVELLY HILL 16
Grayrigg Loops 28C
Great Bridgeford HABD 12B
GREAT CENTRAL RAILWAY (N) 4A
GREAT CENTRAL RAILWAY 17B
Great Crane Brook Bridge 19A
GREAT ORME TRAMWAY 36C
Great Rocks 44A
GREAT WHIPSNADE RAILWAY 10E
GREEN LANE 39B
Green Lane LC (AHBC-X), Stewartby 9C
Green Lane LC (UWC) 23A
Green Lane Tunnel 39A
Green Line LC (AHBC) 22D
GREEN ROAD 31B
GREENBANK 43B

GREENFIELD	45B
Greens LC (UWC)	3B
Greens Viaduct	28B
Gregory Boulevard LC (NET)	6A
Gregson Lane LC (UWG)	33A
Gresley Tunnel	7C
Gresty Green, Crewe	13
Gresty Lane	13
Gresty Road, Crewe	13
GRETNA GREEN	30A
Gretna Jn	30A
Gretton Viaduct	3A
Grimston Tunnel	4C
GRINDLEFORD	44B
Griseburn	34B
Grives Lane LC (AHBC)	5
Groes Viaduct	36C
Dale GF	41A
GUIDE BRIDGE	45A
GUNNERSBURY	1L
Gunthorpe LC (UWC)	3B
GWERSYLLT	37E
Hademore Crossing	12A
HADFIELD	45D
Hafod-y-Wern LC (UWC)	24B
HAG FOLD	48A
HAGLEY	20C
Hagside LC (CCTV) (Metrolink)	47A
HALE	46A
Halesowen Jn	17C
Halewood Sidings & Jn	38A
HALEWOOD	46C
Hall Carleton LC (UWG)	31C
Hall End Jn	18
Hall Farm LC (UWC)	3B
HALL GREEN	15A
HALL I'TH'WOOD	48A
HALL ROAD	41A
Hall Royd	33B
HALTON (Disused)	26B
Halton Jn	26B, 38A
HAMILTON SQUARE	39A
HAMMERSMITH	5
HAMPSTEAD HEATH	1R
HAMPTON LOADE	20C
HAMPTON-IN-ARDEN	14C
Hams Hall	18
HAMSTEAD	16
Hamstead Heath Tunnel	1R
Hamstead Tunnel, Kentish Town	1R
Hamstead Tunnel, Perry Barr	16
HANDFORTH	43B
Handsworth Booth Street (Midland Metro)	16
Hanselmans 1 LC (UWC)	23C
Hanslope Jns	10A
Hanwood LC (UWC)	23C
HAPTON	33B
Harbour City (Metrolink)	47C
Harbury Tunnel	14A
Hardendale Crossover	29A
Hardingstone LC	10A
Hardsough Weir Viaduct	30B
Harecastle Tunnel	43A
HARLECH	24B
Harlescott Crossing LC (MCB)	23A
HARLESDEN	8A
Harlesden Jn	1L, 8A
HARLINGTON	2B
HARPENDEN	2A
Harpers Brook/Geddington Viaduct	3A
Harringay Park Jn SB (H)	1R
HARRINGTON	32B
Harringworth/Welland Valley Viaduct	3A
Harrisons Sidings	29A
HARROW & WEALDSTONE	8B
Harrowden Jn	3A
HARTFORD	26A
Hartford CLC Jn	26A, 43B
Hartford East Jn	43B
HARTLEBURY	20C
Hartshill	11B
HATCH END	8B
HATHERSAGE	44B
HATTERSLEY	45A
HATTON	15A
Haverigg LC (AHBC)	31C
Haw Lane LC (UWG)	33C
HAWARDEN	37E
HAWARDEN BRIDGE	37E
Hawkesbury Lane LC (MCB)	11B
Haybank LC (UWG)	29A
Haydock Branch Jn	26C
Market Tunnel	39A
OXEN LC (UWC)	25C
Oxford GROVE	44A
Oxhey WELL (Disused)	17C
Oxley STONE LANE	8B
Oxley (Staff EN	43B
Oxley T&RS	18
	19
PADGATE CHAPEL	44A

Heaton Norris Jn	44A
Heaton Park (Metrolink)	47A
HEATON PARK TRAMWAY, Prestwich	48D
HEDNESFORD	21A
Hegarty's or Blakeley-bank Wood LC	25A
HELLIFIELD	33C
Helm Tunnel	34B
HELSBY	35A
HEMEL HEMPSTEAD	9A
Henblas LC (UWC)	24A
HENDON	2A
Hendy Halt	24E
Hendy LC (open)	17D
Henfaes Farm LC (UWG)	36D
HENLEY-IN-ARDEN	15A
Hepworth Foot Viaduct	24A
Heritage GF, Crewe	13
Hesketh LC (UWG)	41B
Hest Bank	28B
Hestham Hall LC (UWG)	31C
HESWALL	39A
HEYSHAM PORT	28B
Hicks Lodge Siding GF	7C
High Lane LC (UWG)	49C
High Oaks	11A
High Peak Bridge	5
High School (NET)	6A
High Tor Tunnels	5
Highbury Vale (NET)	6D
Higher Delacre LC (UWG)	43B
Highfields LC (UWF)	12B
Highgate Road Viaduct	1R
HIGHLEY	20C
HIGHTOWN	41B
Hillhouse	49A
Hillmorton Jns	11A
Hills LC (UWC)	3B
HILLSIDE	41B
Hilly Laid LC (TOG)	49A
Hilton LC (MGH)	25C
HINCKLEY	3B
Hinderton Field Tunnel	39A
HINDLEY	48A
Hindlow (OOU) GFs	44B, 44C
Hinds LC (UWB)	3B
Hitchin Branch Jn, Bedford	2C
Hives Farm LC (UWC)	3B
Hockley LC (CCTV)	25C
Hockley Tunnels	16
Hoghton	33A
Holbrook LC (TMO)	5
Holbrook Park	14B
Hollands LC (Streethay)	18
Holliday Street Tunnel	16, 17C
HOLLINWOOD	47A
Holme Tunnel	33B
HOLMES CHAPEL	43B
Holt Lane Tunnel	5
Holts LC (UWC)	3B
Holwell Jn	4C
HOLYHEAD	37B
Home Farm LC (UWG)	43A
Hoods Mill LC	3B
HOOTON	38C
HOPE (Derbyshire)	44B
HOPE (Flintshire)	37E
HOPE EXCHANGE (Disused)	37E
Hopwood GF	30B
Horninglow, Burton	25C
Horninglow Sidings, Burton	25C
Horns Bridge	5
Horrocks LC (UWG)	34C
Horrocksford	33B
Horsfall Tunnel	33B
HORTON IN RIBBLESDALE	34A
HORWICH PARKWAY	48A
HOSCAR	42A
Hospital LC (CCTV)	33A
Hotchley Hill Sidings	4A
HOUGH GREEN	46C
HOW WOOD	8B
Howe & Co's Sdg	34C
HOYLAKE	39B
Hubbards LC (UWC)	3B
HUCKNALL (NET)	6D
Humberstone Road Jn	3B
HUMPHREY PARK	46A
HUNCOAT	33B
Hunsbury Hill Tunnel	10A
HUNTS CROSS	40, 46C
HUYTON	42B
Huyton Viaduct	48A
HYDE CENTRAL	45A
Hyde Lane LC (UWC)	8B
HYDE NORTH	45A
Hyde/Chiltern Green Viaduct	2B
Hyson Green Market (NET)	6D
Icknield Street Viaduct	16
INCE	27A, 48A
INCE & ELTON	35A
Ince Moss Jn & Sidings	27A, 42B

Intersection Tunnel, Willesden	8A
Irchester Viaducts	2D
IRLAM	46A
IRONBRIDGE GORGE	21D
IRONBRIDGE POWER STATION	21D
Ironville GF	5
Irwell Bridge Jn	47A
IRWELL VALE	30B
ISLE OF ANGLESEY RAILWAY	37A
Jack Steele Tunnel	20B
Jacksons LC (UWC)	25B
James Bridge Jn	19
JAMES STREET	40
Jaum Field Farm LC (UWG)	45A
Jericho LC (UWC)	3B
Jewellery Quarter (Midland Metro)	16
JEWELLERY QUARTER	16
Junction Road Junction	1R
Katherine Street Tunnel	45A
KEARSLEY	48A
Keele Tunnel	12D
Keerholme LC (UWG)	28B
Kegworth	4A
Keighley Road Viaduct	33C
KEMPSTON HARDWICK	9C
KENDAL	28C
Kenilworth Jns	14B
Kenrick Park (Midland Metro)	19
KENSAL GREEN	1L
KENSAL RISE	1L
Kent Viaduct	28C
Kent/Arnside Viaduct	31A
KENTISH TOWN WEST	1R
KENTON	8B
KENTS BANK	31A
KETTERING	3A
Ketton	3B
KIDDERMINSTER	20C
KIDDERMINSTER TOWN (SVR)	20C
Kidderminster/Falling Sands Viaduct	20C
KIDSGROVE	43A
KILBURN HIGH ROAD	1L
Kilburn LC (TMO)	5
Kilby Bridge Jn	3B
Kilkewydd Viaduct	23C
Kilsby Tunnel	10B
KINETON MILITARY RAILWAY	14A, 50F
King Street, Blackburn	33A
Kingmoor, Carlisle	29C, 29D
KINGS CROSS THAMESLINK	1R
KINGS LANGLEY	8B
Kings Mill No 1 LC (BW)	5
KINGS NORTON	17C
Kingsbury Jns	18
KINGSLEY & FROGHALL	25B
Kingswinford Jn	20C
Kirby Muxloe LC (UWW)	7B
KIRKBY	41A
Kirkby South Jn	5
KIRKBY STEPHEN	34B
Kirkby Summit SB (KS)	5
Kirkby Thore SB (KT)	34C
Kirkby Viaduct	31B
KIRKBY-IN-ASHFIELD	5
KIRKBY-IN-FURNESS	31B
KIRKDALE	41A
KIRKHAM AND WESHAM	49A
Kirksanton LC (MCG)	31C
Kirtle Water Viaduct	30A
Kitson Wood Tunnel	33B
Knathole Viaduct	44A
Knighton Jn	3B
Knowlesands Tunnel	20B
Knowsley Freight Terminal	41A
KNUTSFORD	43B, 46A
Kronospan	22C
Kynaston LC (UWC)	23A
L & NW Jn, Derby	25C
Lace Market (NET)	6A
Lady Brook Viaduct	44A
Ladywell (Metrolink)	47C
Lambrigg GF	28C
LANCASTER	28A
Landor Street Jn	16
LANDUDNO JUNCTION	36C
LANDYWOOD	21A
Langham Jn	3B
LANGHO	33B
LANGLEY GREEN	19
LANGLEY MILL	5
Langridge No. 2 LC (UWC)	25C
Langton Colliery Branch Jn	5
LANGWATHBY	34C
LANGWITH-WHALEY THORNS	5
Langworthy (Metrolink)	47C
LAPWORTH	15A
Lawley Street Viaducts	16
Lawsing LC (UWG)	28B
LAYTON	49A

LAZONBY AND KIRKOSWALD	34C	
LEA GREEN	42B	
LEA HALL	14C	
Lea Wood Tunnel	5	
LEAGRAVE	2B	
Leaming LC (UWG)	31A	
LEAMINGTON SPA	14A	
LEASOWE	39B	
Leaton LC (AHBC)	22B	
Ledburn Jn	9A	
Leeds Street Jn, Liverpool	41A	
Leekbrook LC (open)	25B	
Leftwich (or Northwich) Viaduct	43B	
LEICESTER	3B	
Leicester Branch Canal	10B	
Leicester Jn, Burton	25C	
Leigh LC (AHBC-X)	25B	
LEIGHTON BUZZARD	9A	
LEIGHTON BUZZARD RAILWAY	9D	
Lenton South Jn	6A	
Leri Bridge LC (UWC)	23E	
Leven/Plumpton Viaduct	31A	
LEVENSHULME	45A	
LEYLAND	27C	
LICHFIELD TRENT VALLEY	12A, 18	
LICHFIELD CITY	18	
LIDLINGTON	9C	
Lifford Jns	17C	
Liggins LC (UWC)	3B	
Lightmoor Junction SB	21D	
Limbury Road	2B	
Lime Street Tunnels	40	
Limestone Hall LC (MCG)	31C	
Linby LC (ABCL)	6D	
Lincoln Street LC (CCTV)	6D	
Lindal Tunnel	31A	
Lindridge Farm LC (UWB)	7B	
Linslade Tunnels	9A	
Lismore Circus Tunnel, Kentish Town	1R	
Little Bowden LC (R/G) (footpath)	3A	
Little Chef LC (UWG)	36C	
Little Eaton Station LC (TMO)	5	
LITTLE SALKELD (Disused)	34C	
LITTLE SUTTON	38C	
Little Viaduct, Settle	34A	
Little Viaduct, Alrewas	18	
LITTLEBOROUGH	47A	
Littlewood Viaduct	5	
Litton's Mill Crossing	26B, 38B	
LIVERPOOL CENTRAL	40	
LIVERPOOL LIME STREET	40	
LLANABER	24B	
LLANBADARN	23E	
LLANBEDR	24B	
LLANBERIS LAKE RAILWAY	24G	
Llanbrynmair LC (R/G) (Manned)	23D	
LLANDANWG	24B	
Llanddaniel LC (MWLG)	37A	
Llanddu Jn	22B	
LLANDECWYN	24B	
Llandegai Tunnel	36D	
Llandre	23E	
LLANDUDNO	36C	
LLANDUDNO JUNCTION	36C	
Llandulas Viaduct	36C	
LLANERCH-Y-MEDD (Disused)	37A	
Llanerchymor Viaduct	36A	
Llanfair LC (MCG)	36D	
LLANFAIRFECHAN	36D	
LLANFAIRPWLL	37A	
LLANGEFNI (Disused)	37A	
LLANGELYNIN (Disused)	24A	
Llanglan Fechan No. 4 LC	23E	
LLANGOLLEN RAILWAY SOCIETY LTD	17A	
LLANGWYLLOG (Disused)	37A	
Llanidloes Road LC (MG)	23D	
LLANRWST	37C	
Llugwy Viaduct	37C	
LLWYNGWRIL	24A	
Llwyn Cadwgan LC (UWC) (Manned)	24B	
Llysfaen Emergency GF	36C	
Lobb Mill Viaduct	33B	
Lock Lane Crossing LC (MCB)	6C	
Lockside Road LC (AOCL)	27C	
Lodge Road West Bromwich Town Hall (Midland Metro)	19	
LONDON EUSTON	1R	
London Road Jn, Carlisle	29C	
London Road Jn, Derby	6A	
London Road LC (Metrolink)	47D	
LONDON ST. PANCRAS	1R	
Long Ashes LC (UWG)	29B	
LONG BUCKBY	10B	
LONG EATON	4B	
Long Eaton Town LC (CCTV)	6A, 7A	
LONG MARTON (Disused)	34C	
Long Meg (or Eden Lacy) Viaduct	34C	
LONG PRESTON	34A	
LONGBRIDGE	17C	
LONGPORT	43A	
Longsight TMD	45A	
LONGTON	25B	
LONGTOWN (Ministry of Defence)	30A	

Lorne Street	39A	
LOSTOCK	48A	
LOSTOCK GRALAM	43B	
LOSTOCK HALL	27C	
Lostock Works, Northwich	43B	
LOUGHBOROUGH	4A	
Lounge	7C	
Low House Crossing LC (MCB)	34C	
Low Mill	32C	
Low Moor LC (CCTV)	33B	
LOWDHAM	6B	
Lower Ashen Bottom Viaduct	30B	
Lower Bentham Viaduct	28B	
Lower Park Street Tunnels	1R	
Lower Portland Farm LC	5	
Lower Radway Green LC (UWG)	13	
Lowgill	28C	
Lowry Centre (proposed)	47C	
Lowther Viaduct	29B	
LOWTON (Disused)	26C	
Loxdale (Midland Metro)	19	
Loxley Lane LC (AHBC-X)	25B	
Luffenham Jn LC (CCTV)	3B	
Lunds Viaduct	34B	
Lune Viaduct	28B	
LUTON	2B	
LUTON AIRPORT PARKWAY	2B	
Lydgate Viaduct	33B	
LYE	20C	
Lyons Wood Farm LC (UWC)	23A	
LYTHAM	49A	
MACCLESFIELD	43B	
MACHYNLLETH	23E	
MADELEY (Disused)	21D	
Madeley HABD	12C	
Madeley Jn	12C	
Madeley Jns	21C	
Madryn Farm LC (UWG)	36D	
MAENTWROG ROAD (Closed)	37D	
Maes LC (ABCL)	24B	
Maes Mawr LC (UWC)	23D	
Maesteg LC (UWG)	36A	
MAGHULL	41A	
Malborough Road LC (BW)	4B	
Malt House LC (UWC)	23C	
MANCHESTER AIRPORT	43B	
MANCHESTER METROLINK	47A	
Manchester North SB (MN)	46A, 48B	
MANCHESTER OXFORD ROAD	46A	
MANCHESTER PICCADILLY	45A, 46A	
Manchester Road, Bolton	48A	
MANCHESTER SHIP CANAL	35A, 38C	
Manchester South SB (MS)	44A	
MANCHESTER UNITED FOOTBALL GROUND	46A	
MANCHESTER VICTORIA	46A, 47A, 48A	
Mann Island Jn	39A, 40	
MANOR ROAD	39B	
MANSFIELD	5	
Mansfield Jn, Nottingham	6A	
MANSFIELD WOODHOUSE	5	
Mantle Lane SB (ML)	7C	
Manton Jn	3B	
Mapperley Goods Branch	7A	
MARCHINGTON (Disused)	25C	
Maritime Way LC	27C	
MARKET HARBOROUGH	3A	
Market Street (Metrolink)	7D	
Marley Green Emergency Crossover (OOU)	23A	
MARPLE	45A	
Marple South Tunnel	44A	
Marsden/Nelson Viaduct	33B	
Marsh Brook LC (MCB)	23B	
Marsh House LC (CCTV)	38B	
Marsh Lane Crossover (North Mersey Jn)	41A	
Marshalls LC (UWC)	33C	
Marshfield Viaduct	34A	
MARSTON GREEN	14C	
Marston LC (AHBC)	9C	
Marston-on-Dove LC (AHBC)	25C	
Marston Vale SCC (MV)	9C	
Martins LC (UWG)	42A	
MARYPORT	32B	
MATLOCK BATH	5	
MATLOCK RIVERSIDE	7D	
MATLOCK	5	
MAULDETH ROAD	45A, 46A	
Mayford Loop	45A	
Meadow Lane LC (CCTV)	6A	
Meadow Sidings, Toton	7A	
Meadows Exchange Sidings, Ketton	3B	
Meaford Crossing LC	12B	
Meir Tunnel	25B	
Melbourne Jn	25C	
Melling Tunnel	28B	
Melrose Avenue LC (UWG)	39B	
Melton Jn	3B	
MELTON MOWBRAY	3B	
Menai (Britannia Tubular) Bridge	36D	
MEOLS	39B	
MEOLS COP	42A	
Mercer's LC (UWG)	46A	

Merchants Quay LC (UWG)	32B	
Merilyn LC (MG)	24B	
MERSEY DOCKS and HARBOUR CO'S LINES	39A	
Mersey Tunnel (Park Branch)	39A	
Merseyrail (IECC) ASC (ML)	41A	
Metro-Cammell GF	16	
Metrolink Intersection Bridge	30B	
Mickle Trafford Jn	35A	
Micklewood No. 2 LC (UWC)	23B	
Mid Cannock	21A	
Middleton Place LC (UWG)	31C	
MIDDLEWICH LOOP (Disused)	43B	
MIDDLEWOOD	44A	
MIDGE HALL (Disused)	49C	
MIDLAND METRO	16	
MIDLAND RAILWAY CENTRE	5	
Midland Yard, Walsall	19	
MILBROOK (Bedfordshire)	9C	
Milburn Grange LC (UWC)	14B	
Miles Platting Jn	47A	
Milford Jn	12A	
Milford & Brocton HABD	12A	
Milford Tunnel	5	
Mill Deeping LC (UWW)	3B	
MILL HILL	33A	
MILL HILL BROADWAY	2A	
Mill Lane Jn, Northampton	10A	
Mill Street LC	27C	
Millers Dale Jn	44A	
MILLOM	31C	
MILLS HILL	47A	
Millwood Tunnel	33B	
Milnthorpe	28C	
Milton Ernest Viaducts	2C	
MILTON KEYNES CENTRAL	9B	
Milton Viaduct, Black Brook, Chinley	44A	
Milverton Jn	14A	
MINFFORDD	4B	
Mintholme LC (CCTV)	33A	
Mitre Bridge LC (CCTV)	1L	
MOBBERLEY	46A	
Moel Llys Tunnel	36C	
Moira West Jn	7C	
Mollington Viaduct	35A	
Mona LC (UWG)	36D	
Monks Siding	38B	
Monmore Green Jn	19	
MONTGOMERY (Disused)	23C	
Monument Lane Jn	16	
Moor Bridge (NET) (Park & Ride)	6D	
Moor Farm 1 LC (UWG)	31C	
Moor Farm LC	6A	
Moor Lane LC (UWC)	4A	
Moor Lane or Bullfields Tunnels	48A	
Moorcock Tunnel	34B	
MOORFIELDS	40	
MOORGATE	1R	
Moors Gorse LC (UWW)	21A	
MOORSIDE	48A	
MORECAMBE	28B	
MORETON (Merseyside)	39B	
MORFA MAWDDACH	24A	
Morfa No. 1 LC (UWC)	24B	
Mortimer Street Viaduct	1R	
Morton	5	
Moseley Tunnel	17C	
MOSES GATE	48A	
Mosley Street (Metrolink)	47D	
Mosley Street GF	25C	
Moss & Plums LC (FP)	6D	
Moss Lane LC (UWG)	45A	
MOSS SIDE	49A	
Mossband Jn	30A	
MOSSLEY (Greater Manchester)	45B	
MOSSLEY HILL	40	
MOSTON	47A	
Mostyn SB	36A	
MOTTRAM STAFF HALT (Disused)	45D	
MOULDSWORTH	35A	
Mouldsworth GF	43B	
Mount Pleasant Tunnel	40	
Mountsorrel	4A	
Mow Cop LC (CCTV)	43A	
Mucky Lane LC (UWK)	3B	
Muirho Farm LC (UWG)	30A	
Munllyn LC (UWC)	23C	
Mywars No. 2 LC (UWC)	23D	
Nadins Swadlincote GF	7C	
NANTWICH	23A	
NANTYRONEN	23E	
Napsbury HABD	2A	
NARBOROUGH	3B	
Navigation Road LC (UWC)		
NAVIGATION ROAD		
Nawlyns LC (UWC)		
Naylors LC (UWC)		
Neasden Jn		
Neilson Street Viaduct		
NELSON		
NESTON		
NETHERFIELD		
NETHERTOWN		

Entry	Code
Nettle Hill Viaduct (M6)	11A
Neuadd LC (UWC)	23D
NEW BIGGIN (Disused)	34C
NEW BRIGHTON	39A
New Cliffe Hill	7B
New Glanyrafon LC (ABCL)	23E
New Hall Hey Bridge	30B
NEW HEY	47A
New House Farm LC (UWC)	23B
NEW LANE	42A
NEW MILLS CENTRAL	44A
NEW MILLS NEWTOWN	44A
New Street Tunnels, Birmingham	16
New Wetmore Sidings, Burton	25C
Newcastle	25B
Newcastle Road LC (AHBC-X)	23A
NEWSTEAD	5
NEWSTEAD (NET)	6D
NEWTON for Hyde	45A
Newton Heath TMD	47A
Newton Jn, Bescot	19
Newton LC (farm) (UWW)	25B
Newton Viaduct, Newton-le-Willows	26C
NEWTON-LE-WILLOWS	26C
NEWTOWN (POWYS)	23D
Newtown Tunnel	44A
Niffany LC (UWC)	33C
Noel Street (NET)	6D
Noose Lane LC (CCTV)	19
Norbury	44A
Normanton LC (10) (AHBC-X)	6B
North Erewash LC (CCTV)	6A
North Jn, Appleby	34B
North Jn, Menai Bridge	36D
NORTH LLANRWST	37C
North Lune Viaduct	29A
North Rode Viaduct	43B
North Stafford Jn, Crewe	25C
North Stafford Jn, Derby	13
North Tunnel Jns, Birmingham	16
NORTH WEMBLEY	8B
NORTHAMPTON	10A
NORTHAMPTON & LAMPORT RAILWAY	10D
Northampton Line Jn, Rugby	11A
NORTHAMPTONSHIRE IRONSTONE RAILWAY	10C
Northchurch	9A
Northenden Jn SB (NJ)	46A
NORTHFIELD	17C
Northgate Street Tunnels	35A
NORTHWICH	43B
NORTHWOOD HALT	20C
NORTON BRIDGE	12B
Norton LC (MWLF) (R/G) (bridleway)	26B
Norton SB	26B
NOTTINGHAM	6A
Nottingham Road Viaduct, Derby	5
Nottingham Transport Heritage Centre	4A
Nottingham Trent University (NET)	6A
NUNEATON	11B
Nuttall Tunnel	30B
OAKENGATES for TELFORD	22A
OAKHAM	3B
Oakley HABD	2C
Oerffrwyd LC (UWC)	23D
Oil Sdgs GF, Burn Naze	49C
Old Chapel LC (R/G, Manned)	23D
Old Chapel Viaduct	24A
Old Colonial (Birkenhead Tramway)	39A
OLD HILL	20C
Old Market Square (NET)	6A
Old Mill LC (UWC)	23B
Old Oak Sidings, Willesden	1L
OLD ROAN	41A
OLD TRAFFORD	46A
Old Trent Dyke Viaduct	6B
Oldbury Branch	19
Oldbury Viaduct	20C
OLDHAM MUMPS	47A
OLDHAM WERNETH	47A
Olive Mount Cutting	42A
OLTON	15A
O'Niels' LC (UWC)	3B
Orams LCs	33A
Ordsall Lane Jn	46A
Oriel Road Tunnel	41A
ORMSKIRK	49B
ORRELL	27A, 41A
ORRELL PARK	41A
Orston Lane LC (11) (MCBR)	6B
OSWESTRY (Disused)	22B
Oubeck	28A
Overbury Street Tunnel	40
OVERPOOL	38C
...NHOLME: LAKE DISTRICT	28C
...d Road Jn, Manchester	46A
...s Loop	28A
...SB (OY)	21C
...ord Road Jn)	21B
...SMD	21C
	46B
Padge Hall Farm LC (UWC)	3B
Padiham	33B
Pages LC (UWG)	49C
Pant y Peron LC (UWC)	23E
PARADISE Jn	40
PARBOLD	42A
PARK (Disused)	45A
Park Farm LCs	15A
PARK HALL (Disused)	22B
Park Hall Viaduct	18
Park House Farm LC (MWLO)	31B
Park Jn, Coventry	14B
Park Lane Jn	18
Park South	31B
PARK STREET	8B
Park Street Jn	45A
Parkhead Viaduct	19
Parkside Emergency GF	46A
Parkside Jn	26C
Parrot's LC	12B
Parrott's LCs	21B
Parry Green LC (UWC)	23C
Partington Jn	46A
PARTON	2A
PATRICROFT	46A
Pattersons LC (UWC)	3B
Peak Forest	44A, 44E
Peakstone PS GF	44A
PEARTREE	25C
PEMBERTON	27A
Penarth LC (UWC)	23D
Pendlebury Tunnels	48A
PENDLETON (Disused)	48A
Pendleton Sidings	48A
PENHELIG	24A
Penketh Hall LC (UWG)	38B
PENKRIDGE	21B
Penllyn	24G
Penmaenbach Tunnel	36C
PENMAENMAWR	36D
Penmaenrhos Tunnel	36C
Penrhos LC (UWC)	24A
PENRHYN	24B
PENRITH North Lakes	29B
PENSARN	4B
Penstrowed LC (UWC)	23D
Pentre Clawdd LC (TMO)	22B
Pentre Ddu LC (UWG)	36D
Pentre LC (UWG)	36A
Pentre Mawr LC (UWC)	23D
PENYCHAIN	24C
Pen-y-Clip or Penmaenmawr Viaduct	36D
PENYFFORD	37E
Pen-y-gelli LCs (UWC)	23D
Peover Viaduct	43B
PERRY BARR	16
Pershore Road Tunnel	17C
Peto/Betts Viaduct	19
Petteril Bridge Jn	29C
Philips Park Jns	45A, 47A
Phoenix Park (NET) (Park & Ride)	6D
Pic Tor Tunnel	44A
Piccadilly (Metrolink)	47D
Piccadilly Gardens (Metrolink)	47D
Picko Tunnels	40
Pikins LC (UWC)	23D
Pilkington Viaduct	42B
Pinfold LC (MCB)	25C
Pinnox Branch	43A
Pinxton	5
Pitts LC (UWC)	22C
Plas Newydd LC (UWC)	23D
Plasau Clatter No. 1 LC (UWC)	23D
Plas-y-Court LC (AHBC)	23C
PLEASINGTON	33A
Pleck Jn, Walsall	19
Plemstall LC (UWG)	35A
PLUMLEY	43B
Plumpton	29B
Poachins LC (UWC)	3B
Point of Ayr Colliery (closed)	36B
POLESWORTH	11B
Pomona (Metrolink)	47C
PONT-Y-PANT	37D
Pool Hey LC (AHBC)	42A
Port Carlisle Branch Jn	29C
Port of Heysham LC (UWG)	28B
PORT OF WORKINGTON	32B
PORT SUNLIGHT	38C
Porth Hir LC (UWC)	24B
PORTHMADOG	24B
PORTHYWAEN (Disused)	22B
Portland Street LC (CCTV)	41B
Portobello Jn 1	9
Portsmouth LC (MWLB)	33B
Post Office LCs	23D
Potters Lock No. 1 LC	7A
POULTON-LE-FYLDE	49A
POYNTON	43B
PREES	23A
PRESCOT	42B
PRESTATYN	36B
PRESTBURY	43B
PRESTON	27C
Preston Brook	26A
Prestwich (Metrolink)	47A
Priestfield (Midland Metro)	19
PRIMROSE HILL (Disused)	1R
Primrose Viaduct	33B
Prince of Wales LC (UWC)	22B
PRINCESS ROYAL DISTRIBUTION CENTRE	8A
Prologis Park	14B
Proof House Junctions	16
Pulford LC (AHBC)	22D
Punch Bowl Viaduct	28B
PWLLHELI	24C
Pye Bridge Jn	5
Quay Ward LCs	23E
Queens Head, Birmingham	16
QUEEN'S PARK	1L
Queens Road Jn	47A
Queensville	12B
Quintinshill	30A
Radcliffe (Metrolink)	47A
RADCLIFFE (Notts)	6B
Radford Jn	6A
RADLETT	2A
RADWAY GREEN (Disused)	13
Radwell Viaducts	2C
Raikes Viaduct	48A
Railway Age Heritage Centre, Crewe	13
RAILWAY TECHNICAL CENTRE	4B
RAINFORD	41A
RAINHILL	42B
Rallt LC (UWC)	23D
RAMSBOTTOM	30B
Ramsden Dock	31B
RAMSGREAVE & WILPSHIRE	33B
RAMSLINE HALT (Disused)	25C
Ratcliffe-on-Soar	4A
RAVENGLASS AND ESKDALE RAILWAY	34F
RAVENGLASS for ESKDALE	31C
Ravenhead Jn	42B
Ravenhead Works	42
RAWTENSTALL	30B
Ray Street Gridiron	1R
Rearsby LC (AHBC)	3B
Rectory Jn	6B
Red House LC (UWC)	23D
REDDISH NORTH	45A
REDDISH SOUTH	45A
REDDITCH	17C
Redhill Tunnels, Trent	4A
Rednal Farm LC (UWC)	22B
Reed's Farm LC (UWC)	23A
Reeds Lane LC (CCTV)	39B
Regent Road LC (AOCL)	41A
Regents Canal Jn	1R
Rheilffordd TALYLLYN Railway Company	24E
RUABON	22C
Rhosfach LC (UWC)	23E
RHOSGOCH (Disused)	37A
RHOSNEIGR	37A
Rhowniar LC (UWC)	24A
Rhydwhimen LC (R/G)	23C
RHYL	36B
RHYL MINIATURE RAILWAY	36E
Ribble or Sherif Brow Viaduct	34A
RIBBLE STEAM RAILWAY	27C
Ribble Viaduct, Preston	27C
Ribble Viaduct, Settle	34A
RIBBLEHEAD	34A
RICE LANE	41A
Rickerscote	21B
Riddings Jn	5
RIDGMONT	9C
Riggmoor LC (UWG)	30A
Rippings LC (UWC)	3B
Rippins Main LC (UWC)	3B
Risehill Tunnel	34A
RISHTON	33B
River Carno & River Severn Viaduct	23D
River Derwent Viaducts, Ambergate	5
River Douglas Viaduct	49B
River Dove Viaduct	25C
River Great Ouse Viaduct	2C
River Nene Viaducts	10A
River Ribble Viaduct	28B
River Trent Viaduct	6C
River Trent Viaduct, Drakelow	7C
River Yarrow Viaduct	27B
Roade	10A
ROBY	42B
Roch Viaduct	30B
ROCHDALE	47A
ROCK FERRY	39A
Rock Ferry Jns	38C
Rockcliffe Hall SB (RH)	36A
Rocks LC (UWC)	25C
Rodidge LC (MGH)	18
ROLLESTON	6B
ROMAN BRIDGE	37D

Name	Ref
Roman Bridge Tunnel	37D
ROMILEY	45A
Rood End Yard	19
Roodee Jn, Chester	35A
ROOSE	31B
ROSE GROVE	33B
ROSE HILL MARPLE	45A
Rosewain LC (MWLG)	32C
Rossett LC (Bridle & cycle way) (MWLF)	22D
Round Oak North GF	19
Rowes LC (UWC)	25C
ROWLEY REGIS	20C
Royal Centre (NET)	6A
RUABON	22C
Ruabon Road Tunnel	22D
Ruckley Viaduct	21C
RUFFORD	49B
RUGBY	11A
Rugby Trent Valley Jn	11A
Rugeley 'B' Power Stn Jn	21A
Rugeley Jns	12A
RUGELEY TOWN	21A
RUGELEY TRENT VALLEY	12A
RUNCORN	38A
RUNCORN EAST	26B
Russell Street Tunnel	40
RUTLAND RAILWAY MUSEUM	50A
RYDER BROW	45A
Ryecroft Jn, Walsall	19
RYLSTONE	33C
S & T Sdg GF, Derby	25C
Saffron Lane GF	7B
St. Mary's Jns, Derby	5
ST. ALBANS	2A
ST. ALBANS ABBEY	8B
St. Andrews Jn, Birmingham	16, 17C
ST. ANNES-ON-THE-SEA	49A
ST. BEES	32A
ST. HELENS CENTRAL	42B
ST. HELENS JUNCTION	42B
St. James Tunnels	40
St. Luke's Jn, Southport	42A
ST. MICHAEL'S	40
ST. PANCRAS EASTERN INTERIM STATION	1R
St. Paul's	16
St. Peter's Square (Metrolink)	47D
SALE	46A
SALFORD CENTRAL	47A, 48B
SALFORD CRESCENT	46A, 48B
Salford Hope Street	46A, 48B
Salford Quays (Metrolink)	47C
Salop Branch Siding, Stafford	12B
Salop Goods Jn, Crewe	13
Salop Sidings, Stafford	12B
Saltcoats LC (MCG)	31C
Salthouse Jn	31B
Salthouse No. 1 LC (UWG)	31C
Saltley SB (SY)	16
Saltney Jn, Chester	22D, 35A
SALWICK	49A
SANDBACH	43B
Sandbanks Road LC (UWG)	36B
Sandbourne Viaduct	20C
SANDHILLS	41A
Sandicare Sidings	7A
Sandilands LC (ABCL)	24A
Sandringham Avenue LC (UWG)	39B
Sandscale/British Cellophane LC (AOCL)	31B
SANDWELL & DUDLEY	19
Sandy Lane LC (UWG)	36B
SANKEY for Penketh	46C
Sankey Viaduct, Earlestown	42B
Sankey Viaduct	46C
Sark Viaduct	30A
Sarn LC (UWC)	23D
Sawley LC (AHBC)	4B
Saxelby Tunnel	4C
Saxondale LC (UWC)	6B
Scarrington Lane LC (19) (AHBC-X)	6B
Scholes Tunnel	42B
Scout Tunnel	45B
Scropton LC (MGW)	25C
Scropton SB	25C
SEAFORTH & LITHERLAND	41A
SEASCALE	31C
Seaton Tunnel/Viaduct	3A
Sefton Jn	41A
SELLAFIELD	31C
SELLY OAK	17C
Serjeants LC (UWC)	25B
SETTLE	34A
Severn Bridge Jn	22A
SEVERN VALLEY RAILWAY	20C
Severn Viaduct	22A
Shap Summit GF	29A
Sharnbrook Jn	2D
Sharnbrook Viaducts	2C
Sharpes LC	3B
Sharston Jn	46A
SHAW & CROMPTON	47A
Shaw's LC (MWLG)	42A
Sheepwash Viaduct	5
Sheet Stores Jn/Trent West Jn	4A, 4B, 6A, 6C
Shell GF	5
SHENSTONE	18
Sherbourne Viaduct	14B
SHIFNAL	21C
Shilton HABDs	11A
Shipman & Greens LC (UWC)	3B
Shipstone Street (NET)	6D
SHIREBROOK	5
SHIRLEY	15A
Shore House Farm LC (UWG)	33B
Shotlock Hill Tunnel	34B
SHOTTON HIGH LEVEL	36A, 37E
SHOTTON LOW LEVEL	36A, 37E
Shotwick GF	37E
Shrewbridge Road LC (AHBC-X)	23A
SHREWSBURY	22A
Shudehill (Metrolink)	47A
Shugborough Tunnel	12A
Shuttlewoods Top LC (UWC)	4A
Sideway Jn	12D
SILEBY	4A
SILECROFT	31C
Silkstream Jn	2A
Sillesbourne Farm LC (UWC)	15A
Silver Birch Crossing LC	19A
SILVERDALE	31A
Silverdale Colliery	12C
Silverdale Tunnel	12D
Sims McIntyre GF, Beeston	6A
SINFIN CENTRAL (Disused)	25C
SINFIN NORTH (Disused)	25C
Skeffington Road LC (TMO)	27C
Skelly Crag LC (MCG)	31B
Skew Bridge Jn, Preston	27C
SKIPTON	33C
Slade Lane Jn	45A
Sleights East LC	5
Slutchers Lane LC (FP)	26B
SM & BP GF, Whittington	22B
SMALL HEATH	15B
Smardale Viaduct	34B
SMETHWICK GALTON BRIDGE	16, 19
SMETHWICK ROLFE STREET	16
SMETHWICK WEST (Disused)	16, 19
Smithdown Lane Tunnel	40
Smithfield Tunnel	1R
Smiths Lower Cefn LC (UWC)	23C
SMITHY BRIDGE	47A
Sneinton LC (MCB)	6A
Snelson's LC (UWC)	21B
SNIBSTON COLLIERY RAILWAY	7C
Snow Hill Tunnel, Birmingham	15B, 16
Snow Hill Tunnel, Farringdon	1R
SNOWDON MOUNTAIN RAILWAY	24F
Sod Hall LC (UWG)	49C
Soho Benson Road (Midland Metro)	16
Soho South Jn	16
Soho T&RSMD	16
SOLIHULL	15A
Songar Grange Farm LC (UWC)	15A
Sough Tunnel	48A
SOUTH ACTON	1L
SOUTH HAMPSTEAD	1L
South Hampstead Tunnels	1R
South Jn, Southport	1B
South Jn, Menai Bridge	36D
SOUTH KENTON	8B
South Tunnel Jn, Birmingham	16
South West Sidings, Willesden	1L
SOUTH WIGSTON	3B
South Yard, Crewe	13
SOUTHPORT	42A
Southport Sidings, Wigan	27A
Southwaite	29B
Sow Viaduct	14B
Specklies LC (UWC)	3B
Speke Jn & Sidings	38A
Spekeland Road	40
SPELLOW (closed)	41A
SPITAL	38C
SPONDON	4B
Spring Gardens Viaduct	44B, 44C
SPRING ROAD	15A
Springs Branch Jns	27A, 27B
Square River Bridge	30B
SQUIRES GATE	49A
Staff Halt (Metrolink)	47A
STAFFORD	12B
Stainforth Tunnel	34A
Stainton Jn	29C
Stallington LC (CCTV)	25B
STALYBRIDGE	45A
STAMFORD	3B
Standedge Tunnel	45C
Stanfield Farm LC (UWG)	30A
STANLOW & THORNTON	35A
Stansfield Hall Spur	33B
Stanton Gate	7A
Stanton Tunnel	4C
Stapleford & Sandiacre SF	7A
Star LC (UWG)	37A
STARR GATE	49A
Stathams LC (UWC)	25B
Station Street (NET)	6A
STAVELEY	28C
Staythorpe Crossing	6B
Steamtown, Carnforth	28B
STECHFORD	14C
STEEPLE GRANGE LIGHT RAILWAY	50C
Stenson Jn, Derby	6C, 25C
Stenson Raynors LC (UWC)	25C
Sterns LC	20C
STEWARTBY	9C
Stockbeck Viaduct	33B
Stocking Farm LC (UWC)	21C
STOCKPORT	44A
Stockton Brook Tunnel	25B
Stockyard LC (UWC)	5
Stoke Hammond HABD's	9A
Stoke Jn	12D, 25B
Stoke Lane LC (AHBC-X)	6B
STOKE-ON-TRENT	25B
STONE	12B
Stone Jn	12B, 12D
Stonebridge Jn	8A
STONEBRIDGE PARK	8A
Stoney Low Tunnel	12D
Stoneyfield/Deans Brook Viaduct	2A
Stoneyford GF	5
Stores Siding GF	8A
STOURBRIDGE JUNCTION	20C
STOURBRIDGE TOWN	20C
Stowe Hill Tunnel	10A
STRAND ROAD	27C
Strand Road LC, Preston	27C
Strand Road LC, Bootle	41A
STRATFORD-UPON-AVON	15A
STRETFORD	46A
Stretton GF	5
Stretton Heath LC (AHBC)	23C
STRINES	44A
STYAL	43B
Substation LC (UWC)	1L
Sudbury Jn, Willesden	8A
Sudbury, Tutbury	25C
Sullivan Works	38A
SUMMERSEAT	30B
Summit Tunnels	47A, 47B
Sunny Hill	25C
Sutton Bridge Jn	23B
SUTTON COLDFIELD	16, 18
Sutton Forest LC (AHBC)	5
Sutton Jn LC (CCTV)	5
Sutton Oak, St. Helens	42
SUTTON PARK (Disused)	18
SUTTON PARKWAY	5
Sutton Tunnel	26B
Sutton Weaver	26B
Swains Park Sidings	7C
Swainsley Viaduct	5
Swan Lane LC	19
Swan Side Viaduct	33B
Swan Village Hill Top Tunnel	19
Swanbourne Siding	9B
Swannington LC (AHBC)	7C
SWANWICK JN	5
Swing Bridge, Barmouth	24A
SWINTON	48A
Switches Farm LC (UWC)	33C
Sydney Bridge Jn, Crewe	13
Syke Foot LC (UWG)	34C
SYSTON	3B
Tai'r Meibion Farm LC (UWG)	36D
Talacre SB (TE)	36B
TALSARNAU	24B
Talwrn Bach LC (AOCL)	24B
TALYBONT	24B
TAL-Y-CAFN	37C
TAME BRIDGE PARKWAY	19
Tame Viaduct	45A
Tamper Siding GF	36C
TAMWORTH (HIGH LEVEL)	11B, 18
TAMWORTH (LOW LEVEL)	11B, 18
Tan Lan LC (UWG)	37C
Tanhouse Lane	38A
Tanyrallt LC (OC)	23E
Tarn Gate LC (UWG)	49A
Tasker Street, Walsall	19
Tattenhall Emergency GF	35A
Tatterwaite LC (UWG)	28B
Taylor Street GF	33A
Taylors LC (UWC)	6B
Tebay	29A
Teigh LC (FPG)	3B
TELFORD CENTRAL	22A
TELFORD STEAM RAILWAY	21D
THATTO HEATH	42B
The Bryn LC (UWC)	23C
The Crescent (Midland Metro)	19
'The Delta'	47D
The Forest (NET) (Park & Ride)	6A

The Hawthorns (Midland Metro) 16, 19
THE HAWTHORNS 16, 19
THE LAKES 15A
THE LAKESIDE and HAVERTHWAITE RAILWAY 31D
The Oaks LC (UWG) 48A
The Royal (Midland Metro) 19
Thomas Street, Crewe 13
Thorneyfields LC (UWS) 3B
THORNTON CLEVELEYS (Disused) 49A
Thornton South Sidings 35A
Thorpes Bridge Jn 47A
Three Spires Jn 14B
THURGARTON 6B
Thurmaston Wheelchex 3B
TILE HILL 14B
Tilford Road LC (AHBC) 5
TIMPERLEY 46A
Tinwell LC 3B
TIPTON 19
Toadmoor Tunnel 5
TODMORDEN 47B
Tolans LC (UWG) 39B
TONFANAU 24A
Tonge Viaduct 48A
Topley Pike 44A
Totley Tunnel 44B
Toton 7A
Tottenham North Curve Tunnels 1R
TOWN GREEN 41A
Towneley 33B
Townsend Fold LC 30B
Traeth Bach Viaduct (Bridge 79) 24B
Traeth Mawr Viaduct (Bridge 83) 24B
Traethmawr LC (AOCL) 24B
TRAFFORD BAR 46A
TRAFFORD PARK 46A
Trafford Park Jns 46A
Trafford Park Freight Complex 46A
Trafford Road LC 47C
TRAWSFYNYDD (Closed) 37D
Treffeddian LC (UWC) 24A
Trent SB (TT) 6A
Trent Fields Viaduct 6B
Trent Lane LC (R/G) (footpath) 6A
Trent Lane LC (UWW) 6A
Trent South Jn 4A, 6A
Trent Valley Jn, Rugby 11A
Trent Valley Jn No. 1, Stafford 12B
Trent Valley Jn No. 1, Stafford 21B
Trent West Jn 4A, 4B, 6A, 6B
Trentham Jns 12D
Trer'ddol River Viaduct (Bridge 247) 23E
Trewin Sands Viaduct 37A
TRING 9A
Trinity Way (Midland Metro) 19
Trowell Jn 7A
Tuebrook Sidings 40
Tulketh Viaduct 49A
Tunnel Road Tunnels, Edge Hill 40
Tunnicliffs No. 1 LC (UWC) 25C
Tunstead Sidings 44E
Turton LC (AOCL) 48A
TUTBURY & HATTON 25C
TY CROES 37A
Ty Mawr Fm LC (UWC) 23D
Ty Pella LC (UWC) 23D
Tyddyn-y-Pwll LC (UWC) 23D
TYGWYN 24B
Ty'n Llan No. 1 LC (UWC) 24A
Ty'n-Ddol LC (UWG) 37C
Tyn-y-Morfa LC (MG) 36B
Ty'n-yr-Wtre No. 2 LC (UWC) 23D
TYSELEY 15B
TYSELEY LOCOMOTIVE WORKS
(Birmingham Railway Museum) 15B
TYSELEY WARWICK ROAD 15B
Tywyn GF 24A

Uffington 3B
ULVERSTON 31A
Underhill LC (UWG) 31B
UNIVERSITY 17C
UPHOLLAND 41A
UPPER HOLLOWAY 1R
Upper Leigh LC (AHBC-X) 25B
Upper Llegodig LC (UWC) 23C
Upper Park Street Tunnels 1R
Upper Portland LC (AHBC) 5
Upperby, Carlisle 29C
Uppermill Viaduct (Saddleworth) 45C
UPTON 39A
URMSTON 46A
UTTOXETER 25C
Uttoxeter Line Jn No. 5, Stafford 12B

VALE OF RHEIDOL LIGHT RAILWAY 23E
Vale Royal Viaduct 26A
VALLEY (Y DYFFRYN) 37A
Vauxhall Jn, Birmingham 16
Victoria (Metrolink) 47A
Victoria Bridge 20C
Victoria Sidings (TOG) 6B

Victoria Tunnel Portal 40
Village LC (TMO) 5
Village Viaduct 23D
Virtual Quarry GF, Kingmoor 29D
Vitriol Works SB (VW) 47A

Wade Works, Northwich 43B
Wagon Repair GF, Carlisle 29C
WALKDEN 48A
WALLASEY GROVE ROAD 39A
WALLASEY VILLAGE 39A
WALSALL 19
WALSDEN 47B
Waltham Nurseries LC (UWG) 31B
WALTON & ANFIELD (closed) 41A
WALTON (Merseyside) 41A
Walton Old Jn & Sidings 26B
WARCOP (Disused) 34B
Wards LC 3B
Warren House LC (MWL) 5
WARRINGTON BANK QUAY 26B
WARRINGTON CENTRAL 46B
WARWICK 14A, 15A
WARWICK PARKWAY 15A
Wash Green GF 5
Washstones LC (R/G) (UWCM) 3B
Washwood Heath 16
Waste Bank Tunnel 34C
WATER ORTON 18
Water Works LC 3D
WATERLOO (Merseyside) 41A
Waterloo Branch Jn 40
Waterslack Quarry LC (UWG) 31A
Waterworks LC (UWC) 18
Watery Lane, Tipton 19
WATFORD HIGH STREET 8B
WATFORD JUNCTION 8B
Watford Lodge Tunnel 10B
WATFORD NORTH 8B
WATFORD STADIUM (events only) 8B
WATFORD WEST 8B
Watkins LC (UWC) 3A
Wavertree Jn & Viaduct 40
WAVERTREE TECHNOLOGY PARK 42B
Wavertree Yard 40
Weaste (Metrolink) 47C
Weaste Jn 46A
Weaver Jns 26A
Weaver or Frodsham Viaduct 35B
WEDGWOOD 12D
Wednesbury Great Western Street (Midland Metro) 19
Wednesbury Parkway (Midland Metro) 19
WEDNESBURY TOWN (Disused) 19
Wednesfield Heath Tunnel 19
Weedon Viaduct 10A
Weer Lane LC (UWC) 25C
Weig Lane LC (AOCL) 23D
Weightmans Viaduct 6B
Welland Valley/Harringworth Viaduct 3A
WELLINGBOROUGH 2D
WELLINGTON (Shropshire) 22A
Welsh Harp/Brent Viaduct 2A
WELSH HIGHLAND RAILWAY 17D, 50H
WELSHPOOL 23C
WELSHPOOL & LLANFAIR LIGHT RAILWAY 24D
WEM 23A
WEMBLEY CENTRAL 8A
Wembley Central Jn (former Sudbury Jn) 8A
Wembley Mainline SB (WM) 8A
Wembley Traincare Depot 8A
Wembley Yard SB (WY) 8A
WENNINGTON 28B
Werneth Tunnel 47A
WEST ALLERTON 40
West Bromwich Central (Midland Metro) 19
West Coast Control Centre 16
West Deviation Jn 38A
WEST HAMPSTEAD 1L
WEST HAMPSTEAD THAMESLINK 1L
WESTHOUGHTON 48A
WEST KIRBY 39B
WEST LANCASHIRE LIGHT RAILWAY 48C
West Lune Viaduct 28B
Westbury LC (AHBC) 23C
Westminster Tunnel 41A
Weston LC (TMO) 22B
Weston Rhyn LC (AHBC) 22C
Weston Viaduct 35B
Westons LC (UWC) 25B
Wetmore Jn 25C
WHALEY BRIDGE 44A
WHALLEY 33B
Wharfside Metrolink (not in use) 47C
WHATSTANDWELL 5
Wheelwright Lane LC 14B
Whissendine LC (MCB) 3B
WHISTON 42B
Whitacre Jn 18
Whitbeck LC (AOCL) 31C
WHITCHURCH 23A
Whitefield (Metrolink) 47A
WHITEHAVEN 32A

Whitehouse Jn 12A
Whitehurst LC (UWC) 22C
Whites LC (UWC) 6C
Whitley Village 33B
WHITLOCKS END 15A
Whittington 22B
Whittle International GF 33A
Wichnor Jn 18
WICKSTEED PARK LAKESIDE RAILWAY 50D
WIDNES 46C
Widnes Intermodal Rail Depot 38A
WIDNES SOUTH (Disused) 38A
Widnes, Tanhouse Lane 38A
WIDNEY MANOR 15A
Wig Farm LC (UWC) 36D
WIGAN NORTH WESTERN 27A
WIGAN WALLGATE 27A
Wigan Springs Branch 27A
Wigston Jn 3B
WIGTON 32C
Wilkinson Street (NET) (Park & Ride) 6D
Wilkinson Street Tram Depot & Control Rm (NET) 6D
Willaston LC (CCTV) (Gresty Lane) 23A
Willersley Tunnel 5
Willesden (Acton Branch) Jn (Willesden No. 7) 8A
Willesden Yard Sidings 8A
Willesden Euro Terminal 1L
WILLESDEN JN HIGH LEVEL 1L
WILLESDEN JN LOW LEVEL 1L
Willesden Traincare Centre 1L
WILLINGTON 25C
Willow Vale Bridge 19A
WILMCOTE 15A
WILMSLOW 43B
WILNECOTE 18
Wilpshire Tunnel 33B
Wiltshires LC (UWC) 25C
WINDERMERE 28C
Windmill Lane Tunnel 35A
Windridge LC (UWC) 18
Windsor Bridge Jns 46A , 48B
Wing LC (UWC) 3B
Wing Tunnel 3B
Wingfield Tunnel 5
WINSFORD 26A
Winston Green Outer Circle (Midland Metro) 16
Winterbutlee Tunnel 47B
Winwick Jn 26C
WIRKSWORTH BRANCH (Wyvern Rail plc) 5
WIRRAL TRANSPORT MUSEUM 39A
Wishbone Bridge 19
WITTON 16
WOBURN SANDS 9C
WOLVERHAMPTON 19
Wolverhampton North Jn 21B
Wolverhampton St. George's (Midland Metro) 19
Wolverhampton Steel Terminal 19
Wolverhampton Viaducts 19
WOLVERTON 9B
Wolverton Works 9B
WOOD END 15A
Woodlands LC (UWC) 23B
Woodlands Road (Metrolink) 47A
Woodley Jn 45A
WOODLEY 45A
Woods LC (UWK) 3B
Woods Tenement Farm LC (UWG) 43B
WOODSMOOR 44A
Woolascott LC 22B
Woolton Road Tunnel 40
Wootton Broadmead LC (AHBC-X) 9C
WOOTTON WAWEN 15A
WORKINGTON 32B
Worleston Viaduct 35C
Wormleighton LC (UWB) 14A
Wraysholme LC (AOCL) 31A
WREXHAM CENTRAL 22D
Wrexham Exchange Jn 22D, 37E
WREXHAM GENERAL 22D
Wribbenhall (Bewdley) Viaduct 20C
Wyfordby LC (MGH) 3B
Wyke Cop LC (AHBC) 42A
Wykey LC (UWC) 22B
WYLDE GREEN 16
Wymington Tunnel (also known as Sharnbrook Tunnel) 2D
Wymondham LC (MGH) 3B
Wyre Viaduct 28A
WYRLEY & CHESLYN HAY (Disused) 21A
WYTHALL 15A

YARDLEY WOOD 15A
Yarrow Viaduct 48A
Yew Tree Farm LC (UWC) 15A
Ymlwch LC (UWC) 24B
Ynys LC (UWC) 24A
Ynyslas LC (AHBC) 23E
YORTON 23A
Ystrad Fawr LC (UWC) 23D

ACP	Avenue Coking Plant Branch (Clay Cross)
AEG	Allerton East Junction - Garston Junction
AFE	Abbey Foregate Junction - English Bridge Junction (Shrewsbury Curve)
AFL	Aintree Fork Line (Sefton Jn - former Metal Box Siding)
AHX	Allerton Jn - Hunts Cross West Jn (Hunts Cross Chord)
AJM	Ambergate Junction - Matlock (and Peak Forest Jn)
ALC	Aston North Jn - Lichfield City Jn
AMJ	Ashton Moss Curve (Ashton Moss South - North Junctions)
AML	Attenborough - Meadow Lane Junction
ANL	Acton - Northolt Line (via Greenford East)
ACW	Acton Canal Wharf Jn - Willesden Jn
AWL	Acton East - Acton Wells Jn
AYS	Ashburys Yard Sidings
BAG	Birmingham New Street - Gloucester
BBB	Bolton - Blackburn
BBM	Bletchley - Bedford Midland
BBS	Blackburn Sidings
BCJ	Birmingham Curve Junction - Branston Junction (Burton-On Trent)
BCP	Stubbins Jn - Bacup
BCR	Blackpool Carriage Sidings
BCS	Bletchley Carriage Sidings
BCV	Bordesley Curve Junction - Tyseley Line
BDH	Brent Curve Junction - Dudding Hill Junction
BDN	Bridge Street Junction - Duston North Junction (Northampton)
BDS	Bidston West Junction - Seacombe Junction (siding only)
BEA	Barnt Green, Evesham - Ashchurch Line
BEJ	Buxton - Edgeley Junction
BEN	Birkenhead - New Brighton Branch
BFO	Bletchley Flyover Jn to Fenny Stratford
BFG	Wembley Repair Shop
BHI	Basford Hall Independent Lines (Basford Hall Jn to Sydney Bridge Jn)
BIK	Bickershaw Colliery Branch (Wigan)
BJW	Bescot Junction - Wichnor Junction (via Walsall)
BLT	Bletchley Sidings
BNN	Bedford - Northampton Jn
BOK	Broad Street - Old Kew Jn via Hampstead Heath (North London Line)
BPC	Bestwood Park Jn - Calverton Colliery
BPH	Blisworth - Peterborough via Northampton Bridge St
BPP	Brewery Jn - Philips Park West Jn
BSC	British Steel Corby Branch
BSD	Bescot Sidings
BSJ	Bootle Junction Crossover
BSN	Brunthill Stainton Sidings (Carlisle)
BUX	Buxton - Hindlow
BYK	Bewdley - Kidderminster
CAW	Cricklewood Curve Jn - Acton Wells Jn
CBC	Carnforth - Barrow - Carlisle
CBR	Castle Bromwich - Ryecroft Jn (Walsall) via Sutton Park
CCB	Cotgrave Colliery Branch
CCG	Colne Jn - Croxley Green
CCS	Rock Ferry - Cathcart St Branch
CDM	Castleford Jn - Dee Marsh
CEC	Carnforth, Station Jn - East Jn
CEH	Castleton East Junction - Heywood
CGJ	Crewe (159Mp) - Carlisle (Gretna Jn) (part WCML)
CHW	Chester - Warrington
CIL	Chester Independent Lines (Salop Goods Jn - Crewe North Jn)
CMD	Colwich Junction - Macclesfield
CMP	Crewe - Manchester Piccadilly
CNB	Chinley North Junction - Buxton (via Peak Forest)
CNH	Crewe North - Holyhead
CNN	Coventry - Nuneaton
COL	Manchester Piccadilly East Jn - Ordsall Lane Jn
CPC	Codnor Park Curve (Codnor Park Jn - Ironville Jn)
CPI	Castleton, North Jn - South Jn
CRC	Camden Road Junction - Camden Junction
CRF	Camden Road East Jn - Copenhagen Jn (North London Incline)
CRR	Chester - Rock Ferry
CSD	Castleton Depot
CSG	Crewe Sorting Siding - Gresty Lane
CTA	Clifton Junction To Accrington Line
CVL	Churnet Valley Line (Leek Brook Junction - Oakamoor)
CVS	Chester South Junction - Chester North Junction
CWJ	Camden Jn - Watford Junction (DC Electric Lines)
CWK	Canning St Jn (Hamilton Square Jn) - West Kirby
CYC	Chinley Chord (Chinley East Junction - South Junction)
DAP	Dalton Junction - Park South Junction (Barrow avoiding Line)
DBP	Derby - Birmingham (Proof House Junction)
DCL	Didcot - Chester Line (Didcot to Handsworth Jn via Birmingham Snow Hill)
DEX	Derbyshire Extension (Rectory Jn - Derby Friargate)

DHF	Denbeigh Hall Flyover South Jn - Flyover Jn (Bletchley)
DJH	Daisyfield Junction (Blackburn) - Hellifield
DJO	Denton Junction - OA&GB Junction
DJP	Dovey Junction - Pwllheli
DJW	Duffield Junction - Wirksworth
DPJ	Dudley Junction - Pleck Junction (Walsall)
DSD	Dinting South Junction - Dinting East Junction
DSE	Deal Street (Manchester) - Edge Hill (Liverpool) (Chat Moss Line)
DSS	Euston Down Side Sheds
ECM	East Coast Main Line (London Kings Cross - Edinburgh)
EDE	Eden Valley Junction - Kirkby Stephen via Appleby West Junction - Warcop
EEE	Liverpool Curve (Earlestown South - West Junctions)
EHW	Edge Hill Junction - Park Lane Goods (Wapping Branch)
EJN	Edgeley Junction (Stockport) - Northenden
EPS	Earles Private Sidings
ETC	Edinburgh - Carlisle Line (Waverley Route)
EWG	Edge Hill Junction - Waterloo Goods
FCO	Farington Curve Junction - Ormskirk
FHR	Farington Curve Junction - Hall Royd Junction via Blackburn
FJH	Frodsham Junction - Halton Junction
FTL	Farringdon - Ludgate (Blackfriars)
GBS	Guide Bridge Sidings
GDW	Glossop - Dinting West Junction
GJC	Gannow Junction - Colne
GLA	Gaerwen - Amlwch
GMC	Greater Manchester Council Branch (Woodley - Bredbury)
GNQ	Gobowen - Nantmawr Quarry
GOJ	Gospel Oak - Junction Road Jn
GSG	Gresty Lane Jn - Salop Goods Jn
GSJ	Galton Junction - Stourbridge Junction (Galton Branch - Stourbridge Extn Line)
GSM	Glendon South Jn (Kettering North Jn - Manton Jn, Melton Jn, Syston South Jn (also Old Dalby Line)
GSW	Glasgow - South Western Line (Kilmarnock GBK Jn - Gretna Jn via Dumfries)
HAJ	Hadfield - Ardwick Junction
HBL	Hest Bank Junction - Bare Lane Junction
HCM	Silverdale Colliery - Madeley Jn
HCN	Hartford Curve (CLC Junction - LNW Junction)
HEG	Hartford East Goods Curve (Northwich)
HGC	Hazel Grove Chord (Hazel Grove East - High Level Junctions)
HHJ	Hooton - Helsby Junction
HHW	Hatton North Junction - West Junction
HND	Halesowen Branch (Longbridge)
HNO	Hartford Northwich Oakleigh Sidings
HNR	Hanslope - Northampton - Rugby
HNS	Heaton Norris - Guide Bridge
HOB	Haydock Park Branch (Ashton-in-Makerfield)
HOK	Horrocksford Branch
HOM	Holwell Branch (Asfordby)
HSA	Hatton - Stratford-on-Avon
HSJ	Handsworth Jn - Smethwick Junction
HTW	Heath Town Junction - Walsall Lichfield Road Junction (Closed)
HWG	Hartford West Goods Curve
HXS	Hunts Cross West Jn - Southport
IMG	Ince Moss Goods Lines (Ince Moss - Bamfurlong Sidings Junction Curve, Wigan)
JRT	Junction Road Jn - Carlton Road Jn
KBC	Kingsbury - Birch Coppice
KBS	Kirkham North Jn - Blackpool South
KCS	Kidsgrove - Crewe South
KGC	Kensal Green Jn via City Lines - Harlesden Jn
KGW	Kensal Green Junction - Surburban Jn
KJW	Kingsbury Junction - Whitacre Junction
KMG	Kingmoor Jn - Mossbound Jn via Goods Lines
KSL	Knighton South Junction - Leicester Junction (Burton)
KWD	Kingswinford South Jn - Pensnett
LCN	Lostock Junction - Crow Nest Junction (Hindley)
LCS	Liverpool Edge Hill - Crown Street Goods
LEC	London Euston - Crewe 159Mp (part WCML)
LED	Little Eaton Junction - Denby
LEL	Lifford West Junction - East Junction
LHL	Lostock Hall Lines (Farington Jn - Lostock Hall Jn)
LJT	Llandudno Junction - Blaenau Ffestiniog and Trawsfynydd
LLG	Low Level Goods (Willesden West London Jn - Wembley Central Jn)
LLI	Liverpool Independent Lines (Crewe) (Salop Good Jn - Crewe Coal Yard Jn
LLJ	Llandudno - Llandudno Junction
LMD	Longsight Depot Sidings
LSC	Leamington Spa - Coventry
LSN	Lenton South - North Junctions
LSS	Landor Street Junction - St Andrews Junction (Birm...

LTV	Lichfield Trent Valley Curve
MAJ	Manchester, Castlefield Jn - Hunts Cross West Jn (CLC Line)
MAS	Totley Tunnel East - Chinley North Junction (Manchester - Sheffield Line)
MCG	Maryport - Carlisle Goods Lines (Currock Jn - Forks Jn)
MCH	Macclesfield - Cheadle Hulme
MCJ	Marylebone - Claydon L&NE Junction (also Ruddington)
MCL	Midland City Line (Moorgate) - Carlton Road Jn
MDH	Mold - Denbeigh
MHH	Morecambe Jn - Heysham
MIA	Manchester International Airport Rail Link Line
MIR	Mersey: Liverpool Loop Line and Mann Island Jn to Rock Ferry
MJI	Madeley Junction - Ironbridge Line
MJS	Melbourne Junction - Sinfin Branch
MJT	Mansfield Junction - Trowell Junction
MLN	Main Line (Paddington - Penzance via Bath)
MPR	Miles Platting Jn - Rochdale East Jn via Oldham
MRH	Marple Wharf Jn - Rose Hill Marple
MSM	Morecambe South Junction - Morecambe
MVB	Manchester Victoria - Bury (Superseded by Metrolink)
MVE	Manchester Victoria - Euxton Junction via Bolton
MVL	Manchester Victoria, Mile Platting Jn - Heaton Lodge Jn, also Leeds
MVM	Manchester Victoria - Miles Platting Jn
MVN	Manchester Victoria, Thorpe Bridge Jn - Normanton, Goose Hill Jn via Rochdale
NAJ	Neasden South Jn - Aynho Junction via Bicester North
NBS	Norton Bridge - Stone
NEC	Newcastle - Carlisle
NGC	Netherfield - Gelding Colliery
NGD	Newcastle Goods Lines (Carlisle, London Road Junction - Bog Junction)
NGJ	Newton-le-Willows Jn - Golborne Jn (Parkside West Curve)
NJN	Neasden South Sdgs and Neasden Jn
NLI	North London Incline
NMB	North Mersey Branch (Aintree, Fazakerly - North Mersey Jn)
NMC	New Mills - Cheadle Branch
NMH	Northampton - Market Harborough
NMM	North Mersey Branch - Marsh Lane Junction
NOB	Nottingham - Barnetby via Lincoln
NOG	Nottingham - Grantham
NSA	Nuneaton South Jn - Abbey Jn
NSN	Northwich South Junction - Northwich West Junction
NSS	North Stafford Junction (Derby) - Stoke-on-Trent
NTM	Northampton Sidings
NWO	Nuneaton - Whitacre Jn
OLD	Oldbury Branch
OLL	Ordsall Lane - former Liverpool Road Stn
OLW	Ordsall Lane Junction - Windsor Bridge Junction (Salford) (Windsor Link)
OOS	Old Oak Sidings, Willesden
ORG	Miles Platting Junction - Oldham Road Goods
OWW	Oxford, Worcester and Wolverhampton Line
OXC	Oxley Chord (Oxley Stafford Road - Bushbury Oxley Junctions)
OXD	Oxford Branch (Oxford - Bletchley)
OXW	Oxenholme - Windermere
PBC	Pinxton - Bentinck Colliery
PBJ	Proof House Junction (Birmingham) - Bushbury Junction via Bescot
PBL	Perry Barr West Jn - North Jn
PBN	Preston - Blackpool North
PBS	Pye Bridge Jn - Mansfield Woodhouse (143M40c)
PDB	Preston Deepdale Branch
PJL	Parkside Junction - Lowton Junction (Parkside East Curve)
PJW	Portobello Junction - Wolverhampton (also known as Portobello Loop)
PMJ	Peterborough - Manton Junction
PPA	Philips Park West Jn - Old Midland Jn (Ardwick Branch)
PPP	Philips Park South Junction - Baguley Fold Junction (Parks Fork)
PRG	Padiham - Rose Grove
PSE	Mansfield Woodhouse 143M40c - Shireoaks East Jn (Worksop)
PSR	Preston Strand Road Branch
QLT	Queen's Park LUL
RAC	Radford Junction - Kirkby Lane End Jn
RBS	Rugby - Birmingham - Stafford
RDB	Runcorn Dukes Dock Branch
RDK	Ramsden Dock Branch
RGY	Rugby Sidings
RRN	Ryecroft Jn (Walsall) - Rugeley North Jn
RTS	Rugby - Leamington Line
RUD	Ruddington Chord (Loughborough)
RYH	Romiley - Hyde Jn
SAC	Settle And Carlisle Line
SAG	St Andrews Junction - Grand Junction (Birmingham)
	Stalybridge Junction - Guide Bridge West Junction

SAR	South Acton - Richmond
SAS	Stechford - Aston
SBA	Shrewsbury (Sutton Bridge Jn) - Aberystwyth Line
SBH	Springs Branch (Wigan) - Huyton
SCG	South Carlisle Goods Lines (Bog Junction - Forks Junction)
SCL	Soho Curve Line (Soho North Junction - East Junction)
SCN	Ship Canal Branch (Eccles to Weaste)
SCQ	Stoke-on-Trent - Caldon Low Branch (Waterhouses Branch)
SCR	Speke Junction - Church Road Junction (Garston)
SCT	Seaforth Container Terminal Branch (from Bootle Branch Junction)
SDJ	Latchford - Ditton Junction Line
SEN	Syston East Junction - Syston North Junction
SHL	Shrewsbury and Hereford Line
SHS	St Helens - Sutton Oak
SIL	Stock Interchange Line (Liverpool Central) (Paradise Jn - Derby Square Jn)
SJC	Wennington - Carnforth Furness and Midland Junction
SJD	Skelton Junction - Deansgate Junction (Navigation Road)
SJO	Sandhills Junction - Ormskirk
SJS	Stourbridge Junction - Stourbridge Town
SJT	Stratford-on-Avon and Midland Jn Line
SKN	St Andrews Junction - Kings Norton (Camp Hill Line)
SKS	Skipton Middle Junction - Grassington/Skipton & Swinden
SKW	Skipton North Jn - Wennington
SLT	Stonebridge Park LUL Depot
SMA	South Manchester Airport Chord
SNJ	Sandbach - Northwich West Junction
SPC	St Pancras - Chesterfield, Tapton Jn via Derby (Midland Main Line)
SRD	St Helens - Rainford (Gerards Bridge Jn - Cowley Hill)
SSJ	Sheet Stores Junction - Stenson Jn
SSP	Soho South - Perry Barr South Jn
STY	Styal Line (Wilmslow Junction - Slade Lane Junction)
SVB	Severn Valley Branch
SYC	Shrewsbury - Crewe
SZS	South West Sidings, Willesden
TAH	Tottenham And Hampstead Line
TCC	Trent East Jn - Clay Cross South Jn
TES	Trent East Junction - Sheet Stores Junction
THL	Toton High Level Goods Line
TJC	Tapton Junction (Chesterfield) - Colne
TPS	Trafford Park Sidings
TSB	Tyseley South Jn - Bearley Jn
TSN	Trent South Jn - Nottingham
TTA	Chinley North Jn - Ashburys Line via Romiley
UCJ	Upperby Bridge Junction - Caldew Jn via Rome Street
UHL	Up High Level (Wembley Central Jn - Harlesden Jn via Wembley Yard)
USS	Up Side Sidings, Euston
WAR	Appleby North Junction - West Junction
WAW	Willesden LL Goods Jn - Acton Wells Line
WBS	Windsor Bridge North Junction (Salford Crescent) - Southport via Wigan
WCG	Watford High St - Croxley Green Jn
WCL	Willesden Carriage Lines (Harlesden Jn - Willesden Carriage Shed North)
WCM	West Coast Main Line (Carlisle - Glasgow Central)
WDB	Wrexham Central - Bidston
WDJ	Walsall Pleck Jn - Darlaston Junction
WEE	Winwick Jn - Earlestown East Jn
WGL	Wednesbury Goods Loop (Bescot Jn - Bescot Curve Jn)
WGP	Wigston South Jn - Glen Parva Jn
WGS	Willesden Sidings
WHM	Stanton Works Siding (former West Hallam Colliery Branch)
WHT	Washwood Heath Sidings
WJK	Walton Junction - Kirkby
WJL	Weaver Junction - Liverpool
WJP	Woodley Junction (Cheadle Jn) - Partington
WKL	Wigan - Kirkby
WKS	Wolverton Works
WLL	West London Line (includes West London Extension Line)
WMB	Willesden High Level Junction - Mitre Bridge Junction
WMO	Wavertree Junction - Downhill Carriage Sidings
WNS	Wigston North Jn - Nuneaton South Line
WOA	Walton Old Junction - Arpley Junction (Warrington)
WOP	Water Orton West Jn - Park Lane Junction Curve
WPS	Wyre Dock (Fleetwood) - Poulton-le-Fylde
WSA	Watford - St Albans Abbey
WSJ	Wolverhampton North Jn - Saltney Junction (Chester)
WTS	Willesden Through Sidings (Sidings Jn - Sudbury Jn)
WYM	Wymington Slow Line (Sharnbrook, Midland Main Line)
WZS	Willesden TMD